BISON
BOOKS

CRIPPLE
CREEK DAYS

Mabel Barbee Lee

Foreword by
Lowell Thomas

University of Nebraska Press
Lincoln and London

Copyright 1958 by Doubleday & Company, Inc.
All rights reserved
Manufactured in the United States of America

First Bison Book printing: August 1984
Most recent printing indicated by the first digit below:
                          7   8   9   10

Library of Congress Cataloging in Publication Data
Lee, Mabel Barbee.
  Cripple Creek days.
  Reprint. Originally published: 1st ed. Garden City,
N.Y. : Doubleday, 1958.
  "Bison."
  1. Lee, Mabel Barbee. 2. Cripple Creek (Colo.)—
Social life and customs. 3. Cripple Creek (Colo.)—
Biography. I. Title.
F784.C8L4 1984   978.8'58   84-5204
ISBN 0-8032-7912-4 (pbk.)

∞

Reprinted by arrangement with Doubleday & Company, Inc.

For
LOWELL THOMAS

In Remembrance of
The Golden Years

Acknowledgments

COUNTLESS stories have been told about the world-famous Cripple Creek District. Many yarns have become legendary, passed along by word of mouth but never recorded. In spite of the difficulty of sifting fact from hearsay, several reliable histories have been written which serve as guideposts for reminiscent authors and students of Western Americana. Among the books most helpful to me were *Midas of the Rockies*, (revised) Frank Waters, Denver University Press, 1949; *Money Mountain*, Marshall Sprague, Little Brown & Company, 1953; *Rails around Gold Hill*, Morris Cafkey, World Press, Denver, Colorado, 1955; *Labor History of the Cripple Creek District*, Benjamin McKie Rastall, University of Wisconsin Press, 1908; *Stampede to Timberline*, Muriel Sibell Wolle, University of Colorado Press, 1949; *A History of American Mining*, T. A. Rickard, McGraw-Hill Book Company, 1933; *The Confessions and Autobiography of Harry Orchard* (*Albert E. Horsley*), McClure Company, 1907. I also found invaluable, *Variety Music Cavalcade*, a chronology of vocal and instrumental music popular in the United States, 1620–1950, compiled by Julius Mattfeld, Prentice-Hall, 1952.

I am grateful to Mr. Blevins Davis and Mr. Richard W. Johnson, publishers of the Cripple Creek *Gold Rush*, for giving me access to the early issues of the Cripple Creek *Morning Times* and the Victor *Daily Record* which were stored in the fireproof attic at the Carlton Mill. I never could have handled these weighty volumes, however, without the patient help of Mr. A. N. (Bob) Ragle of the mill staff, who arranged with the management for me to use one of the mill offices. These fascinating old newspapers brought back vividly many of the stirring events which had slipped my memory. Mr. Tom Rolofson was kind in lending me his rare miniature copy of the Cripple Creek *Morning Times*, issued the day after the first great fire had destroyed most of the plant.

My sincere thanks go to Mr. Gene Fowler for letting me read his valuable collection of clippings about Otto Floto, Cripple Creek's colorful, enterprising carnival and prize-fight promoter during the nineties who later became noted as sports writer for the Denver *Post*. Newspapers deserving bows for feature stories of special interest to me were the Colorado Springs *Gazette;* the *Rocky Mountain News;* the Cripple Creek *Gold Rush;* and the former San Francisco *Call-Bulletin* for its graphic account of the Corbett-Fitzsimmons championship fight in Carson City, Nevada, March 17, 1897.

The stories of Cripple Creek days, however, were drawn largely from my own recollections, vivified now and then by those of other old-timers. The passing years have shed a glow on some of the episodes, while others have been toned down in the softening light of perspective. The names of Jim and Molly Letts are fictitious, but the people were real although they did not actually live next door to us on Golden Avenue. Some of the dwindling group of pioneers may take issue with me, claiming that I have brushed over important incidents too lightly or omitted them altogether. But this is a matter of opinion, interpretation, and point of view. Scarcely any two old Cripple Creekers saw the Golden Era through identical lenses or in precisely the same detail, but all were agreed on the essence and spirit of the turbulent events.

My visits with old-timers brought dividends in the discovery of long-lost friends and acquaintances. The stories they remembered were often highlighted with drama and humor that I might otherwise have missed. Many went to endless trouble to help with information. Among those to whom I am particularly grateful are Mrs. Margaret Burns Ackelbein; Mrs. Alice Baltzell Addenbrooke; Mrs. Albert E. Carlton; Mr. Richard A. Hart; Mrs. Martha Albert Stephenson, daughter of Hans Albert; Mr. Lowell Thomas; Mrs. Pherbia Thomas Thornburg; Mr. and Mrs. A. W. Oliver; the late Harry J. Gehm; Mr. Sam Cohen; Mr. David P. Strickler; Dr. W. W. King; and Mr. Wayne Mackin.

Also Mr. Jack Dempsey; Dr. Frank Healy; the late Bill Kyner; Mrs. Humbolt Emens; Miss Mae Dunn; Mrs. Eleanor Finn LaDuke; Mrs. Louie Olsen; Mrs. Electa Franklin Mc-Combs, daughter of Victor's former mayor, Nelson Franklin; Mrs. Leonie Leighton Rinker, beloved teacher at the Golden Avenue School; Mrs. Grace Arkins Page; the late William Arkins and Mrs. Arkins, formerly the widow of Harry Woods; Mrs. Lester Rogers; Miss Minnie Zimmerman; the late Tom Sharkey; Mr. George Coplen; Mr. Leslie Wilkenson; Mr. and Mrs. Richard Roelofs, Jr.; Miss Miriam F. Carpenter; Mrs. Ishbel MacLeish Campbell; Mrs. Norman Titus; Mr. Wallace Irwin; the late Ben Hill; Mrs. Norris Eads; Mr. Harry Mac-Donald; Dr. John Vincent, Director of the Huntington Hartford Foundation, and Mrs. Vincent; Mr. Huntington Hartford; Mrs. Minnie Welty McInturf, daughter of Alonzo Welty.

I wish to thank Mr. Bill Hosokawa, former editor of the *Empire Magazine* of the Denver *Post,* for permission to reprint parts of "The Great Cripple Creek Fires," published April 2, 1950, as well as excerpts from a later article, "Camp Bird Honeymoon." The Chapter titled "Uncle Si's Jack Pot," embodies, together with additional material, the article "The Most Unforgettable Character I've Met," which appeared in the *Reader's Digest,* January 1949. It has been reprinted by kind permission of the editors.

I should like to express appreciation for their interest and co-operation to the following: Mrs. Alys Freeze of the Denver Public Library; Mr. Glenn H. Johnson, Jr., of the State Historical Society of Colorado; Miss Dorothy E. Smith of the Pioneers Museum of Colorado Springs; Mr. H. L. Stubbs, Trustee of the Myron Stratton Home; Miss Louise Kampf of the Coburn Library at Colorado College; Mrs. A. C. Denman of the Cripple Creek Museum; and to the Library of Congress.

Finally I wish to acknowledge my indebtedness to the Huntington Hartford Foundation, without whose generous fellowships it would not have been possible for me to develop and complete the Cripple Creek stories. I could not end these tributes without a word of gratefulness to my daughter Barbara, whose pertinent, sometimes pitiless, but always constructive criticisms have led to the deletion of many a precious adjective or phrase. And my warmest thanks go to Mrs. Margaret A. Griswold, who proved her competence as my first secretary at Bennington College, and then, after more than twenty-five years, with ability undiminished, she consented to type my manuscript and launch me on another exciting venture.

Mabel Barbee Lee

Pacific Palisades, California
March 1958

Foreword

IT had always seemed a bit odd to me that "the world's greatest gold camp," the richest eldorado of them all, had no Homer to chronicle its epic story. The California gold rush had its Bret Harte; early Nevada had its Mark Twain; the trail of '98 to the Klondike was immortalized by Jack London and Robert Service; and Rex Beach was the chronicler of the stampede to Nome. But Cripple Creek produced no writer of importance—until now.

Of course a number of books about the old days in Cripple Creek have been written, such as Frank Waters' *Midas of the Rockies* and the excellent *Money Mountain* by Marshall Sprague, New York *Times* correspondent, who settled in Colorado Springs for his health. However, now at long last a true Cripple Creek writer has emerged.

In a way I suppose you might say this book by Mabel Barbee Lee is a sort of sequel to *Timberline*, a story of another part of Colorado that brought fame to a brilliant Colorado reporter of my era, Gene Fowler.

For years, Rocky Mountain newspapermen of my vintage

—Damon Runyon, George Creel, Gene Fowler, Ralph Carr, Ford Frick, and others—had urged me to tell the Cripple Creek story. But, instead of looking back, I kept on hunting for other eldorados, all over the world, always more curious to see what was beyond the next horizon. I'm glad I did so, for I never could have written one half as good as this story of Cripple Creek days by Mabel Barbee Lee. Of course I may be a little prejudiced because I lost my heart to her when her name was Mabel Barbee. So did all the other fellows in our class.

There's only one *first* day of school that I can recall. That was one September when we were all surprised to find that we had a young and stunning redhead for a teacher, a girl who obviously was only a few years older than we were. Most of my teachers made less of an impression on me than did the men I met in the mines and the gambling halls, except two: one of them an amazon who sat on me, and there on the floor gave me a licking I'll never forget, and the other the lovely Mabel. None of us ever wanted to play hooky from her class, and playing hooky was a thing we all dreamed of and occasionally did, so that we could explore the scores of abandoned mines and caves that made our part of the high Rockies a place of magic for youngsters. How any boy could get good grades in a roaring gold-mining camp like Cripple Creek in its heyday, with all the diversions we had, I don't know. Maybe that's just my alibi for the near-flunking record I racked up year after year.

On our way to school in the morning we all had to pass Dingman's gambling emporium, and the swinging doors of Diamond, the Monarch, and other saloons that never closed. Then there was the lurid red-light district almost next door to the schoolhouse. And just outside our windows was a mine boiler repair shop. The man who ran it had the most colorful variety of purple profanity I have ever heard. In English class perhaps we would be reading William Cullen Bryant's *Thanatopsis* or James Russell Lowell's *Vision of Sir Launfal*, or our history teacher would be telling us the story of the Crimean War and the story of Florence Nightingale, when through the window would come an oath usually including a string of brand-new words that would curl the hair of a Ute Indian.

After school hours, on our way home, when we were not doing our own fighting, we would talk about the classic championship battle between John L. Sullivan and Gentleman Jim Corbett, or maybe it was a little later, when our heroes were Jim Burns, Stanley Ketchel, Joe Gans, or Ad Wolgast. We knew far more about them than we did about our own colonial history, or ancient Greece and Rome. Or we would hear about the latest discovery of rich ore on the Golden Cycle, the Tornado, or the Doctor-Jack Pot; or a disastrous cave-in on the Molly Kathleen, the Anchoria-Leland, or the Gold Coin; or of a miner's battle on Tenderfoot Hill or in Poverty Gulch.

Beautiful Mabel Barbee was one of the few teachers who could always hold our attention. She had a gift for storytelling, and then we just liked to look at her.

When I went away to college and came back to work in the mines and later take over the editing of a couple of daily papers in the Cripple Creek District, I lost track of her for a dozen years or more, except occasionally when I would hear that she had become a dean at some college. I knew she had married a young mining engineer and that something had happened to him. And that her life had been touched with tragedy, as is so often the case with people whose lives have anything to do with the search for gold. Gold miners are a special race. They seldom if ever will have anything to do with mines that yield coal, lead, zinc, or any of the base metals.

In fact, a gold miner never wants to admit that he works for wages. For when he does, it is simply to get the wherewithal for another grubstake so he can go on looking for the end of the rainbow. Since the beginning of time, gold has had that effect on man.

Finally, after she had been associated with the faculties of four or five institutions of higher learning—Colorado College, Radcliffe, the University of California, and Bennington —our trails crossed again. By now she was doing some writing, which led to this. And the only part I played in her book was to urge her on.

While this is not in any sense a chronological history of "The World's Greatest Gold Camp," it tells the story in the way that those of us who lived there would like to have it told. I'm sure she can tell one hundred more tales just as exciting as these. And I hope she will. Mabel Barbee Lee, the Bret Harte of Cripple Creek!

Lowell Thomas

CONTENTS

CONTENTS

CRIPPLE CREEK DAYS

1

Up the Long Trail

F A R away among the sandstone ridges of southwestern Utah, word of the fabulous gold strike in the Cripple Creek District reached my father, Johnson R. Barbee, and wakened a familiar, slumbering urge in him. Once he would have dropped everything to pull up stakes and join the great rush, but that was before he married Kitty. For a decade, now, he had been mining in Silver Reef, the longest he had ever settled in one place. Until then he had been a prospector, free as the air, roving the land wherever excitement called and whenever the spirit moved him.

Restlessness was in his blood. While still a boy in Kentucky his family, under the threat of Civil War, left the large plantation where he had been born, and went to live on a small farm near Weston, Missouri. He was seventeen and in his first term at Liberty College when hostilities finally started. Without consulting his father, he ran away from home to become a standard bearer with the Confederate Army. Four years later the defeated South lay in ruins. Bitter, discouraged and unable to find work he struck out for the West and arrived, at last, in Virginia City, Nevada.

He was a hardened veteran and strong of body, but his outspoken hatred of "damnyankees" made it difficult for him to get or keep a job. He was far too stubborn and individualistic to be under the thumb of a mine boss. Somehow he managed to pick up considerable knowledge of ore formations and mining practices and, more important still, discovered the use of the divining rod for locating underground deposits of precious metals. It marked a turning point in his life and led to the calling that exactly suited his temperament.

He roamed over most of Nevada, prospecting mountains, valleys and blistering desert, and his hands became sensitive to the slightest quiver of the "forked stick." He grew to understand the language of the earth and stone and could spot from afar a significant outcrop of rock and knew the meaning of its colors. Occasionally he lingered in some mushrooming camp long enough to take up a claim and sell it for a few needed dollars. It began to look as though he were destined to be a nomad forever and that change was the only unchangeable thing on which he could count.

Then one day a passing sheepherder told him of a big silver strike in the sandstone bluffs across the border in southern Utah. It was near a small Mormon town named Silver Reef. He was skeptical at first, saying that he had never heard of silver occurring in a sandstone formation, but he was enough of a gambler to take a chance. Luck was with him this time and he located a claim that developed into a moderately rich property. For some reason, he didn't try to sell it as usual, and take to the hills again.

There was something appealing about the little village with its stately poplars shading the streets, and neat, white cottages surrounded by lawns, gardens and fruit trees. It was different from the Nevada mining camps. The deeply religious people had never permitted saloons to sully their town; and their Mormon faith had forbidden them to work in mines. The well-run stores and markets were booming as a result of the silver discoveries and recently a fine new Wells Fargo bank had been built on Main Street. The feeling of stability and promise seemed to fill the newcomer with a strange, baffling wish to remain there and perhaps find a wife to make a home for him.

With plenty of money coming from the Barbee Shaft, and a rather handsome, weatherworn face, set off by captivating manners, he soon became a catch among the young women of the village. But it was a pretty, auburn-haired Scotch girl, one of the few non-Mormons, who finally won his heart. Her name was Kitty and although she was twenty years his junior, everybody spoke of it as an ideal match. He built her the nicest house in town, with a broad veranda across the front, reminiscent of Kentucky, and enclosed it with a white picket fence. Because of the scarcity of water, he followed the custom of sinking several barrels in the back yard for catching and storing rain. An extra one was put down near the wood-shed with a boardwalk leading around the house so that Kitty would have enough moisture for the peach tree by the dining-room window and the moss roses climbing on the gate trellis.

The birth of two little girls, two years apart, completed the idyllic picture. I was the elder and resembled my father with my reddish-blond hair and blue eyes. I was like him, too, in disposition, always running away from home to explore the wonders of Silver Reef. My mother was constantly looking for me, calling me up and down the streets. Nina, with her brown curls was Kitty's image and clearly my father's favorite. She was contented to play all day long with her dolls and other toys and never gave anyone a moment's worry. I loved Nina and often wondered why I was so unlike her, causing Kitty to scold when I climbed trees and ran off, while my sister was happy just sweeping the front porch with her little broom.

Then a sudden blow fell upon the household one morning and filled it with desolation. My father had gone to the mine; Kitty was inside cleaning and dusting and I was swinging on the front gate waiting for the stage to Saint George to rattle by. I heard my mother calling Nina several times but thought nothing of it, knowing that she would soon come running. But when she didn't answer or come, Kitty told me to go and look for her. As I started around the walk toward the back I noticed wet broom marks on the boards all the way to the woodshed. I called, "Nina—Nina!" but she was nowhere within. I ran to the barrel which was half-hidden by a large, yellow rosebush. The cover had been pulled off and there I found Nina, her head submerged in the water, her hand still clutching the toy broom.

After her death my father was never the same. He began to drink heavily at the saloon across the state line in Nevada, and often talked of padlocking the Barbee Shaft and getting out of the Reef. But Kitty did not want to go away. I heard him arguing with her many times, and once he threatened to leave without her if she persisted in clinging to her house and garden. The ore at the mine had already begun to pinch out, he declared, and in a few months there would be nothing left and he would have no way of earning a living. But his words seemed only to drive Kitty's roots deeper. If she weren't there, she said, who would lay fresh flowers on Nina's grave every day? She swore that she would rather die than abandon the baby forever to the lonely, desert graveyard. Because of her insistence he delayed making a definite move until his mine had become exhausted and only a few hundred dollars were left of his nest egg. It was the early summer of 1892;

4

he was on the sunny side of fifty. He would have to make up his mind soon where to go and what to do, or else resign himself to a woman's foolish whims.

It was almost at that moment that he heard the news of Cripple Creek's gold field. He told Kitty it was as if the finger of the Almighty had pointed the way. Now there was no question about his next step; he apparently had steeled himself against my mother's objections. "A miner has no choice but to go where the mines are," he said, "and that's what I intend to do. You can stay here and I'll try to send you money as I get it, or I'll take you with me as far as Salt Lake City. From there I can arrange for you and Mabs to go to Kansas City and stay with my brother Graham's family until I can find a house in Cripple Creek and send for you." Kitty pleaded and argued and wept, but he remained firm and unshakable. At last she gave in, exacting only one promise, that as soon as he struck it rich he would bring her back again to Silver Reef.

The day we left, the young peach tree by the dining-room window was a mass of delicate pink blossoms. Kitty gave it a lingering glance and her chin quivered as she pulled her shawl over her eyes. But for me the exciting journey was anything but a time of sadness. Now I myself was riding on the stage to Saint George, as I had often longed to do, and every sight, smell and sound along the road was a part of an endless adventure. And I wanted to fly with joy at the thought of seeing my real cousins in the strange, distant place called Kansas City!

2

Windfall

M Y father's relatives lived in a large house with many rooms for me to explore. Kitty and I were greeted warmly at first, and made to feel at home. But when weeks passed without word from Cripple Creek our welcome began to cool Uncle Graham, the youngest of my father's brothers, was away a great deal on business, and my aunt made no bones of the fact that we were an imposition. Her own three children, she hinted, were enough without adding one more to the confusion. She often made disparaging remarks about my father, calling him a ne'er-do-well and the black sheep of the family. She even predicted that he might desert us, the way he had done with the rest of his kinfolks. Kitty tried to defend him but she was not equal to my aunt's quick, sharp tongue, and usually went to her room where I often found her in tears.

When the long-expected letter came at last, the whole family gathered around after dinner to hear Kitty read it. Jonce excused himself for not writing sooner, saying that the politicians were still squabbling over the name of the camp Some wanted it called Hayden, others claimed it should be Fremont, but the old-timers in that area insisted on Cripple

Creek. The government had shifted the post office so often that mail got lost—it was better to wait until things were more settled before sending letters.

He described his stiff climb to the District from Colorado Springs, over the north shoulder of Cheyenne, a dragon-shaped mountain that reared straight up from the plains. The trail twisted through almost impenetrable country. He passed many folks on the three-day trip, tenderfeet from Missouri, farmers from Iowa and Kansas. Others had turned back exhausted, glad to be heading for home. He hadn't come across one experienced prospector so far, and nobody who had ever heard of the forked stick.

He went on then to tell about conditions in the camp. They beat anything he had ever seen in the worst days of early Nevada. Food and beds were as costly as they were scarce. Every night men could be seen sleeping on billiard tables and saloon floors. Newcomers often paid four bits just to sit in a hotel lobby chair a few hours at night. Luckily he had packed his own tent and bedding from the Springs. "It's a godforsaken hole up here at present—no place for you and Mabs. Arrange with Graham and his wife to stay on there a while longer if possible. Enclosed is a money order for expenses." Kitty sat for a moment looking off into space. Then she folded the letter and put it in her apron pocket.

"Is that all?" my aunt asked anxiously. "Didn't he even mention finding a house? Surely there must be *something* . . ."

"You heard what he wrote," Kitty said huskily, "but don't worry, we're going no matter what he says. I intend to take things in my own hands!" And she hurried from the room.

"Kitty, Kitty—come here!" Uncle Graham called. "Ella didn't mean to offend you. . . ." But she didn't answer and in a moment I followed her upstairs to our bedroom.

That night, as I leaned against the dresser watching her

brush her long, wavy hair, she talked to me as though I were a grownup. "Jonce has no right to pawn us off on his relatives like this," she said, her eyes flashing indignantly. "We've worn out our welcome and I hate being here—I can't endure it any longer!" She reached for a handkerchief and blew her nose.

"But he said Cripple Creek was a hole—a godforsaken hole," I ventured.

"There are worse things!" she snapped. Her defiance mounted with each stroke of the hairbrush. "He can put us up in his tent until something better can be found. At least it would be our own to live in as we pleased. I am going to telegraph him the first thing in the morning that we're leaving just as soon as I can get packed!" And she started pulling boxes and grips from the closets and emptying dresser drawers.

My uncle, a generous and kindly man, tried to dissuade her from taking what he called "an impulsive, dangerous journey." He upbraided her for being too sensitive and swore again that my aunt didn't mean to hurt her. "Jonce may not even get your telegram," he argued, and urged her to wait at least until she heard further from him. "It would be serious if you arrived alone in that wild outpost and found yourself stranded among strangers."

"I've considered everything," she said flatly, "and my mind is made up. Tell Ella I hold no grudge against her—it's hard for a woman to accept another in her home—and with an extra child, at that—it's likely to put anybody's nerves on edge."

No reply came from my father but we left as planned. Uncle Graham had relented, finally, and my aunt was kinder than she had been for a long time. They brought the children down to the depot to see us off and we all cried a little bit. As the train started to move, Uncle Graham gave me a bright silver dollar and ran along by the open window, warning me to beware of card sharks and bandits, and to take good care of my mother. I had come to love him and wished through my tears that he might have been my father instead of my uncle.

We traveled in a chair car and for a long time I was fascinated trying to count the telegraph poles as they flew past. Then children began to run up and down the aisle and some stopped to stare at me over their all-day suckers. People started to eat, it seemed, as soon as they were seated, although it was only the middle of the morning, and they bought fruit and cookies from the candy butcher whenever he made the rounds. The air smelled so temptingly of peanuts and oranges that Kitty broke down and let me have a piece of fried chicken from the lunch that Aunt Ella had made for us. Shortly I too had fallen into the routine of getting endless drinks of ice water and rushing to the toilet, which was usually already occupied. Kitty took many cat naps, but too much was going on for me to waste the hours in sleep.

It was chilly and daylight had just begun to break when we arrived in Florence two days later, several hours before the stage was due to leave for Cripple Creek. We huddled on a bench in the depot waiting room, surrounded by our many bundles and wicker telescopes. The big trunk which Kitty had checked had come through safely but it would have to be held over for the next freighter into camp. After the sun came up, people gathered on the platform and strolled in and out of the waiting room. Kitty was the only woman around. The roughly dressed men stared brazenly at her and two or three tried to make conversation. She looked fresh and pretty, in spite of the long, tiring trip. Her brown cashmere basque with feathered toque to match, and her dainty, opera-heeled shoes were in strange contrast to the heavy, high-laced boots and corduroy outfits of the men. I too felt very spruce in a new red coat and fur-trimmed bonnet; and I managed to toy conspicuously with my silver dollar so that the passers-by might briefly turn their eyes to me instead of Kitty.

The big Concord coach at last lumbered up to the platform. I had never seen such an odd, top-heavy stage outside of pictures in fairy tales. Its body was closed, with doors and windows on both sides and a driver's seat so high that it made me dizzy just to look at it. Three span of horses were needed to haul the cumbersome vehicle up the steep Shelf road to the District, thirty miles north. Everybody, lugging knapsacks and other possessions, made a scramble to get inside or climb on top. By the time Kitty and I had gathered our belongings no space was left in the coach. The busy driver was in and out of the depot, apparently getting his orders. He was about to jump on the seat when he suddenly noticed my mother alone, crowded out and looking as if she didn't know what to do next, and he walked back to us.

"Was you aimin' to go to the Crik, lady?" he asked, smiling good-naturedly. She told him that she certainly was but the menfolks had taken up all the room. "Well, we'll just see what can be done about that," he said. "Lord knows, the crazy, stinkin' camp needs decent women more'n it does a lot of shysters and slickers and tenderfoot prospectors! Sorry boys," he said, going over to the coach, "cain't 'low no strap hangin' —my load's limited to fourteen, provided a couple are lightweights." One or two fellows protested and cursed and he yanked them by the heels. "Don't like to be rough," he laughed, "but it's the law—guess it'll have to be shanks' mare for some of you guys."

He opened one of the doors and counted the passengers jammed inside. "Cain't let more'n six medium-sized folks on them two seats," he said, spitting and wiping his mouth on his sleeve. "Here, you two big bruisers, get up on the seat with me; make room for this little lady and her girl. Come on, git amovin'; ain't got all day for gabbin'!"

Almost before we realized it, my mother and I were sitting back comfortably on one of the two cushioned seats that faced each other. I could hear the driver cracking his long bullwhip, and swearing at the sixes. "Gee—Doc, giddyap there, Prince—steady—steady, Jerry!" he shouted, snapping the whip again and again. The heavily loaded coach lurched and the wheels creaked and whined; and the horses began to gallop until it seemed as if they were running away. The town soon vanished behind in clouds of dust.

It was early afternoon and warm for mid-October when we started, but as soon as we reached the foothills a chilly wind came up and the shadows began to deepen until only the tips of the mountains could be seen catching the last rays of sunlight. I sat close to the window and a man squeezed on the other side of Kitty. He went to sleep at once and hardly moved. The three passengers facing us scowled and grumbled while Kitty dozed fitfully, glancing at me now and then as if to make sure that I was all right.

I was never more wide awake, and kept my face pressed against the window, trying to make out the landscape or to catch the glimmer of a lamp in some lonely cabin. But everything was inky-dark; woods, mountains and sky were indistinguishable, one from the other. I lay back, sniffing the fragrance of pine and sagebrush and listening to the wailing wheels as they slipped endlessly into ruts and over stones. I began to feel drowsy at last and was about to go to sleep when one of the men across began to talk loud enough for me to hear.

"Un'erstan' we're takin' that new Shelf road through Phantom Canyon," he said. "Sure feels like it—dug right outa the cliffs, they say, 'cept for a stretch along the bottoms of Eight Mile Crik." He struck a match on his boot and lit his pipe. "Lotsa accidents, I hear," he went on, "up above, where the lead team has to be onhitched to make it around the hairpin curves—one slip an' yer name's mud!"

"Lucky it's dark," another said; "what can't be seen won't hurt nobody."

"Can't be too sure of that," the third spoke up. "Fella in Florence was tellin' me that only a coupla weeks ago the brakes failed in broad daylight an' the whole outfit, men, horses an' stagecoach, went rollin' backwards down the mountain and over a cliff."

"Guess the worst was the flash flood that come roarin' outa clear sky, down a piece where the road follows the crik bed," the first man said; "washed everything clean to the Arkansas River, never found a trace of nobody, only a single cottonwood tree jammed against a big boulder."

"Life's pretty goddamned cheap, any way you take it," put in another. "If you ain't a gittin' drownded or kilt in a wreck, a bandit's likely to fill you fulla bullets before a fella even gets to Cripple Crik. I hear say this road's plagued with bandits, remnants of Quantrill's rebel guerillas. . . ."

My heart raced and I clutched the silver dollar in my coat pocket. I peered through the window but saw nothing except shadows cast by the lantern hanging from the driver's seat. Kitty had slumped against me, asleep, and the man next to her was snoring. The others had lapsed into silence. Now and then someone coughed and cleared his throat, or lit a pipe. Beyond that, only the joggling stagecoach and the uneven thud of the horses' hoofs broke the stillness of the night. All at once a wail like a woman's scream, high and thin and faraway, pierced the air, and then came gradually closer until it seemed as if it were following us. "What's that—what's that——?" I cried, tugging at my mother. She stirred and mumbled something about being quiet and fell back to sleep. One of the men across chuckled. "Let your mama rest," he said; "there ain't nothin' to be scairt of—just a wildcat or a coyote maybe, asparkin' his best girl." I felt weak and trembly, and sank wearily against the window.

I must have been asleep a long time, for the next thing I knew the stage had stopped, and Kitty was shaking me hard and telling me that we had come to halfway house. "They're changing horses," she called, trying to button my coat. "Come, wake up! We're going to get a cup of coffee!" But it wasn't the prospect of food that brought me to life; it was the thought of my dollar. I groped for it frantically, but there it was, still safe in my pocket.

The lunchroom, a large tar-papered cabin set back in a widening of the road, was already crowded with people who had tramped in from the trails, or driven their own carts. The heavy odor of tobacco smoke, whisky and sweaty corduroys sickened me. Luckily most of the customers headed for the long, plank bar. Kitty found a table over in a corner but no sooner had we sat down than a portly, ruddy-faced man took the chair next to her and began to talk. He introduced himself as Oscar Burnside and said that he was in business in Cripple Creek. She told him our name and asked if he knew my father, Johnson Barbee. "Everybody in the District knows John," he said. "I don't mind telling you that he's a fine man. I consider him one of my good friends, as well as my best customer." Kitty seemed pleased to hear such nice things about her husband and talked more easily. She spoke of having heard about the dreadful living conditions in camp and that it was almost impossible to get a house of any kind, and wondered if it were really true.

"I'm sorry to say things are even worse than the reports,"

he admitted, pouring his coffee in the saucer to cool it. "I happened to get hold of a fairly comfortable shack for my family. But we're not immune to epidemics, and they sweep through the District with deadly results. If it ain't pneumonia or smallpox, it's typhoid or scarlet fever. Right now it's diphtheria." He looked over at me solemnly. "Your girl looks to be about the same age as my Blanche. Has she ever been sick with diphtheria?" Kitty's face turned pale as she said that I'd never had any contagious diseases. "Well, if you'll make John do what my wife insists on me doing, your girl probably won't catch it. I change everything from the skin out when I come home at night from the saloon."

I thought my mother would faint. It was hard to tell which had shocked her more, the chance of my dying of diphtheria or the discovery that Oscar Burnside was a saloonkeeper and that my father was his best customer! But I knew for certain what was in store for me as soon as she could unpack one of the telescopes. She would force me to swallow a big dose of castor oil and to wear an asafetida bead constantly on a string around my neck. This treatment was always my mother's "ounce of prevention" for every childhood disease. But I couldn't even imagine what she would say to my father, for she considered liquor a devil's concoction, and any man who made his living selling it was a pariah and the scum of the earth.

It was a relief to climb back into the coach for the final lap of the trip. Barring accidents and other unforeseen events, the driver said, we should arrive in camp between ten and eleven o'clock that night; it was now about seven. Several miles of hard pulling still lay ahead before we reached the next stop at a settlement called Limekiln. The road seemed to be even steeper than it was below halfway house. The horses snorted and the coach lurched and slipped as we struggled out of deep mudholes; and once, just as the man had said, the lead team had to be unhitched to get around a sharp bend. It had grown colder, too, and I wrapped my coat tighter over my knees and plunged my hand into the pockets. Soon a warm, cozy feeling stole through me and in spite of my efforts to stay awake, I dropped off to sleep.

What happened next was more of a bad dream than an actual occurrence. I felt drugged and couldn't open my eyes; and my mind whirled in a confusion of voices. People were cursing and arguing; and it seemed as if I were being pushed and shoved about like putty. Then I became conscious of Kitty yanking my arm and trying to drag me out of the stage. "What's the matter—where we going?" I whined drowsily.

"Sh—be still—just hang on to me," she whispered. "It's bandits!"

I clung to her skirts for dear life as we milled around in the lantern light, watching the masked robbers line up the other passengers. They had left Kitty until the last and when they came to her they seemed to grow polite, all at once, as though it was against their principles to frisk a woman. But apparently there was no time for quibbling and we were lined up along with everybody else. My heart thumped with fear but curiosity burned my mind. I felt vaguely like a spectator watching a thrilling play which was partly real but mostly nightmare. I could see the two burly thieves with bandanas covering all but their eyes. Their caps were pulled down and instead of corduroy coats they wore heavy shirts. A lantern hung from the cartridge belt of each, together with a pistol holster. The bandits worked fast but smoothly, one covering the victims with his six-shooter while the other searched them for money and jewelry. Only the wind rustling through the pine trees and the tinkle of silver and gold dropping into a satchel broke the mountain stillness.

As the holdups stepped closer and closer to us, I clutched my dollar tighter in my pocket. Panic gripped me as I tried to think of a safer place to hide it. They would see me if I stooped over to slip it in my stocking; and there was nothing to keep it from falling to the ground if I tucked it in my corset-waist. Then, just as the men approached Kitty, inspiration struck me. Pretending to scratch my nose, I slid the silver cart wheel, quick as a dart, into my mouth. It choked me and tickled my throat until it was all I could do to keep from coughing. Then I felt a heavy hand on my shoulder. "Git in line there, you young whippersnapper!" a gruff voice said. "This stick-up means you too!" And he flourished his gun to show me that he meant business. I could hardly breathe, and saliva drooled from the corners of my lips.

"Please, please, mister," Kitty begged, "spare her; don't scare her to death!"

He scowled at her for a second, and then winked as he leaned toward me and squinted as if he couldn't believe his eyes. "Well, I'll be gol-durned!" he said, as if flabbergasted, and beckoned to his partner. "Take a blinker at this sassy-faced kid," he said, pointing with his pistol. "Don't it beat all how she was atryin' to cheat on us?"

"Guess we oughta learn her a lesson as a warnin'," the other said, pursing his lips seriously and nodding.

"Don't you dare touch her," Kitty shouted, "or I'll——"

"Hold your tongue, missus," the first put in, "if you know what's good for you! I might just get the notion to make you hand over them garnet earrings you're wearin' and take a peek at what you got in that big, fat pocketbook."

This threat seemed to strike both men as being very funny, and they motioned the rest of the passengers to come over and see what was about to happen. They too began to snicker and even my mother seemed to be holding back a smile. I hadn't been able to close my jaws and it came to me all at once that they were laughing at the dollar lying there in plain sight! Tears of shame and terror mingled with the saliva pouring down my chin. One of the fellows reached over and patted my head. Then, without saying a word, he pulled another dollar out of the heavy satchel and slipped it on top of the one in my wide-open mouth.

"Next time, pug-nose," he said, chuckling and fastening the the satchel again, "better keep your little trap shut. Don' try no more funny tricks; you moughtn't fare so well with a fella who ain't been brung up so gentleman like!"

When the bandits were well out of sight down the road, the passengers began to compare losses and to boast about their cleverness in hiding their wallets. But everybody agreed that I had been the luckiest of them all. "I'll bet ten grand," the driver said, "it's the first time a body's ever been knowed to double his stakes in a gold rush 'fore ever settin' foot in camp!"

Before long we could see lights at the mines, shimmering high above like stars in the sky. Occasionally the faint, yellow flicker of a candle showed through a cabin window, and then came clusters of little shacks and tents with people out in front swinging lanterns. A thin layer of snow lay on the frozen ground and the coach wheels skidded and whined around the curves. It must have been well past midnight when the sixes galloped across the flats below camp and pulled to a stop at the Continental Hotel on Myers Avenue. The street was crowded with men and out of the uproar of yowling dogs and pistol shots we heard yells of "Hello, Sucker!" and "Ah, there, Yokels!" and "Welcome, Tenderfeet!" It was far more terrifying than being held up by desperadoes on the Shelf road in the deep of night!

Kitty scanned the faces anxiously, for she was not at all sure that my father had received her telegram; he might not be there to meet us. But I never doubted Kitty's ability to handle any situation with success. After what seemed like eternity, I heard my father's familiar voice calling and saw him pushing his way through the mob toward us. It was no time or place for greetings, and he picked me up in his arms and half carried my mother into the hotel lobby, and then hurried back to help unload our luggage.

"What's all the commotion about?" Kitty asked, when we were safely in our room upstairs. "Is there a special celebration or something?"

"It's this way with every stage that comes in," my father replied, "but tonight the crowd's bigger and noisier than usual —news of the holdup was telephoned from Limekiln." He looked down at me with a knowing grin. "Understand you're pretty flush right now," he laughed. "How about staking me to a couple of dollars?"

I felt shy and couldn't think of anything to say. It was hard to get used to him again, as my father. I was disappointed to see the most thrilling adventure of my life disposed of so quickly, but apparently he and Kitty had more pressing matters to discuss. I sat on one of the wicker telescopes watching and listening as they talked. I was surprised to find that he and Uncle Graham resembled each other. Both had fine, blond hair that receded from the forehead, and their eyes were the same color of blue. But my uncle had more warmth in his manner; he was not afraid to show tenderness and affection. My father acted embarrassed if Kitty tried to put her arms around him, saying that sensible folks didn't wear their hearts on their sleeves. But with my sister Nina it had been different; he always picked her up and cuddled her when he came home from work. After she died he seemed to grow more and more remote toward my mother and me.

"You took a great chance," he was saying now, "coming here

without letting me know ahead of time. Your telegram came only this morning." He looked around the room quickly. "This place ain't much," he said apologetically, "but at that, I was in luck to get it. I managed to find a good-sized tent, with a lean-to. You can go there tomorrow."

"But it's not big enough for three of us in here," Kitty said. Why can't we go to the tent tonight?"

"Folks haven't moved out yet. Don't worry about me. I'll sleep on a cot at Burnside's."

Kitty bit her lip, but said nothing.

As soon as he was gone she yanked the blankets from the bed and began to examine the mattress and the cracks of the wooden bedstead.

"Uh-huh," she muttered, squeamishly, "just what I expected —bugs! The place is alive with bedbugs! I wouldn't lie on that mattress for all the gold in Cripple Creek!" She unstrapped the heavy plaid shawl from one of the telescopes and wrapping it around me, told me to lie down on the floor. "I'll sit here in the chair by the window; don't be afraid!"

It was almost as light after she had blown out the lamp as it had been before. Wheezing and snoring could be heard through the muslin-covered walls, and the shuffle of heavy boots shook the door as people passed up and down the creaky stairs. The odor of whisky seeped from the saloon below and over and over a woman's nasal voice sang the same unforgettable ditty on a scratchy gramophone:

> "As I walk along the Bois Boolong
> With an independent air
> You can hear the girls declare
> He must be a millionaire!
> You can hear them sigh
> And hope to die,

19

You can see them wink the other eye
At the man who broke the bank
At Monte Car—ha—ha—lo!"

The monotony lulled me to sleep at last and nothing aroused me, neither the raucous laughter in the hall nor the mine whistles screeching from the hills beyond. Only the shock of my father's holding me up in his arms, and the sudden realization that the long journey had come to an end brought me back to life again. What excitement lay ahead! I was going to have my own lean-to in a tent over on Freeman's Placer!

Cripple Creek to me was anything but a godforsaken hole. It opened out as a world of mysterious, fascinating adventure, waiting for me to explore its every hill, gulch and alley!

3

No Life for a Lady

O U R tent was one of several scattered over the level stretch of ground at the camp's western edge. Like the others, it was patched and dirty, but differed from them by having a store-door with an adjoining half window. The former tenants had barely left when we arrived. Ashes still smoldered in the cook stove; empty cans of condensed milk and unwashed dishes were on the homemade table. A lumpy mattress sagged on an old wooden bed in a corner and a thin pad covered the cot in the lean-to which I proudly called "my room." A cracked, marble-topped washstand, or commode, and a few nonde-script chairs, including a low rocker, completed the furnish-ings.

Kitty began at once to clean and scour the place. The bed-ding was aired, the floor boards scrubbed with lye, the ceilings and walls wiped down, and the stove scraped and polished. My father and I carried water from the community well—we had to buy what we drank from the water wagons—and made trips to Roberts' Grocery for food supplies. There was little to choose from but Kitty could make the plainest things taste good; and by suppertime the tent smelled appetizingly of steaming coffee, hot baking-powder biscuits and fried sow-belly. "You've made it feel homelike already," my father said, reaching over and patting Kitty's hand. "It's been a coon's age, seems like, since I've eaten one of your hot biscuits. I'm damn glad you didn't let me have my way—about you and Mabs coming to camp." It was quite an admission for him to make. But instead of "telling him a thing or two," as she had threatened in Kansas City, Kitty just smiled and blushed happily; and her dark eyes glistened in the lamplight.

Early the next morning I set out to give the neighborhood a more thorough going-over than had been possible the day before. Within sight of us, but separated by a high chicken-wire fence, was a smug-looking clapboard house with perhaps three or four rooms. Geranium plants bloomed in the sunny windows, and a plank walk led to the woodshed and pad-locked privy. Just outside the kitchen a private cistern supplied pure drinking water. Then, to my amazement, I heard someone practicing scales on a piano! I hurried back to tell Kitty. "They must be moneyed folks," she said, "maybe a rich prospector. We'll get a piano for you too when your father hits the jack pot!"

I waited eagerly to see if there were any children. But three days passed before a girl of about my age came out and began to skip rope up and down the plank walk. She was very pretty, with an uptilted nose and blond braids tied with red ribbons; and a scarlet dust ruffle flashed beneath her blue coat. I edged toward the fence, smiling warmly, hoping to catch her eye, but she never looked my way. Suddenly a stern-faced woman appeared in the doorway. "Blanche! How often do I have to tell you to stay in the house!" she screamed. "Get in here this minute and don't let me find you outdoors again!"

My heart sank; now we would never get acquainted! But the

following day I saw her tiptoe out to the front porch and then
stand there gazing at me as if I were an ogre. I decided to use
bold tactics and buy my way, if necessary, into her good
graces. With my precious hoard in hand, I ambled casually
over to the gate. "Want to see my two silver dollars?" I asked,
holding them out. "A bandit gave me one of them—honest he
did! He put it right in my mouth, like this—see?" But she never
budged. "Here," I said brashly, "you can have it if you'll come
and play." She hesitated a moment, glanced around furtively,
and then started toward me, staring curiously at the dollar in
my outstretched hand. As she reached to take it the door was
yanked open and this time the angry mother began to shriek
at me while Blanche vanished into the house. "Go home . . .
go home!" she said, shaking her finger at me and scowling.
"Never let me catch you around here again. Blanche Burnside
can't play with you . . . do you hear?"

It was the first time I had ever suffered the humiliation of
being sent home and I ran with tears streaming down my face
to tell my mother. "So, that's where the Burnsides live!" she
said, ignoring my shame. "I might have guessed it! Well, we
don't have to take snubs from any saloonkeeper's family," she
went on indignantly. "I'll go over and give her a piece of my
mind!" I could hardly wait to see my mother make Mrs.
Burnside cringe and apologize. But by the time she had
combed her hair, powdered her face with Pozzoni's and put
on a fresh apron, she had cooled off considerably and looked as
calm as though she were making a neighborly call.

"Come along," she said, taking my hand. "Sometimes you
get things twisted." Mrs. Burnside barely opened the door and
we were not asked to come in. Blanche, who struck me now as
being anything but pretty, peered from behind her mother's
skirts. After introducing herself as a newcomer, Kitty went
directly to the point, without mincing words.

"My daughter says that you sent her home," she began, without any show of anger, "and told her never to come near again. I'd like to know what she did wrong. If she has been unladylike . . ."

"It's not that," Mrs. Burnside said, narrowing the opening, "nothing of that kind."

"But Mabs claims that you won't let Blanche speak to her— even through the fence!" she said with a trace of resentment. "You must have some reason . . ."

"Being a stranger, maybe you don't know about the diphtheria epidemic raging all over camp." Mrs. Burnside's voice lowered, as if the germs might overhear. "Children're dying like flies. They're burying them night and day, carrying them in boxes, without a funeral. Pretty soon no room'll be left in Pisgah graveyard!"

Kitty's face turned the color of ashes. "Has Blanche been exposed?" she asked, squeezing my hand tighter.

"It's in the air and gettin' closer an' closer," Mrs. Burnside said shakily. "In that tent where you live a baby came down with it only last week. It was gone in a few hours—choked to death. Your girl'll likely catch it an' I don't want her giving it to Blanche." She shut the door, and the key clicked in the lock. My mother stood for a moment, aghast, as if paralyzed by the dreadful disclosure.

"Well—I never——!" she fumed, hurrying from the yard. "Jonce must have been out of his mind, letting us live in a pesthole! We'll move, even if I have to tramp up and down myself looking for another place!"

I knew what she intended to do to me when she got out the castor oil bottle, but I had no idea what lay in store for my father. He had barely taken off his hat when Kitty's pent-up fears and resentments flew at him like arrows. He confessed that he had known of the baby's death of diphtheria, but the tent had been fumigated immediately afterwards and Dr. Whiting assured him that there was little danger of contagion. He hadn't told her because he knew she'd worry. His failure to trust her common sense seemed to heighten her bitterness; and the darts came from every direction. She spoke of meeting Oscar Burnside at halfway house, and how he had described John Barbee as one of his best customers. "And here we are," she went on breathlessly, "existing in a disease-ridden tent while our savings provide the saloonkeeper's family with comforts—even a piano!" She was struggling for self-control. "It may be too late but you must find us another place, at once!"

"Hold your tongue around the girl!" he said, pouring water into the wash basin.

She looked at me sharply for a moment as though I had no business watching and listening. "Put on your coat, Mabs," she said, "and run down to the grocery for a pound of margarine."

I hesitated on the step outside, eavesdropping, but the quarrel had spread to matters I didn't understand; and I dawdled downtown and back, puzzled by the strange ways of grownups. Everything had quieted by the time I returned. Supper was on the table and my father was stirring sugar in his coffee. Kitty drooped in the chair across from him, and I knew by the trapped, defeated look in her eyes that my father had won the battle—we were not going to move from the tent.

Neither Blanche nor I came down with the diphtheria. Kitty gave the heavy dose of physic full credit for my escape. But my father declared it was sheer contrariness that saved me, together with the "iron constitution of the Barbees." Whatever the reason, I was immune to most of the diseases that made perennial rounds of the camp, dealing death to the children.

Because of the severity of the epidemic, opening of the first school had been delayed until shortly after Christmas. Classes were to be held in a big, one-room log cabin on Main Street over in Old Town. I had been promoted to the fourth grade in Silver Reef, and my mother wanted to go along and talk with my teacher. But she had been ailing much of the time lately and seldom went out. It was just as well; seeing the musty schoolhouse might have finished her. The dirt floor and roof gave off a dank, mushroomy odor. Light filtered through a weather-stained window at one side. The fourteen pupils, ranging from six to sixteen, sat huddled on boxes and benches around a potbellied stove to keep warm while they studied; and often, when blizzards swirled across the mountains from Pike's Peak, the smoking chimney smothered the fire and the pupils had to be sent home.

My father said that we were lucky to have even one classroom and told me not to complain. Few people in the booming camp had time to think about schools. Many spoke confidently of not being there "next year" and meanwhile their children could study at home or get jobs. An attorney named W. G. Alexander objected to the do-nothing attitude toward education. He tried to organize a school board; and ended by being the sole member. Undaunted, he called himself president and appointed his well-educated wife as the first teacher. It was a labor of love, with no aids such as a blackboard, map of the United States of America or globe of the world. Most of the books came from the Alexander library, or had been brought by the pupils from previous schools.

Attendance increased so rapidly that soon half-day sessions became necessary and another teacher volunteered. But these measures proved to be inadequate, and one day Mr. Alexander announced that we were moving to larger quarters. The new location was upstairs in a sheet-iron building on Myers Avenue, an area that already showed signs of developing into the red-light district. It was a thrilling experience, at first, to amble past the one-story cribs on the way home in the afternoon. All the blinds were up at that hour, and scantily dressed women might be glimpsed sitting at the wedge-shaped windows, smoking cigarettes. The boys would snigger and wink at each other knowingly; and the older girls, glancing sideways, would blush and quicken their steps. Before long we came to know by sight such gaudy characters as Mexican Jennie, Leo the Lion, French Blanche, and Two-bit Lil; and sometimes they enlivened our recess periods with their noisy brawls.

My knowledge of their after-dark activities was sketchy and full of gaps. Mostly it was what I had gathered in whispered gossip on the school grounds. I might have asked questions of my mother, but I doubted whether she knew the answers, and besides, it seemed better to keep my curiosity secret. She had been sick a great deal lately and often had to stay in bed several days. I didn't want to add to her worries. Already I had heard her urging my father to send me away, "down below someplace," for a while; and that was a frightening prospect. I had never been separated from her and the very thought of it made me achingly homesick.

Then one afternoon in early March I heard the fateful decision. My father had arranged for me to go with Mrs. Loretta Riley to Rocky Ford. She was a "lady prospector," who lived up in Poverty Gulch. She also owned a melon ranch just outside Rocky Ford and had agreed to let me stay with her and go to school for a couple of months. I rebelled loudly, and threatened to run away, until she promised me a pony to ride back and forth to classes every day.

Kitty had never met Mrs. Riley, and seemed taken aback when she came to get me in her two-wheeled cart. She looked more like a man than a woman in her overalls and boots and canvas coat. To me she was the image of Leo the Lion, with short, brick-red hair; and her voice sounded like the shrill disaster siren at the Gold King Mine. Only the thought of the pony kept me from hiding in the tent and refusing to leave; and even Kitty seemed on the verge of changing her mind. Instead, she drew me aside and whispered, "Make the best of it, Mabs . . . maybe it won't be for long. Write me often, and if things get bad, we'll send for you."

We were starting down the other side of Carbonate Hill, just out of camp, when Mrs. Riley reached under the seat and pulled out a bottle of whisky. Then she handed me the reins and told me to drive. "But I don't know how," I objected; "they might run away . . ."

"You heard me!" she muttered. "Take them lines an' drive, like I tol' you, or I'll wring your neck!" There was no choice; before long she had passed out and her head was wabbling loosely against my shoulder.

But the worst blow was the discovery that Loretta had never owned a pony. Her only horses were the two we had driven down from Cripple Creek. Since the melon ranch was fully four miles from town, my attendance at school depended on Mrs. Riley's need of supplies. As it worked out, a hired man plowed the field; I cleaned the house and did most of the cooking; while Loretta lay, much of the time, in a drunken stupor on the sofa. I lived in dread of her waking because she would likely find fault and give me a "skunning." I wrote Kitty every day for a while, but I found that the letters had been opened and torn up; and no word ever reached me from home.

One morning when I happened to go to school, the principal called me to his office. He wanted to know why I had been absent so much. I told him that I had no way of getting there except when Mrs. Riley drove in from the ranch. "But it's the law that you attend school until you are fourteen," he said, looking concerned. "Mrs. Riley is aware of it; once before we had trouble with her." He pulled a chair over beside him at the desk. "Come, sit here. You look pale and thin," he said; "tell me what's wrong?" I glanced fearfully at the doorway. "No one will overhear," he added in a fatherly way; "you can trust me."

Somehow I managed, between sobs, to pour out the whole story. When I had finished, he wrote down my father's full name. "Make the best of it for a few days more," he said, putting his arm around me, "and don't worry." A great burden seemed to lift from my heart; I no longer felt alone in the world.

Loretta was different from that day on. I couldn't understand it. She stopped drinking and was kind; she even made me a new calico dress; and said that the hired man would take me back and forth to school every day. It was too good to be true; it was also too late. Within a few days an unexpected telegram came from my father telling her to put me on the next train for Colorado Springs, where he would meet me for the stage trip home. "It's all the doings of that nosy school principal," she said angrily. "First, he threatened to report me to the authorities; now he's gone and lied to your old man. I ought to horsewhip him!" But she did what my father had told her and soon I was peering through a car window, watching the last straggling cottages of Rocky Ford fly by.

I had been gone about four weeks but it seemed as if it had been a lifetime. When we reached the top of Carbonate Hill, the stage driver stopped to rest the horses and to give us a bird's-eye view of the District. It was late March and snow still covered the mountains. Cripple Creek lay three or four miles below us, a patchwork of mud and melting drifts. I hardly recognized it. Tents and car-roofed cabins spilled over the rim of the basin, pushed up Poverty Gulch and down past the hummocks of Mound City to string through Squaw Gulch and over Raven Hill.

The skyline of the camp also looked unfamiliar. Several two-story buildings, and many others with tall, false fronts, had gone up in the business section of Bennett and Myers avenues as far east as Fifth Street; substantial boarding and lodging houses clung to the sunny side of Carr Avenue. St. Peter's Catholic Church, with the "loftiest steeple in the world," had been completed, and perched securely on the summit of Golden Avenue Hill. "A sure test," my father said, "of the parishoner's religion!" Not far away, on the same rocky heights, the Golden School, due to open in the fall, had begun to take shape. Already plans were being made, according to my father, to build another down on Warren Avenue in the southwest part of camp. "Looks like they can't put 'em up fast enough," he added. "I've heard say that in the past few months the population has doubled from twenty-five hundred to five thousand!"

I sensed vaguely another baffling change—the absence of familiar mining camp sounds. In that rare atmosphere it was possible, on a clear day, to hear the brakes of the big freighters screeching down far-off mountain roads; and a bur-ro's braying at night would shatter sleep all over town. But now a kind of foreboding stillness hovered in the air. No rocks spilled over the dumps; no smoke belched from the huge mine-stacks; and although it was time for the day shift to end, no whistles blew, and no miners scuffed down the trail from tthe Anchoria-Leland. I asked my father in amazement what had happened. He said he thought my mother had told me about the strike that had been called soon after I went to Rocky Ford. But the letter had never reached me.

Then he and the other passengers began to talk about the critical situation in Colorado, and in the Cripple Creek District. Much of it was over my head, but now and then I understood enough to realize that times were bad and that President Cleveland was to blame. He had "gone along with the Wall Street gang," it seemed, and signed the repeal of the Silver Purchase Act, which restored the gold standard as a basis for repaying loans. The huge sums borrowed by western capitalists were to have been repaid in silver; and now it had dropped in value from a dollar and a quarter to sixty-five cents an ounce. It meant crashing banks and closed factories all over the country. Colorado, the largest producer of the nation's silver, faced economic disaster.

Mines in the state's great camps such as Leadville, Aspen and Silverton had shut down and thrown hundreds of men out of work. They naturally flocked to the fabulous gold-mining district where, they had been told, the big producers were running full blast and new discoveries were being made every day. But the truth was that production had been curtailed because of the panic.

The job hunters from other mining towns were considered inferior to the pioneer Cripple Creek miner. They came mostly from Italy and Middle Europe with lower standards of living and were willing to work for a pittance. When the Cripple Creekers realized what was going to happen to their jobs, they organized the Free Coinage Union and affiliated with the Western Federation of Miners. Their first act was to run all the "dagoes, bohunks and hunkies as well as chinks" out of town, with orders never to return. Then they demanded a minimum wage of three dollars for an eight-hour day. The mine owners refused and a walkout was called. "There's no

telling how long it'll last," my father said; "the public is on
the side of the miners and lots of money is pouring into the
union till to help 'em win."

I was on edge to ask him a question. I had often heard him
express his opinion about "joiners," folks who never felt secure
enough to "go it alone." At last I screwed up my courage and
asked if he were a member of the union.

"*Me?*" he said in astonishment. "Not on your life! I'm neither
a mine owner nor a miner. I'm a prospector and my own boss.
There's only one thing worth belonging to and that's my lodge.
I figure that a good Mason who believes in God Almighty is
going to do right by his fellow men."

We had turned the corner on Bennett Avenue, and all
conversation stopped. The sidewalks were lined with idle
people but no one waved or yelled at us the way they had
the night Kitty and I arrived from Florence little more than
a year before. The stage pulled up at the Palace Hotel on
Second Street and my father and I walked in silence up the
hill where we lived. As we approached our tent he told me to
go on in, explaining that he wanted to chop some wood before
dark.

Apparently my mother didn't hear me enter, and I leaned
against the door for a moment, dumbfounded by the sight
that met my eyes. She was sitting in the low rocking chair
by the stove, gently fondling an infant that lay whimpering
on a pillow in her lap. So this was why they wanted to get
rid of me, I thought bitterly, on the verge of tears! Resentment tore at me. There was no room for a new baby in the
family and so they sent me away with that cruel Loretta
Riley! Well, I'd show them! I'd never take care of it—never!

Then another idea suddenly struck me—maybe the baby
wasn't my mother's after all; perhaps some stranger had left
it on our doorstep. I had learned from schoolmates that the

story about storks' bringing babies was humbug; we knew from a woman's shape when she was "in the family way." But Kitty's figure had never changed, noticeably; it was as trim and slender as ever when I left for Rocky Ford. The notion that the infant didn't belong to her heartened me; and I tiptoed closer.

"Hello. I'm back," I said simply. "Papa's outside chopping wood."

She looked up, startled. "Mabs! How did you creep in so quietly, without making a sound?" She reached out and drew me nearer. "My, it's good to see you again! I wanted you home sooner but Mrs. Riley said you were fine, and Jonce wouldn't let me take you out of school. Then the letter came from the principal—oh, you poor child! Whoever would have thought she—and to think you never told us!" The infant stirred and she turned it tenderly on its stomach. "Take a peek," she said, lifting a corner of the blanket a bit. "I'll bet you never guessed that you were coming home to a little brother!"

I stiffened and pulled away. "What's his name?" I asked coldly.

"William Johnson, but I call him Billie." She must have sensed my disapproval. "Aren't you pleased? Here—touch the silky hair. . . ."

"When did you get him?" I asked, ignoring her question.

"Ten days ago," she said, covering the baby's face again. "Only a miracle saved him, but perhaps you're not old enough to understand. . . ."

"I'm older than you think, maybe. Tell me."

I could hear my father, still splitting wood and throwing the chunks on the pile. Not much time was left before sunset. Already it was dusky in the tent and I lit the lamp, put another stick in the stove, and sat down on the floor to watch the bright-red ashes sift through the grate. Kitty's voice

seemed far away at first, and I only half listened. It had been
snowing all day, before he was born, she began, and the
drifts were window-high. Jonce had carried in extra wood
to keep it dry, but even the roaring fire was no match for
the freezing wind that whined through the cracks. Before
long she was burning the chips in the bottom of the box,
and wondering what she would do when they were gone.

"Your father went to Beacon Hill, as usual, to work on his
claim," she continued; "any day he expected to come into
ore. But no sooner had he got there than he turned around
and came home. He had a premonition, like the one before
Nina died, that some fearful thing was about to happen."
She began to speak haltingly, as if not sure that she should
talk so intimately to me. "The first pains had started when
he reached here. I huddled in the bed trying to keep warm.
Oh, I was so sick—so sick I thought I would die. You see,
child, the little one was on the way—a woman never knows
how soon. It's hard to explain to you." Her voice had grown
husky and she coughed and cleared her throat. "I'll never
forget the way the wind howled and smoke blew down the
stovepipe, choking me; and the tent whipped until it seemed
as if it would tear loose from the ropes and be swept away.
It was the hand of Providence that brought your father home,
for my hour was not far—without him I would surely have
died."

She recalled, dimly, seeing Dr. Whiting washing his hands,
and feeling someone move the lukewarm flatirons from her
feet and put them on the blanket at the edge of the bed.
Then she must have fainted. "When I came to," she went on,
"and asked for the baby, the doctor told me it had been born
dead." He laid the tiny body aside on the bed while he
worked to save her life. "All of a sudden," she continued,
"there was a feeble wail, the unmistakable cry of a newborn

34

infant gasping for breath. His tender body had been laid, inadvertently, against one of the sadirons and the warmth had given him life." She turned away her face as if to hide the tears. "But a blister sears the full length of his back," she added, adjusting the pillow softly. "It will be a long time healing. He may carry the scar to his grave."

I moved closer and leaned my head on Kitty's knee. When I saw her pale, thin hands, and thought of her courage, and how near I had come to losing her forever, a tender, protective feeling stole over me. "Now you needn't worry any more," I said, groping for words. "I can help you take care of . . ."

"Billie," Kitty said, smiling, "but maybe you'd like better to call him Brother."

"Yes," I said, touching the tiny fingers, "I shall call him Brother."

4

The House on Golden Avenue

A M A R K E D change came over my father after Brother's birth; it seemed to give new meaning to his life. Once he had ridiculed men who caressed their wives in public but now he seemed unafraid to show his affection for Kitty. He often laughed and joked and sometimes, when he had pushed me too far with his teasing, he would catch me up in his arms suddenly and call me the "sugar on his apple dumpling." But most noticeable of all was the lightness in his step. When he set out mornings for the Little May, he walked with the confident stride of a person who expected to uncover a bonanza with the first round of shots, that very day!

Despite opinions of mining experts and other prospectors that pay dirt would never be found on Beacon Hill, he stubbornly persisted in working his claim. His friend W. S. Stratton, who discovered the Independence Mine on Battle Mountain only the year before, urged him to explore the Raven Hill or Bull Cliff areas farther east. "If a couple of drugstore clerks," Stratton said, "can find the Pharmacist vein where their hats fell when they tossed them in the air, you and your forked stick ought to have no trouble hitting a Golconda!" Even this rosy forecast went unheeded. "One of these fine days," he told Kitty, "I'll make every wiseacre in camp eat crow!" It looked as if his prophecy had come true when a few weeks later he brought home some gray, crystallized specimens and laid them on the table where Kitty was making biscuits. "Take a look at these," he said with a wide grin; "they're good for what ails you!"

She glanced up at him, annoyed, and pushed the rocks away. "Jonce—watch what you're doing—you're getting dirt on my breadboard!"

"Be careful, woman, how you treat that stuff," he said; "it's gold, fresh out of the Little May!"

"If that's gold," she replied airily, "then I'm Mrs. Vanderbilt! It looks like tin to me; even a child knows gold's yellow."

"Come over here a minute," he said, picking up one of the glistening rocks. "I'll show you a miracle!" And he scraped the silvery crystals on the red-hot stove lid. "Wait and see what happens."

Kitty wiped the flour from her hands impatiently and we both stood by, staring at the hocus-pocus. Suddenly, before our very eyes, the flakes began to curl and turn yellow. "Well, of all things," Kitty said, still a little skeptical. "Are you sure it's gold?"

"That's the form it comes in, up here in the District," he said importantly. "It's called sylvanite—a telluride of silver and gold. Just give me a few carloads of it," he went on, "and the Barbees are fixed for life!"

"How you talk, Jonce!" Kitty said, going back to her biscuit making. "With this terrible strike going on and on, you couldn't ship a load if all of Beacon Hill turned to gold. Who are *you?*"

"*Me?*" he fairly shouted at her. "I'm free, bound to no man, neither miners nor mine owners. Give me the ore; I'll find a way to get it to the mill in Florence if I have to carry it sack by sack!"

But the expected bonanza failed to materialize. The rich samples of ore had come from a small pocket; and the lode vein still eluded him. The discovery had proved, however, that Beacon Hill was not just a mound of sagebrush and granite debris. Other prospectors began to take an interest in the region, and promoters, knowing that my father was heavily in debt, made a few small offers. He finally let the claim go for a thousand dollars cash. When Kitty upbraided him for not hanging on and working it himself, he explained that it took big money to develop a mine and that he didn't have that kind of dough yet. "I'm primarily a prospector," he said, "with no capital to risk. Others who are better heeled will have to do the development. I'll make my stakes in my own way; don't you worry!"

It had been a long time since he had felt dollars jingling in his pocket and he behaved as if he were a millionaire. After celebrating with his friends, and paying his bills, he deposited the rest within easy reach, in Burnside's café. Kitty flew into a rage when she finally wormed it out of him.

"I'm tired of hearing your promises," she said bitterly, when he tried to pacify her, "and I'm sick of living in a tent. It's time you considered your family and found us a decent home. If you don't, you may open your eyes some day and find that we've gone!" She seldom threatened him so boldly, but it seemed to take effect. Not long afterwards he bought a house on West Golden Avenue.

It was a four-room place with unpainted sidings and a shingled roof, something rarely seen on the camp's makeshift buildings. The front was level with the ground but the back had to be stilted against the slope, and several steps led up to the kitchen porch. Beacon Hill could be seen from here and on a clear morning, the hazy mountains this side of Florence, twenty-five miles distant. My father told us there was talk of a railroad's being built pretty soon, connecting with the Denver and Rio Grande Railroad in the Arkansas Valley. "If that goes through," he said, "we could watch the train from our back door pulling around the curve of Raven Hill!"

Golden Avenue started in Old Town and trudged up and down across the lower slopes of Mineral Hill, a sizeable mountain distinguished by one solitary pine halfway to the top. It was believed at first that the mother lode would be found here and prospectors had left it pitted with innumerable holes and abandoned shafts. The street in most places was nothing more than a burro trail. It climbed steadily until it reached St. Peter's Catholic Church. Then the road narrowed and pitched sharply down the other side and continued westward past our house to join the well-worn highway to Pisgah graveyard.

No vehicles or pack animals ever ventured on the perilous West Golden Avenue Hill; miners going to and from work always avoided it as a short-cut. It was at its best in winter, from November to the last blizzard in May, when children of all ages flocked there to coast. Little girls bundled in heavy coats and bright stocking caps stopped on their way to school to make butterfly wings in the feathery snow. Older youngsters coasted over the ice-slick run on every imaginable device—barrel staves, scraps of sheet iron, dishpans and homemade sleds. And when the big boys yelled, "Clear the track!" everybody scrambled out of the way and watched breathlessly as the fearsome double-rippers flashed by, swaying, bouncing, striking sparks and coming to a stop not far from our house.

But for me, the immediate neighborhood turned out to be

equally fascinating. Except for Jim and Molly Letts, the child-less couple who lived next door, every house around was filled with children of various sizes and ages. My favorite family was the Baltzells with six, all under sixteen. They lived only two back yards down from us and I was there most of the time, especially when they were about to have supper.

Mr. Baltzell, like my father, was called Jonce. He had once been a successful pharmacist but was now bedridden with rheumatism; and his wife earned the living by taking in sewing. She had a beautiful, tranquil face and a heart that was as warm and roomy as her lap. Alice, the eldest, helped with the housework and was known as the best student in school. My father was always holding her up to me as an example of "fine young womanhood," which only drew me closer to Laura, the pretty, harum-scarum sister who was about my age.

On the corner below the Baltzells lived the Richard Roelofses. Their house was painted gray and among the nicest in camp. It looked out of place on Golden Avenue and, as if to make up for the mistake, the blinds on that side were kept drawn. Mr. Roelofs was the most intelligent and best-educated man in camp, my father said, and I always felt flattered when he called me over from play to chat with me. He was very proud of his six-month-old son, Dick. "Some day, when he has grown a bit more," he said seriously, "he will be out here yelling and playing hide-and-seek just as you are doing now. I wouldn't be surprised if you came to know him." Often he and my father walked up the hill together and they would sit for a while talking on our back steps. He never failed to ask about Brother's health, and Kitty said that he had the manners of a true gentleman.

But in my opinion, the most exciting gentleman on Golden Avenue was Joe Moore. He passed our house every day and must have known that I was sitting on the front porch but he

was too uppity to glance in my direction. He was a bartender
at Tom Lorimer's saloon and the leader of the Elks Band.
I often watched him marching at the head of funeral proces-
sions. His dark hair curled at the edge of his gold-braided
cap; his eyes were the color of lupines in midsummer and he
carried himself erect as though molded into his royal-purple
uniform. Once I almost swooned at a big Fourth of July
parade when his band struck up "Dixie Land." Oh, the way
his cornet swayed and glistened in the sun! How the golden
fringe on his epaulettes danced to the rhythm!

I often talked with Laura Baltzell about him but she said
he must be at least twenty-five and far too old for me. "You'd
better not let your mother find out that you have a crush on
a bartender," she warned; "you know how she hates saloon
people." When the burden of my smothered infatuation became too heavy to bear, I would wander up to the Lone Pine
Shaft on Mineral Hill and sit on the dump or lie in the tiny oat
patch I had planted at the side of our house and look up at the
blue sky and dream of Joe Moore and me walking hand in
hand through a lifetime of lovely green oats. I vowed that even
if Joe Moore never knew of my existence, I would always be
true to him.

While I mooned away the days in fantasy, trouble loomed
in the world of reality. I often caught snatches of the talk
among grownups. It was the middle of May and the strike had
not ended, but was getting more and more bitter. Charges
and countercharges flew back and forth between the mine
owners and the miners' union. Sometimes I couldn't make
out whether the District was in the throes of a labor war or
in the heat of an election campaign. One side was fighting
to keep the Western Federation of Miners from organizing
the camp and to oust the prounion Governor Waite. The
miners were even more determined to unionize the District

and establish a closed shop and a minimum wage of three dollars for an eight-hour shift.

Kidnapings and murders had become so common that the chief of police advised women and children to stay at home, indoors, after dark. Few families escaped hardship and poverty. We suffered more than most of the others because my independent father boasted of being a prospector and sympathized with neither side. Both had committed crimes in his opinion. His stand disqualified him for financial help from any source and we lived mostly on what food he could slip into his pockets from Burnside's free lunch counter. If my mother had known where the bread came from, she would have starved rather than eat it.

One morning while I was playing in our back yard, Richard Roelofs called to me from the alley. "Would you like to earn a dollar?" he asked, coming toward me. I grinned happily. To me a dollar was still a fortune. "Fine!" he said, handing me a key. "This will unlock my kitchen door. Nobody's there—Mrs. Roelofs has taken the baby and gone on a little trip. I'm not much of a housekeeper. Go in and wash up all the dirty dishes you can find. If you do a good job I'll give you the money when I get home this afternoon." The blinds were drawn, as usual, and I tiptoed through the rooms fearfully, half expecting a ghost to jump out at me. Then I rushed into the kitchen and closed the door to the rest of the house.

Only the promised dollar kept me from making a beeline for home when I saw the pile of dishes stacked on the table, and I wondered why men were so helpless as I scoured the stewpans and skillets. It seemed as though I'd never finish, and my stomach began to ache from hunger. But at last everything was clean and in order when Mr. Roelofs returned. He looked around carefully and examined the cupboards, and then, nodding with satisfaction, gave me a silver dollar.

"You've done a fine job." he said, patting my head. "I think you'll be a credit to your father and mother when you grow up."

The Roelofses moved away from the neighborhood shortly, and new people settled in the gray-painted house on the corner. Now the blinds were never drawn and lace curtains hung at the windows. Several young girls were in the family and there were parties almost every night. We could hear them singing and laughing long past bedtime. Molly Letts said, "They must be easterners"—her favorite description of people whose conduct mystified her—"to bang that piano like they do."

"I love to hear them playing the piano," Kitty replied. "I only wish we had one. Maybe then Golden Avenue wouldn't seem so ugly."

Not long afterwards, as if in answer to her wish, a delivery wagon backed up to our front door and two men began to unload a huge concert grand piano. Kitty refused to believe it was for us until they assured her that John Barbee had ordered them to pick it up at Burnsides' and take it to his house on Golden Avenue. It required a lot of pulling and pushing to get it through the narrow doorway and then set it up on the squat, fat legs. All the neighborhood children came in to watch the curious operation and stood around with Kitty and me long after the men had left, gazing at the monstrous instrument.

What a miserable object it was to crowd into our parlor! From the way it had been scratched and stained Kitty vowed it must have come through the Civil War. The ebony finish had faded into a muddy brown. Most of the yellowed keys were chipped and some were broken. We propped up the lid to see what was inside. Several of the hammers had lost their padding; strings were snapped and torn; crumpled sheet music lay scattered about. "Of all things," Kitty said, reaching for a piece and blowing off the dust. "Here's a song I used to know when I was a girl!" She held it on the rack and tried to pick out the notes on the piano, humming as she went along, "Where, oh where is my wand'ring boy to-night . . ." She stopped suddenly and wheeled around on the stool. "There's not a tune left in this old crate," she said. "It's not even fit for the woodpile. I hope Jonce isn't out any money for it!"

When he came home we were in for an even greater surprise. The delivery men had overlooked another musical instrument which he had acquired and he carried it under his arm. "Didn't know, I reckon, that your old man used to be quite a fiddler back in his sparkin' years," he said, laying a scuffed leather case on the kitchen table. Then he lifted the violin out carefully and began to plunk at the loose strings. "Needs a little tightenin' and polishin' but I've been told it's a good make an' has a right nice tone."

"You must have lost your senses, Jonce," Kitty said, looking aghast, "buying this cast-off junk from Burnside when we need food and clothes."

"Wait a minute," he told her. "Don't go off half-cocked. Burnside offered to wipe out all my debts for a triflin' interest in the Little Rosebud. I told 'im he was throwin' his money away but he said he knew what he was doin'. So I let 'm have it."

"What about the piano and this fiddle?"

"I'd had my eye on 'em for some time. Figured Mabs ought to begin takin' music lessons pretty soon," he said, almost shyly. "Burnside wasn't usin' 'em, said he was gettin' a new upright as soon as the railroad come in. I asked 'im what he'd take for the two of 'em, and I'll be damned if he didn't up and say I could have 'em for haulin' 'em away!"

44

"You're hopeless!" she said disgustedly. "Maybe I can use the piano for kindling wood. That's about all it's good for!" But somehow she didn't sound convincing and I felt that she had no intention of getting rid of it.

The next day she scrubbed and polished the concert grand from top to bottom, "to get the smell of whisky out," and she brought her treasured Paisley shawl from the trunk and draped it across a corner of the lid, "to give it an air of respectability." Then she dusted the shabby violin case and laid it well toward the back on the piano. And when the tuner came from Colorado Springs, in a week or two, to put in new strings and tune them, he swore that he had never heard a piano with a sweeter tone. "You've got a rare antique here," he said, as she paid him, "and some day it ought to sell for a lot of money!"

Life in the house on Golden Avenue became different and happier. I gave up going to the Baltzells' around suppertime and my father seldom spent his evenings downtown. I learned quickly to play by ear so that I was able to accompany Kitty when she sang the old songs, such as "In the Gloaming" and "Oh Promise Me." My father would try to follow along on the fiddle but he was more at home with the jigs and polkas he had known as a boy in Kentucky. My fingers would fly over the keys, hitting sour notes, trying to keep up with him. "Give it more thump," he'd call out, "and lay off that loud pedal—I can't hear myself play!" Sometimes he made me laugh so hard I fell from the stool. "Hush, Mabs," Kitty would say, "you'll disturb the neighbors and Molly Letts will accuse us of being easterners!"

But with the approach of summer we seemed to lose interest in the piano and fiddle and seldom played in the evenings. An endless round of excitement kept me out of doors until Kitty made me go to bed. There were games to quarrel over—

45

hopscotch, jacks and kick-the-can; and donkeys to race, rope to jump, stilts to make and walk on, and Kitty's long skirts to dress up in. When there were no picnics to Spring Creek or Box Canyon, I tagged after my father to Beacon Hill. I watched him laboriously windlassing the heavy buckets of waste, and often he let me climb down the ladder to the bottom of the shaft, to sit in the candlelight and sniff the pungent odor of freshly dug earth.

Now and then I wandered off to look for Indian paint-brush or mushrooms after a shower, or strolled to the top of the hill hoping to see signs of the new railroad that was being rushed up through Phantom Canyon from Florence. Then one day I heard the shriek of a locomotive whistle, high and thin and faraway, and ran back, stumbling, to tell my father. "It won't be long now," he said, sorting some ore and throwing it in a canvas sack. "Most any time now, one or the other of those steam horses'll be reaching camp. What a great day that'll be for Cripple Creek!"

5

The Race of the Iron Horses

I t was July 1, 1894. The sun seemed to sparkle brighter than usual and the air tingled with excitement. Flags decked Cripple Creek from Poverty Gulch to Freeman's Placer, from Old Town to the flats above the Broken Box ranch. A celebration had been planned that promised to make even the Glorious Fourth pale in significance. For it was the day that the first train was due to pull around Gold Hill into camp.

A turning point in the District's growth had been reached. From this time on, wrote the editor of the *Weekly Crusher*, Cripple Creek would no longer be known as a crude, uncivilized outpost shut off from the rest of the world. She was about to take her place as Colorado's most famous city. The mayor foretold that the population would increase by leaps and bounds. Hundreds of homes would have to be built and fine business blocks would line Bennett, Carr and Myers avenues. Rumors had spread that a department store "as big as Daniels and Fisher's down in Denver" was going to be erected and that ladies would have a wide choice of dresses, coats and materials without having to wait for catalogs from

Chicago. Molly Letts, our next-door neighbor, hoped that Roberts' Grocery would get in step and carry fancy canned goods, fresh fruit and a variety of meats. "I'm clean stumped," she said, "tryin' to think of things for my old man's lunch bucket; and I've ate so much sowbelly myself that I'd be ashamed to look a hog in the eye!"

But my father was unimpressed by such speculations. He agreed that thousands of newcomers would flock to camp. "But they ain't going to build fine houses 'til they strike it rich, and then it'll be down in the Springs." All the District wanted of a railroad, he said, was cheap haulage so that the mines could ship low-grade as well as high-grade ores to the mills at a profit. "When that happens," he declared, "it will signal the beginning of the greatest decade in the history of gold mining!"

Now the momentous event was at hand. But it was not going to be the Midland Terminal's huge Mogul that we would see down yonder on the flats. Cripple Creekers had known for several weeks that the Midland Terminal couldn't win the race but they never stopped betting on it. After all, it was the most logical route into the District. The broad-gauge Colorado & Southern, running up Ute Pass to the Western Slope, came within eighteen miles north at Divide, the summit of the continental watershed. This road had incorporated the Terminal spur in 1892, at the start of the gold rush, but construction failed to get under way because of the panic threatening the country.

Meanwhile, traffic bound for the District continued to be hauled over the main stage route from the transfer point at Divide. It was unsatisfactory, slow and costly; and the future of the camp looked dark. Without adequate transportation, development of the rich gold field would come to a standstill. Everything hung in the balance until the coming of the railroad which, of course, would be the Midland Terminal.

Finally in early summer of 1893 sufficient capital was raised to start grading for a narrow-gauge line, the kind that had proved successful in reaching other mountainous camps in the West. Cripple Creekers were jubilant and mining stocks skyrocketed when it was announced that the road would be ready to operate by the following July Fourth. Work pushed ahead at phenomenal speed and some were offering odds that if that rate kept up, the girls at the Old Homestead would be feasting on Christmas turkey brought in by Midland Terminal express. Then a shocking discovery came to light. Nine miles of track had been laid before it was revealed that traffic would still have to be transferred at Divide unless a third rail were added to the Colorado & Southern's equipment. The staggering cost was out of the question, but the alternative of abandoning the undertaking was equally forbidding.

Everybody in camp was up in arms at the railroad's fumbling leadership and the mayor appointed a committee to seek elsewhere for a solution to the transportation problem. My father and his friends talked about it so much that I came to know the story word for word. The Denver & Rio Grande, it seemed, had already been considering the feasibility of running a narrow-gauge spur into the District from Florence, the closest connection thirty miles south in the Arkansas Valley. Cripple Creekers gave the idea only halfhearted support. The distance was too great and the intervening country presented problems impossible for engineers to meet. But the railroad's promoters, led by David C. Moffatt, one of Colorado's highly respected silver barons, were not dissuaded by the prophets of failure. They began quietly to incorporate and make plans for the venture.

When the Midland people got wind of it, they lost no time

in raising additional capital and announced shortly that surveys had begun for a different, broad-gauge route to the District. The new roadbed would lead through wild, precipitous territory, skirting the northwest slopes of Pike's Peak. Several high wooden trestles would have to be built, including a pair of twin bridges and one tunnel four hundred and fifty feet long. Even so, the company said, it was expected to complete the project as originally scheduled by the Fourth of July. Crews labored night and day. No attempt was made to put up stations at the small settlements along the way; boxcars on sidings served as ticket offices and waiting rooms. Such dynamic courage and determination won back public confidence. Once again miners coming off shift crowded around the bulletins posted on saloon windows to note the Midland's daily progress and to gamble hundreds of dollars on their hunches. They seemed to have lost sight of what was going on down by the Arkansas River.

One morning at breakfast late that fall my father glanced over the *Weekly Crusher*. "Well, I'll be damned," he said. "Looks like we're in for a race of the iron horses!"

"What do you mean," Kitty asked.

"Dave Moffatt says that grading is well advanced for that new railroad into the District. Humph—claims it'll be in operation by next Independence Day. Says she'll be a narrow gauge connecting with the three-rail Denver & Rio Grande—they're calling it the Florence & Cripple Creek. . . ."

"Who's Dave Moffatt?" Kitty interrupted, peeking over his shoulder at the headlines.

"He's the fellow who made a mint of silver in Aspen and Leadville," he said, getting up and taking his corduroy coat from a nail on the wall. "But it won't take 'im long to lose it, feeding the hungry maw of a railroad!"

After he had gone to work I read the piece aloud to Kitty

while she dressed Brother. It went on to tell that the promoters had decided to run their line over the shortest and quickest route—directly north through Phantom Canyon. The engineers were aware of the hazards but these were offset by certain advantages. Part of the track, the story read, could be laid on the hard gravel bottoms of Eight Mile Creek, the little brook with a long name, that was dry most of the year, and a channel at one side would take care of the high waters in spring.

"Imagine," Kitty said, "riding through Phantom Canyon in a train! We'll take the trip someday, just to see what it looks like in the light."

The frenzied struggle of the two railroads became the talk of the town and as the weeks passed, people went wild in an orgy of betting. Scandals, robberies and murders gave way in the news to speculations on which railroad would be the first to reach camp. A plum richer than a bonanza dangled before the competing roads. The monopoly of the District's lush shipping and traffic business would fall into the hands of the winner. They were running neck and neck much of the time, with the narrow gauge easily overcoming its handicap of extra mileage on the fairly level stretch before reaching the canyon.

But setbacks frequently confounded the gamblers. The Midland battled against gravel slides and cave-ins, while the Florence & Cripple Creek repaired burned trestles and widened channels where Eight Mile Creek had already begun to show her temper. And as winter deepened, blizzards assailed them both, howling through the passes and canyons and piling high drifts where rails were to be laid. These delays and others kept Cripple Creekers in a continuous state of betting fever.

Sometimes in spring when the snow was about gone, I went with my father as far as Beacon Hill, and then climbed to the top of Straub Mountain, not far beyond. From there I could see the Wilbur Loop of the Florence & Cripple Creek winding like a snake from the mouth of Phantom Canyon, coiling around the hills between as if getting ready to strike at Alta Vista, only a few miles distant. And on warm Sundays the Baltzell girls and I would go picnicking to the summit of Hoosier Pass to watch the Terminal engines switching cars back and forth, or emerging in a cloud of vapor from Waters Tunnel.

The stages were already meeting the train at Midland, a tiny settlement at the far side of the tunnel. In another two weeks passengers would transfer at Gillett for the steep wagon ride over Tenderfoot Hill, four miles from camp. This town, one of the earliest in the District, had been named for W. K. Gillett, a leading spirit behind the new railroad. He proposed to make it the metropolis of the area, chiefly because of its location in a valley of Upper Beaver Park on the only level stretch of ground anywhere around. But the idea never took fire. Miners wanted to live closer to their work and they were not concerned about the lay of the land. Besides, Cripple Creek was celebrated, even then, as "the greatest gold-mining camp on earth" and the people meant to keep their townsite.

The Midland directors were well aware of the rich discoveries that had been made in the southeast region, and new strikes were being reported almost daily. At the risk of losing the race, a fourteen-mile detour was charted around Bull Cliff and Battle Mountain, to tap such producers as the Pharmacist, Stratton's Independence, the Strong and Portland mines. It was to back into the bustling new camp of Victor, some ten thousand feet high, to let off passengers, then coast in and out among the mines on Raven Hill. After a brief stop at Anaconda in Squaw Gulch it would cut over Gold Hill and cross the high trestle at Poverty Gulch to pull up at the head of Bennett Avenue, where its fine brick depot would stand in Cripple Creek. The company reaffirmed its aim to reach there by the Fourth of July.

Many townspeople were skeptical and the odds in the saloons might have shifted to the Florence & Cripple Creek if that road hadn't run into serious trouble. As spring approached, melting snows sent muddy torrents down Eight Mile Creek and flash floods washed away several trestles. Another roadbed, high above the stream, had to be blasted from the cliffs. At last, after a few weeks of good weather and several miles of easy grading, the narrow gauge snatched the lead and pulled to a victorious finish on July first, three days ahead of schedule.

Cripple Creekers were at such a pitch of excitement that they apparently forgot all about the Midland Terminal languishing on a siding just over Tenderfoot Hill in Gillett, and facing still another six months before reaching the goal. The F. & C. C. train was expected around noon and I ran to our back porch every few minutes to watch for puffs of smoke and listen for the whistle. As the hour neared, the air quivered with discordant sounds. I could hear the Anaconda Drum Corps practicing rolls and ruffles behind the City Hall, and the Elks Band warming up cornets, horns and tubas down by Koch's Opera House on Myers Avenue. A merry-go-round, in camp early for the Fourth, had put up its big yellow tarpaulin on the flats, not far from the railroad yards. Now the hand organ was swinging around and 'round, playing "Daddy Wouldn't Buy Me a Bow-Wow, Bow-Wow!" It seemed to me that Kitty was taking forever to get dressed.

"Don't worry," she said, "we'll start in plenty of time to see the sights on Bennett Avenue. Jonce promised to meet us in front of Burnside's at eleven. I'll give him the dickens if he's been showing off that baby in the saloon. Come now," she said, picking up her skirts, "let's hurry!"

My father wasn't in sight, so we strolled up Bennett Avenue to look in the store windows, stopping occasionally to watch the camp's society ladies wearing the latest styles and driving in Welty Bros. shiniest buggies. I glanced appraisingly at Kitty. She was old, I thought, almost thirty, but still pretty. She had on the black basque and skirt with the taffeta lining which she hadn't worn since the day it was bought in Kansas City. Her figure looked trim and slender and her feet appeared tinier than ever in her new patent leather shoes with cloth uppers. When I saw the glint of her auburn hair below her toque and the sparkle in her wide, dark eyes, I thought her far more attractive than any of the prim, aloof women in the carriages.

My father was waiting for us when we walked back down the street. He was holding Brother in his arms and grinning. "The boy made quite a killing," he said. "He didn't want to leave—like to never got 'im away!"

"I told you not to take him into the saloon!" Kitty said, as anger flushed her cheeks. "Sometimes I think you haven't a grain of common sense. He'll get there soon enough without your help!"

"Now, now, old lady," he said, "no harm was done. Don't be such a stick-in-the-mud." He turned to Brother, "Show mamma what you got in your pockets."

The next thing I knew, money was jingling and falling all over the sidewalk, gold coins, dollars, two-bit and four-bit pieces which had spilled from Brother's pockets. "Where did he get all that?" Kitty asked, stooping to pick up what she could. "You'd better take it back—right where it came from!"

"Not on your life," he replied. "The lad won it all at faro— it's his and nobody's goin' to take it away from him!"

Kitty shot him a quick glance, but all she said was, "Jonce, you've had too much to drink again. Why do you always spoil things for me by getting drunk?"

It was noon by the time we reached the flats, and still the train hadn't come. The big crowd waited patiently with people craning their necks as if expecting to see the engine appear at any moment. But when one o'clock came and then two, it began to look as if maybe there wasn't going to be any train after all. Folks began to amble in little groups to the brow of Gold Hill from where the trestle above Anaconda could be seen. My father went back uptown and Kitty, Brother and I sat down on a pile of ties near several old-timers who were talking about their early-day experiences. Most of them had packed in from Florence or over Cheyenne Mountain from the Springs. Others had tramped through passes of the Mosquito range from Aspen and Leadville to catch the stage at Florissant. Brother soon went to sleep in Kitty's arms, and she sat quietly, as though taking in every word while they told of the scarcity of food and cabins, and the terrible epidemics that swept through camp. But she never let on that she too had gone through it all.

"Times're goin'a be lots better now," a man they called Crapper Jack said, winking at Kitty. "Yes sir, it won't be long 'til you pretty gals'll be rustlin' down Bennett Avenue in taffety underskirts, just like they're doin' on Sixteenth Street in Denver!"

Kitty blushed and stiffened self-consciously and acted as though she were about to get up and go away. Then, all of a sudden, the watchers on Gold Hill began to run down toward the flats, and a boy near us started jumping and screaming. "She's comin'—she's comin'," he yelled. "I heard the whistle over there." He pointed toward Anaconda. "It tooted three times—a real locomotive whistle!"

I squinted and shaded my eyes, looking for smoke toward the southern hills, but not even a cloud marred the summer sky. "You got bats in your belfry, kid," somebody called out. "That was a woodchuck's whistle!" And the crowd burst into a roar of nervous laughter.

A tall, skinny fellow who, they said, was the driver of the Cheyenne Mountain Stage, stood up, stretched, and started rolling a cigarette. "Guess that damned woodchuck fooled all them guys up there on the hill too," he said, spitting out a shred of tobacco. "Well, here's one hombre that don't give a goddamn if she never shows up. The camp ain't goin'a be the same when steam horses takes over. No piddlin' narrow gauge apantin' in here'll ever hold a candle to them big Concords aswingin' down Bennett Avenue to the Palace, with the sixes agallopin' an' sweatin', an' folks in the street acheerin' an' wavin' their hats, an' scramblin' fit to kill to git outta the way. God, what a sight!" Nobody said a word and he dug into his pants pocket and fished up a big silver biscuit watch. "Hell's bells!" he ripped out, turning to go. "Time to hitch up my fours. Got a feelin' they ain't agoin' to be many more stage trips to Lil' Ol' Lunnon. Well . . . so long, folks," he shouted back as he hurried away to the stable.

No sooner had he left than the mine sirens and whistles from one end of the District to the other set up such a screeching and moaning that shivers ran down my legs. Everybody started running toward the platform. Kitty clutched Brother in one arm and with the other held up her trailing skirts while I tore on ahead to find a good place to watch. This time, the train was really coming. I could hear the wheels clicking and the engine puffing. In a moment it would be in sight, and the next thing I knew it would pull to a stop right in front of Kitty and me!

What bedlam broke loose! Hysterical men and women

56

shrieked and yelled and hugged each other for joy. Bombs and pistol shots added to the pandemonium. Dogs howled and terrified horses snorted and reared and started to run away. A buggy tipped over and spilled several screaming society ladies on the dusty ground. Policemen were helpless against the pushing throng. "Get off the track, folks!" they shouted. "Step back, step back . . . watch out for cinders . . . she's acomin'!"

The Anaconda Drum Corps boomed and rub-a-dub-dubbed and the piccolos trilled "Ta-ra-ra-boom-der-é!" while the Elks struck up "She'll Be Comin' 'round the Mountain" with the people joining in.

"She'll be comin' 'round the mountain
When she comes;
She'll be comin' 'round the mountain
When she comes;
We can hear that engine pantin'
And the passengers a-chantin'
She'll be comin' 'round the mountain
When she comes!"

The locomotive crept slowly, cautiously, along the glistening new tracks, blowing the whistle continually and ringing the bell. But impatient greeters paid no attention. They jumped on the cowcatcher and clung to the slender, diamond-hooded smokestack. Boys climbed on the cab and leaped to the tender from where they tossed chunks of coal into the crowd, as souvenirs. We watched the dignitaries—mayors, railroad directors and big mine owners—who were the first to make the trip, gather around David C. Moffatt as he drove a golden spike into the last rail. After they had left for the banquet at the Palace Hotel, the onlookers moved in closer. I trailed with other children through the coaches and we bounced on the green plush seats, drank up the ice water and tried in vain to open the locked lavatory doors.

A sudden commotion drew us all scampering outside to the platform. The conductor had opened the baggage car; somebody was handing out presents from the townspeople and farmers, it was said, in the Arkansas Valley. "Hold on there!" the conductor ordered, when some of the older boys tried to rush in ahead. "No need to be greedy—enough's here for everybody in camp!"

There were potted petunias, geraniums, begonias, and fuchsias; and fresh vegetables of every description; and gunny-sacks heavy with oranges, June apples and bananas. Then a bugle sounded and it was announced that the city of Rocky Ford had sent a special gift to Cripple Creek's children —watermelons! After they had been stacked in piles, the youngsters were turned loose to eat their fill. In our eagerness we cracked them open with rocks or dropped them splashing on the ground. We buried our faces in the luscious red pulp, swallowing seeds and all, oblivious of everything else, stopping only long enough for a quick, urgent dash behind the stack of railroad ties where Kitty and I had waited for the train to come.

It was getting late; the setting sun had already left the flats in shadow and it had grown chilly. But few were in the mood to go home. The mayor had decreed beforehand that events usually scheduled for the night of July Fourth would take place, instead, on the evening of Cripple Creek's greatest day, when the first train arrived to link her with the outside world. There would be dancing on the sidewalks of Bennett Avenue to Joe Moore's incomparable band, followed by a display of fireworks such as the camp had never witnessed before— bursting flower baskets, skyrockets of every hue, spinning wheels and Roman candles.

I begged Kitty to stay downtown but she said it was time Brother went to bed and reminded me that the best view was from our back porch. Just then the merry-go-round began to play its one tune, "Daddy Won't You Buy Me a Bow-Wow?" and I blubbered that I was the only child who hadn't ridden on the painted horses, But Kitty wasn't impressed. The merry-go-round, she said unfeelingly would be there until after the Fourth. "Stop pestering, Mabs," she scolded. "Your father is probably home now waiting for his supper."

We hadn't gone far when Jim Letts caught up with us and offered to carry Brother. He was much nicer than Molly, I thought, and good-looking too, with his wavy, light-brown hair and blue eyes. There had been times when I imagined he was a bit sweet on my mother but she kept him at a distance. He said that the fellows downtown were betting that the narrow-gauge road would go bankrupt in a year's time."

"For goodness' sake!" she exclaimed. "Why would they say that?"

"Because it was built in too much of a hurry. All Moffatt and his crowd wanted was to beat the Midland Terminal in here. The grades are too steep, it's said, and some of the curves are so sharp there're bound to be accidents."

"Well," Kitty said, "there are always folks who look on the black side of everything. It strikes me they ought to be thanking their stars that we've got any kind of railroad this soon!"

We had reached our house only to find it dark; my father hadn't come home. I lit the kitchen lamp and got kindling. After we had eaten and Brother was in bed, Kitty and I huddled in coats on the back steps for a long time, watching the thrilling fireworks. Every few moments she'd peer down the alley and listen, waiting to hear my father's footsteps. Then, all of a sudden, she said, "I don't think one train or a dozen coming to this miserable place is going to make it any more

59

bearable. A mining camp is a man's world; it means a hard, lonely life for a woman."

The last Roman candle had sputtered and died; only the stars twinkled in the darkened sky, and the strains of "Home, Sweet Home" floated up from Bennett Avenue. Cripple Creek's glorious day had come to an end. But not for my father; he was still celebrating, apparently, somewhere in one of the street's murky saloons. We didn't see him until late the next morning. Kitty was about to give him a sound berating, but held back when he said he'd been to Anaconda to see the wreck. The train, on its return to Florence, had tipped over from a curved trestle and the coaches had fallen into a ravine, killing one man and injuring several others, "just as folks had predicted."

6

The Father of Beacon Hill

H E had been called the "Father of Beacon Hill" ever since his first discoveries in that generally discounted area. But his failure to strike anything more after almost two years of tramping over the ground with his divining rod caused him to shy away from the title, saying jokingly that he must have "sired a bastard." Other prospectors, some of whom he had once grubstaked, were having better luck. Finally he took a lease on the Orizaba. But it was the same old story; the forked stick had gone dead on him.

Now he was pointed out as a superstitious fool to put so much faith in the black art of a willow switch. But still nothing seemed to shake his confidence. Kitty declared that she was at her wit's end. "You've got to do something soon," she told him, "or we'll starve. Why don't you try to find a job in the mines? You'll never get anywhere with that stick!"

"It's not the stick," he said, "it's me—the magnetism in me seems to have run dry. I guess you're right—I'll see De Lavergne about putting me on at the Raven."

But he never went near the Raven to look for work. Instead, he found a cleaner piece of baling wire, one that was entirely free of rust, and he twisted the center and bent the ends so that they fitted precisely into the palm of his hand. He would leave the house at sunrise and often not return home for supper. Sometimes I would be wakened late at night by Kitty's scolding and accusing him of trying to escape his responsibilities by drinking and gambling with "that no-account crowd at Oscar Burnside's saloon."

Something even more serious than his drinking had begun to trouble her. Occasionally she talked with me about it. For the past year he had suffered from a persistent cough owing to what she called "inflammation of the bronchial tubes." She had pleaded with him to go and see Dr. Whiting but he refused. "He won't even let me rub his chest with hot sweet oil and turpentine," she complained, "and he knows that once it cured Molly Letts of pneumonia." Then matters reached a crisis and I began to suspect that something far more dreadful than a cough ailed him.

The four o'clock whistles had blown and I had gone for chips to start the fire for supper. It had been a rare, sunny afternoon for February, with little snow in the hills, a good day for prospecting. Already Pisgah's long shadow had begun to spread through camp. Kitty said we would eat early, for it was doubtful whether Jonce would be home until late. She had scarcely spoken when I heard him coming up the alley, coughing the hard, dry, body-wracking cough that always frightened me. "That's funny," Kitty said, "sounds like your father. I wonder if something's wrong—run see!"

I found him slumped against a woodshed, gasping for breath. His face was drawn and pale. I took hold of his arm, trying to help him. "I'm all right now," he said, pushing me aside and making his way slowly into the yard. He walked with a stoop, his hands clasped behind his back, his eyes fixed on the ground as though still searching for the elusive float. Faded denim overalls bloused over the tops of his heavy boots. The pockets of his corduroy coat bulged with empty sample sacks; his shirt, as usual, was unbuttoned at the neck. Kitty ran down the steps to meet him. "Here, give me your lunch bucket," she said anxiously. "How many times have I begged you not to hurry up the hill? It always makes you have a spell of coughing. Why can't you remember?" But he went on into the house without speaking.

Molly Letts came over to the fence. "I'd be worried crazy if he was my man," she said. "Why don't you make him go see Whiting? I'll bet anything he's got the miners' consumption——"

"Don't talk like that," Kitty flashed at her angrily; "you've no right to say such a thing!" It was considered a disgrace for anyone to have lung trouble, and a family would keep it secret until the day of death. "It's a bad cold he has," Kitty went on. "It hangs on and on. You know how stubborn Jonce can be; he wouldn't hear to getting a doctor just for a cold!" She sent me inside to look after Brother, but I overheard what she said to Molly. "I'll thank you to be careful not to speak that way in front of Mabs."

He was lying down in the bedroom with the door half closed. Kitty covered him over with a blanket and sat at the kitchen table to pare some apples for frying. All of a sudden she pushed the bowl of peelings aside and buried her face in her apron. She made no sound but I knew she was crying. I wanted to say something to comfort her but couldn't think of the words. I put my hand gently on her shoulder for a moment and then picked up the paring knife to finish the apples.

Kitty always swore that it was an act of Providence when Dr. Whiting came by that night, "just to ask John's advice about a claim he was thinking of buying." But Molly Letts told me later, in deep secrecy, that she had gone herself to ask the doctor to come because she was worried plum sick. He stayed for a long time asking my father questions and examining his chest and then he reached in the black satchel he always carried and gave him some medicine, warning him at the same time that he would have to stay in bed for several days and let the womenfolks wait on him. Kitty followed him to the door and whispered something in his ear. "Might be a good idea, John," he called back, "to let Kitty rub your chest with hot sweet oil and turpentine—won't do you a bit of harm!" After he had gone, my father said sleepily, "That's funny, he never mentioned what it was he wanted to ask me about— nice fellow, Doc——"

Jonce rebeled against restraint of any kind and refused to stay in bed "like a woman," and let Kitty and me wait on him. But he agreed to loaf around the house and take it easy for a few days. He liked Dr. Whiting as much as he had ever liked any doctor, he said, but that didn't mean that he had to take his physic. Even so, he grew more cheerful and his cough seemed improved. He even joked with me and talked about his plans to send me away to school someday so that I could have a fine education. But best of all, he promised Kitty to stop drinking and to stay home evenings and practice on the fiddle.

I always knew that he must have many friends downtown but except for a few like Richard Roelofs and W. S. Stratton, he seldom mentioned them. Now, as the days of his sickness stretched into weeks, visitors crowded our parlor. I never heard anything but their first names—Speck, Chip, Bert, Griff, and an old fellow he called Blind Tom. "I guess there ain't a man in camp's more respected than John," Jim Letts told

Kitty; "even the boys that don't agree with him about Beacon Hill speak well of him. He's known as "Honest John" up and down Bennett Avenue because he's never broken his word and would share his last crust. Take Blind Tom there—before he lost his eyes in that mine explosion, John grubstaked him when I'll warrant he didn't have enough food for you and the kids."

"I never heard him speak of helping out anybody," Kitty said, trying to remember, "but then, Jonce would be the last to speak about such things."

When W. S. Stratton came Kitty left the parlor door partly open so that we could hear his stories. He was a nervous, high-strung man, with snow-white hair, long mustache and deep-set, blue eyes. People said he was "self-contained, silent and solitary." But he talked and laughed freely when he was with my father, recounting his early experiences as carpenter and prospector. One time, he said, he and another carpenter named Dave Lee were building the station house for the Cog Road on top of Pike's Peak. He swore he had never seen such wind and rain. "It was all we could do," he declared, "to hang on. Thunderheads were so thick I'll be doggoned if we didn't nail four feet of the roof on a cloud and never knew it 'til a week later when the sun came out for a few minutes."

Again he told about a prospecting trip he and Dave took over in the San Juan country. They drew straws to see who would do the cooking and agreed that the one who got the job could quit at the first complaint. "Dave was it," Stratton said, "and Lord, how he hated even to boil water! But things went along pretty well for quite a while and then he scotched the works by dumping the can of salt in the sourdough. I bit off a hunk and swallowed it before I knew what was up. I coughed and gagged until I damn near puked. Dave hadn't touched the stuff. 'What'd you put in the bread?' I asked. He looked kinda sheepish and grinned. That made me mad as the devil and I started to give 'im a cussing out when all at once I remembered our bargain. 'It's very tasty,' I said, 'I like it this way. Don't mind, do you, if I help myself to some more?'"

"He's a smart one," Kitty said under her breath. "No wonder he's the richest man in the District—he knows how to hang onto a good thing!"

But sometimes he gave my father serious advice. "If you ever discover a lode worth a hundred thousand dollars," he said once, "take a tip from me—sell it." And he went on to tell how a couple of years back he had given an option on the Independence for $125,000. He had wished a thousand times ever since that the holders had taken it up. "Then I could have retired from mining and lived on my income," he added, brushing his neat mustache with his bony fingers. "Too much money's not good for any man. I have too much and it's not good for me. A hundred grand is enough for anybody who wants to be free from the bitterness and heartache that come with great wealth. It's been the ruin of many a young fellow," he said, getting up to leave. "I would be doing a dear one of mine a positive injury to leave him more money than he is able to take care of."

"It's usually millionaires that talk that way," Kitty said in a whisper. "There's no danger of Jonce ever having to take his advice!"

Soon my father felt so much better that he talked of going to work again. Kitty tried to dissuade him but he argued that it was only a short distance to the shaft from Elkton where the train stopped. His long sessions with Stratton had revived his spirits and he spoke of striking it rich as though it were already an accomplished fact. Then one evening in March everything changed from hope to sudden despair.

A blizzard had been raging all day riffling the shingles and piling high drifts against the house. Inside, it was warm and cozy with the coals glowing cheerfully behind the isinglass in the parlor stove. After putting Brother to bed Kitty picked up her basket of fancywork and moved her low rocker over by the lamp. My father had pulled a chair close to me at the piano and taken his violin from the case. "Give me that A note," he said, tightening the strings. Again and again I sounded it while he listened until the tone rang true.

At last he crossed his legs, straightened his shoulders and with a confident, downward sweep of the bow, broke into "Old Dan Tucker." My hands were not quick enough to keep up with him. He played with his whole body, his head swaying from side to side, his free leg swinging up and down and the fiddle dancing under his touch. To save me, I couldn't find the right chords, and struck frantically, hitting sour notes and flatting others. "Come, come, Mabs," he sang in rhythm, "this ain't a funeral march. Put more zing and zoom into the base and for God's sake cut out those discords!" I pressed so hard on the loud pedal that I couldn't hear either me or the fiddle. "Mabs, Mabs!" Kitty screamed, "not so much noise; you'll wake up Billie!"

He laughed so hard he couldn't play. After catching his breath he began to tune up the fiddle again. "Let's try another," he said, "and don't get so rattled. This will be an easy one; it's a little ditty that Lutie, my black mammy, used to sing when I was knee-high to a grasshopper. She called it 'The Monkey's Wedding,' and made it up, I'll swear, as she went along. You'll catch on, Mabs," he said encouragingly, "once you get the beat." And he lilted the words in a soft southern twang as the bow flew over the strings.

67

"What do you think the bride was dressed in?
A white gauze veil with a green glass breastpin,
Red shoes quite interestin'
She was quite a belle!

"Oh, the bridegroom blazed in blue shirt and collar
And black silk stock that cost a dollar,
Long false whiskers the fashion to foller,
He cut a monstrous swell!

"And what do you think he had for a fiddle?
An ole banjo with a hole in the middle,
A tambourine and a worn-out griddle
Oh, he was——"

A sudden fit of coughing seized him, the first he'd had for many days. He leaned far over, clutching his throat and choking for breath. It seemed as though he would never stop. His face turned purplish red and beads of perspiration stood out on his forehead. Kitty ran to the kitchen to bring a dipper of water. "Drink some quick," she said, patting his back. "Maybe it's bad for you to strain your lungs singing, maybe . . ." She looked helpless and scared, as if not knowing what to do or say. I took the fiddle from his lap and put it on the piano.

"Maybe . . . maybe . . . maybe," he gasped, without glancing at her. "Maybe I'd be better off dead, too." Then he reached for the violin and laid it gently in the leather case. I never saw him take it out again.

It was hours before I could go to sleep that night. Outside, the wind thrummed a mournful dirge in the telegraph wires. "It's not a cold your father has," it seemed to say; "it's something far worse and you will live forever in the shadow of disgrace!" Tears wet my pillow; pity and shame tore at my heart. And I resolved that I must never let on to Kitty that I knew what ailed him.

"You look peekity," she said the next morning at breakfast. "What's the matter—don't you feel well?"

"The storm scared me; I don't know why," I said, trying to avoid her searching eyes. My father was still asleep; she went over and closed the bedroom door.

"I've wanted to talk with you for a long time about Jonce," she began, coming back to the table, "but you were not old enough to understand or to keep things to yourself. Now you must listen, Mabs, and promise that no matter what happens—I mean how sick he gets—you will never look down on him. Promise?" It seemed as though she had read my very thoughts and I squirmed with guilt as I crossed my heart.

"He may not be as refined a gentleman as Richard Roelofs," she went on, "but he was well born. You heard what Jim Letts said about him being respected for his honor—that's something far more important than manners. Don't forget that ever!" She poured herself another cup of coffee and stirred in a little sugar. "Honor is a real mark of quality," she added, "and shows up a person's breeding."

Aunt Ella in Kansas City had told her much about his family. "Jonce is so closemouthed about such things," Kitty said, "you'd think all his forebears were bandits!" His father, Elias, fought in the Revolutionary War and later settled on a big plantation in Kentucky where he owned many slaves. "He was a real blue blood," Kitty continued, "and if Jonce had a mind to, he could claim kinship with some of the best families in the South. One of them, in Louisville—I forget the name—was famous for its beautiful women." She got up and listened at the door. "I wish your father took more pride in his connections," she went on. "For the sake of you and Billie he shouldn't pretend to be an ignorant nobody."

Aunt Ella claimed it was fighting in the Civil War that ruined him. He was a brave soldier—hot-blooded and fearless.

"He was never the same when it ended; seemed restless," Ella said, "alway bent on adventure."

"Was that where he got those scars on his shoulder—in the war?" I asked, remembering how often I had begged him to tell me the story of how he had been wounded; but he had ignored my questions.

Kitty nodded. "He would never talk about his courageous deeds," she went on, "but I heard from your aunt that he had saved another's life at the risk of losing his own, when the shot almost cut off his arm." She sat thoughtfully for a moment as if wondering whether she should tell me more.

"That must have made his family proud," I said.

"I guess it did," she replied, "but his father was angered when his eldest son left home for the West. He wanted him to finish his schooling and become a lawyer or a doctor—somebody who would be a credit to his name. But Jonce defied him—there were no opportunities for young men in the defeated South. And when he married me, just an unknown girl from Utah's desert land, his relatives would have nothing more to do with him."

"If he really did go to school," I asked, still mulling over what I had heard, "why hasn't he ever talked about it?"

"For the same reason he turned his back on his family, I guess," she replied; "he wanted no reminders of the past. Why, he even boasted of being born again out west where folks don't give a hoot where you came from, or if you ever went to school. It's not important, he claims, who you are or how far back your name goes; it's a man's integrity that counts."

I felt closer to Kitty from that morning on, more as though she were my friend than my mother. When spring came and my father had returned to work she insisted that I go with him every day to carry his lunch bucket, just as soon as the school term ended. I suspected that she wanted me to come to know and understand him as she did so that I would not be ashamed if I found out that he had miners' consumption.

The trail from the Elkton depot down across the saddle of Guyot Hill and around Beacon to the Orizaba No. 2 became as familiar to me as Bennett Avenue. I knew where the thimbleberry bush grew, the other side of the Caledonia dump, and how to whistle like a ground hog, and what kind of sage and wild onion dried best for seasoning. Usually I lagged behind to throw rocks in an abandoned prospect hole, or to listen to the scolding of a blue jay, or to tempt a cautious chipmunk with a soda cracker from the lunch pail. And often I just lay on the ground looking up at the cottony clouds curling in the sky; and thinking about Joe Moore.

One afternoon as I was drifting in a web of daydreams, I heard my father calling me. His voice was tense and urgent. I jumped up and ran to see if he were sick, or perhaps had killed a rattlesnake. He was walking slowly over a slight rise in the ground with the divining rod in his hands. It was dipping and trembling as if under the spell of a witch.

"Come here, Mabs, come quick!"

"What's the matter?" I asked breathlessly.

"Matter?" he repeated, without raising his eyes from the stick. "Just take a look at this son of a gun; why, it's almost twisting outa my hands! There's a jack pot down under or I'll eat my shirt!"

I stood for a moment watching the movement of the divining rod, skeptically, half suspecting that he himself was making the wire dance. "Let me try it," I suggested. "I'll bet the wire won't bend for me."

"That depends," he said, hedging a bit. "You've got to have a lota magnetism—we'll see." He folded my fingers tightly over the wire and gave me a gentle shove. "Be careful now," he warned, "go straight ahead . . ."

I stepped gingerly, hardly daring to breathe, never taking my eyes off the witching rod, hoping to see its slightest dip or tremor. But nothing happened. In spite of my doubts I whispered a little prayer and mumbled a hocus-pocus; I didn't want to fail my father. Still no movement—the rod was stiff and dead in my hands. "There's no magic in a forked stick," I said, holding it out in scorn. "It's just a piece of twisted baling wire—maybe you didn't do it on purpose, but it was you that made it point to the earth!"

"Are you accusing me of lying?" He gave me a sharp look and jerked the rod from my grasp. For a moment I thought he was going to strike me with it. No man had ever dared to call him a liar. The insult had come from me, his own flesh and blood. I wished with all my heart that I could take it back, but suddenly it occurred to me that nobody could be truthful all the time and I, too, had an obligation to be honest. He neither knocked me down nor scolded me, but fixed the rod firmly in his fingers and started to walk over the land. "Watch me again," he said; "see how my nails cut into my palms. The harder I grip, the more it resists me! There she goes! I can't hold on any longer. . . . !"

The witching stick quivered for a second and then bowed swiftly downward. I had kept my eyes glued on my father and could have sworn that his hold hadn't loosened. "What pulls it toward the ground?" I asked, plainly baffled.

"Magnetism," he said with an air of authority. "It pours right through my body into the wire and the yellow stuff singing in the earth draws it like a siren."

I thought about that for a moment, wondering if the divining rod had really failed to act for me because I lacked magnetism. "What's magnetism?" I asked, yielding a bit. He picked up a rock and began to examine it as though he hadn't heard me. Then he broke it in two with his sorting hammer, blew away the dust, spit on the facets and polished them with his sleeve.

"Can you see magnetism," I persisted in a louder voice, "or feel it tingle in your fingers?"

"You ask too many questions, Mabs," he replied as if wanting to put an end to them. "You wouldn't believe me anyhow. You think I don't tell the truth." He began to gather up his tools to go home. "One of these fine days you'll sing a different tune. Sooner or later, I'll strike one of the richest jack pots in the District about four hundred feet under the spot you're standing on right now. Mark my words!"

We scarcely spoke on the train back to town and I knew that he was put out because I doubted him. As we reached the corner of Bennett Avenue at Second Street, a strange, fascinating sight stopped me short in my tracks. A woman whom I had never seen before came prancing past on She Devil, the most skittish mare in Welty's Livery Stable. She was a picture to behold in her small Derby hat and dark habit with the skirt billowing to the toe of her boot. The horse capered and wheeled and reared but she seemed sure of herself and the animal. "Look, look!" I said, tugging at my father's sleeve. "Who is the lady on She Devil?"

"Nobody you should be rubbering at," he said gruffly, turning up the avenue. "Go on home now. Tell your mother I'll be late. Got some things to do at Neal's Assay Office." But I stood gazing at the beautiful rider until she disappeared down Third Street toward Myers Avenue.

I ran all the way home, so excited by the beautiful horsewoman that I forgot to tell my mother about the incident over the divining rod and how I had hurt my father's feelings. I even failed to give her his message saying he would be late.

Contrary to my expectations, Kitty became agitated and upset when I described the wonderful person I had seen riding She Devil on Bennett Avenue. "She must be one of those poor unfortunates the new railroads are bringing in by the hundreds, some from as far away as Paris in France, so they say. It's disgraceful!" My heart sank; "poor unfortunate" meant only one kind of creature in Kitty's language. But it was impossible for me to believe that such a lovely woman was just another wench from the tenderloin.

"She's different," I protested, "not coarse and ugly like . . ."

"Decent folks never look at them," Kitty was saying, "because they debauch our men. Next time one comes down the avenue, keep your eyes straight ahead. Do you hear?"

I had heard only too well but I had no intention of heeding. Kitty was unaware that she had put me on the alert for a new kind of denizen of Myers Avenue, the darling of millionaires —the parlor house madam.

7

Good-bye, Little Girl, Good-bye

SHE called herself Pearl De Vere but even I, an eleven-year-old schoolgirl, knew that it wasn't her right name. People said she came of a good family in the East who believed that she was a high-toned dressmaker—the designer of "De Vere Gowns" for the wives of Cripple Creek's millionaires. Actually she was the madam at the camp's fanciest sporting house, the Old Homestead on Myers Avenue.

I saw her from time to time after that first afternoon with my father, but never riding She Devil. Instead, she drove a span of high-stepping black horses and rode in a single-seated phaeton with shiny red wheels. She held the reins firm, with a regal air, looking neither to right nor left as if unconscious of the gawking miners who crowded the sidewalks. Sometimes she wore a changeable taffeta dress and a wide, green velvet hat with a matching willow plume atop her auburn pompadour, and again, she would be a study in brown, or black. Her dark lashes were so long they seemed to brush her pale cheeks, and the shimmering puffs of her leg-o'-mutton sleeves almost touched her delicate pink ears.

Once in a breathless instant when I was staring at her from around a telegraph pole, she glanced down and smiled at me. I was spellbound; never had I laid eyes on such an enchanting vision! From that day, Pearl De Vere became my secret sorrow, the heroine of my fondest daydreams, mysterious, fascinating and forbidden.

Often on my way home from school at noon I would stroll down to the alley behind Fairley Bros. and Lampman's Undertaking Parlors where the back of the Old Homestead was in plain sight. The second-story windows were always shaded against the daylight. Nothing stirred; no smoke curled from the dozen hooded stovepipes that forested the roof. The stillness of death hovered over the bright yellow building and isolated it from the life around—children playing tag in the street, the junkman in a rattling buckboard, squawking "Rags . . . bottles . . . saa—cks," a gramophone, somewhere, screeching,

> "Hello, ma baby
> Hello, ma honey
> Hello, ma ragtime gal . . ."

It was hard to picture dashing Pearl De Vere in this ugly, noisy setting. What must it be like, I wondered, inside that aloof place with the warm, friendly name of Old Homestead? Tales of its extravagant furnishings scandalized Kitty. "Think of it," she flared, "two bathrooms in a house of ill repute when respectable women seldom have *one!* And imagine, crystal chandeliers in a camp where most folks are lucky to have a coal oil lamp!" But it wasn't the bathrooms, or the crystal chandeliers, or even the baby grand piano in the parlor that aroused her greatest indignation. It was the wallpaper in the spacious banquet hall, handpainted in traceries of laurel and especially ordered for the madam from Europe. "It's disgraceful," Kitty

76

went on, "when decent families must live in cabins lined with rusty building paper!"

I was more interested in what went on at the Old Homestead, and speculated endlessly about it. But my rangy musings got me nowhere and I was afraid to ask questions of grownups. The *Cripple Creek Times*, the daily newspaper, printed a whole page of society notes describing in detail such uninteresting affairs as the Klover Klub dances and the Jolly Dozen Five Hundred Club luncheons but nothing was ever mentioned about the social life on Myers Avenue. I tried to figure out just what line of distinction separated the doings of the ladies on Eaton Avenue from those at the Old Homestead. Not money, certainly, not being attractive and stylishly dressed. It was all very confusing.

Then Fate stepped in to enlighten me and forever change the cast of my daydreams.

Rumors had been flying before the winter holidays that one of Pearl De Vere's admirers who had recently struck it rich up in Poverty Gulch was going to celebrate his good luck with a magnificent ball at the Old Homestead on Christmas Eve. The parlors were to be turned into a tropical garden, the report ran, with orchids, gardenias and mimosa shipped in from Mexico. Cases of French champagne, caviar from Russia and crates of wild turkey from Alabama began to arrive by express. It was said that two orchestras, Denver's finest, had been engaged to play the latest cakewalks, schottisches, and two-steps. And as if that were not enough to wag the tongues of school children, news leaked out that Pearl De Vere would wear an eight-hundred-dollar ball gown of shell-pink chiffon encrusted with sequins and seed pearls, sent to her direct from Paris.

I couldn't go to sleep the night of the big event. It was snowing and bitter cold but I raised the window slightly,

77

hoping to catch any strains of music that might be wafted on the air. I tried to visualize a tropical garden interlaced with orchids but it was difficult. I had never seen an orchid. The only flowers around Cripple Creek were wild asters, lupine and Indian paintbrush in the late summer; and sprays of red and white roses sent up from Colorado Springs for funerals. But I knew something about gardenias. I had sniffed the sweet perfume from the atomizer at Griff Lewis's Pharmacy. The fragrance filled my nostrils again as I imagined Pearl De Vere waltzing in the arms of the handsome Midas from Poverty Gulch.

But even as I lay there in the far hours, lost in fantasy, the body of Pearl De Vere, cold in death, was stretched on a marble slab at Fairley Bros. and Lampman's Undertaking Parlors.

The story in the *Times* next morning was tantalizingly brief. Every word was burned in my heart:

Pearl De Vere, madam at the Old Homestead, died early today from an overdose of morphine. According to a denizen in the house, a gay party was in full swing when Pearl excused herself, saying that she felt indisposed. She refused to let anyone go with her to her room. She was in high spirits all evening, a woman said, and never seemed happier or more carefree. No one could offer any reason why the madam should want to end her life. The body was discovered by the wealthy patron of the lavish affair. It was lying across the bed fully clothed in the ball dress that came only last week from a salon in Paris. The name of the patron could not be learned. It was understood that he left suddenly on business in Denver. Funeral arrangements will be announced later pending word from the deceased's relatives in the East.

Kitty's lips tightened as she pushed the paper aside. "Another one of those poor unfortunates has taken poison," she said grimly. "It's just as well. Places like the Old Homestead, together with its inmates, should be wiped from the face of the earth!"

It was the saddest Christmas of my life. I had no interest in the gifts that banked our tree, no desire to help Kitty string cranberries and popcorn. The thought of Pearl De Vere cold in death, forsaken and alone in Fairley Bros. and Lampman's back room pulled at my heartstrings. It was all I could do to keep from crying. My mother had no inkling of my grief and if I wept she would grow suspicious and pry out my secret. So I escaped to my retreat at the Lone Pine Shaft on Mineral Hill, to sit on the dump and mourn over the tragedy of my idol.

Then a daring obsession began to grip me. It was nothing less than a visit to the funeral parlor to gaze once more on Pearl De Vere's lovely face. I had never seen a corpse; the very word made me shiver with horror. I would cross the street any time rather than pass near a house with black crepe on the door. But my urge to see her was stronger than my fear; and besides, the saying came to me that if you touched a dead person his ghost would never return to haunt you. Even so, several days passed before I could muster sufficient courage to take such a bold step. The arrival of Pearl's sister from the East brought things to a head; now there wasn't a moment to lose.

At first glance, the entry of the mortuary was so inviting that it might have been a parlor in anybody's house. An enormous fern hung down from an iron stand in the sunny window. Green Brussels carpet covered the floor and comfortable chairs were scattered around. I waited at the desk a moment for the undertaker to appear but the place seemed empty. A large glass case on a table caught my eye. It contained mementos of people who had met violent death in Cripple Creek and been laid out at the mortuary. Each bore a typewritten label. There was the lunch bucket of a miner who had been struck by lightning, sidecombs of Two-go Ruby who had swallowed strychnine, the pistol of a gambler who shot himself through the mouth, a piece of fuse that another used to blow off his head with dynamite. It was the lock of Pearl De Vere's red hair that made me shudder and try to escape through a back door. But instead, I found myself facing the morgue.

Four shadowy coffins stood along the wall of the dimly lit room and I recalled with a shiver the mine explosion up on Gold Hill. I was tempted to run out before anyone discovered me, but all at once low, insistent voices near a far window caught my ear. A thin, sharp-nosed woman and a man in a dirty oilcloth apron were standing alongside a lavender casket. They apparently didn't notice me as I tiptoed closer.

"She's dead," the man was saying; "her sins won't rub off on you now."

"The stain on our family will never rub off," the woman said bitterly. "It is as red as the dye on her hair! You should have told me what she was, the kind of life she had been leading, before I made the long, futile trip to this loathsome place." And yanking on her gloves, added, "I'll take no further responsibility. I'm washing my hands of the disgraceful business!"

"But she is penniless!" the man urged. "Do you want your sister buried in the potter's field?"

"This harlot is no sister of mine!" the woman shot back, as she started to leave. I was trembling so that I dropped my new purse. "What're you doing here?" she screamed, seemingly aware of me for the first time. "A fine place this is for a child!"

And she flung out, slamming the door so hard the calendar on the wall fell to the floor.

"There's a lot a' mean-hearted folks in the world," the man said, shrugging, "but for my money she takes the cake!"

"Is Pearl De Vere's hair really dyed red?" I asked, struggling with disillusionment.

"Sure," he bantered, "that's nothing. All the girls on the row do it. Sometimes black, sometimes blond, and now and then it's red, like De Vere's. I done my damnedest to bleach it before any of her hoity-toity relations got here, but it was no use—came out a dirty pink—the ungodliest sight I ever seen on a cadaver!"

I leaned over the coffin for a better view. She looked so natural that she might have opened her eyes and smiled up at me slantwise through her long lashes. If there had been any stain of wickedness in her face Death had erased it. She seemed much younger than my mother; the hurt, wistful expression about the mouth was like that of a girl. "Do you care if I touch her?" I asked, reaching over to brush a pinkish wisp of hair from her forehead.

"Go ahead," the man replied, "but make it snappy. I got work to do—can't hang 'round here all day. Say," he eyed me sharply, "ain't I seen you somewheres—whose kid are you, anyhow?"

I turned and ran out of the room, afraid that he was one of my father's friends.

The whole town was in an uproar when word spread that Pearl De Vere's sister had disowned her. The editor of the *Times* wrote, "Cripple Creek can bury its own dead!" The Reverend Jim Franklin preached a sermon called, "Let Him Who Is without Sin Cast the First Stone!" And Johnny Nolon, the owner of the camp's biggest gambling rooms, started a movement to auction off the Parisian ball gown, "and give the little girl the finest funeral that money can buy!" But before the exquisite shell-pink creation could be handed over to the highest bidder, Fairley Bros. and Lampman announced receipt of a mysterious, unsigned letter. It was postmarked Denver and enclosed a thousand dollars in crisp new bills to pay all burial costs. The only request was that Pearl De Vere be laid out in the elegant dress in which she had danced on Christmas Eve.

A throng turned out the day of the funeral, mostly children and miners. I watched from the top of a barrel in front of Roberts' Grocery. Somebody claimed he saw ladies from up on the hill sitting in the shadows of upstairs office windows. The Elks Band headed by Joe Moore led the procession, playing the "Death March." Then came the heavily draped hearse with the lavender casket almost hidden by a blanket of red and white roses. Just behind, a man walked solemnly beside the empty rig with the shiny red wheels, driving the span of restive black horses. A large cross of shell-pink carnations lay on the seat.

My throat ached; I swallowed hard to choke back the tears. Now four mounted police were coming down the avenue, pushing back the crowd to make way for all the lodge members in brilliant regalia trying to keep in step. The sight of their red fezzes, feathered helmets and gold braided scabbards sent thrills of ecstasy through me. Bringing up the rear were buggies filled with thickly veiled women who, a man said, were Pearl's friends from the row.

I ran along the alley to the edge of town where Bennett Avenue narrowed into the road to Pisgah graveyard. Except for a few squatters' cabins, that part of camp was barren and windswept. I climbed on a rock from where I could get a clear view of the cemetery. It was late afternoon and the sun had begun to slant toward Pisgah Mountain. I watched a man chopping wood in front of a tar-papered shack. Not far away a boy was trying to hitch an obstinate burro to a cart while a dog yelped and snapped at the animal. A chicken hawk soared and dipped above an acrid, smoldering dump ground. My feet were getting chilly and I hugged myself to keep warm.

The last of the procession had passed by and the marchers were gathering around the freshly dug grave. I wondered uneasily if the services would be long. Soon the train would be coming in from Beacon Hill and Kitty would call me up and down the neighborhood to help her with supper. The thought had scarcely crossed my mind when I saw some of the mourners scattering and climbing back into the rigs. But a few of the lodge members had moved in closer to the grave and one of them seemed to be reading from a book. All at once, through a break in the ranks, I caught a glimpse of the flower-laden casket being lowered into the ground; and then came the sad sweet notes of Joe Moore's cornet playing "Good-bye, Little Girl, Good-bye." That was too much for me to bear; my heart was broken and I buried my face in my coat and sobbed.

When I looked up again, the long line of carriages and men had begun to file through the cemetery gate and down the slope back to camp. But the order had been reversed. The women, coming first, had thrown the veils off their faces and were laughing merrily as the trotting horses kicked up dust. Lodge members hurried willy-nilly, flapping their arms up and down, crossing them from side to side to get warm. The driver of the buggy with the shiny red wheels had jumped on the seat and the frisky steeds galloped wildly while he held the reins with one hand and pulled for a bottle from under the seat with the other. Even the hearse had picked up speed and the wheels rattled clumsily over the stones. The musicians came last and as they approached me, dapper Joe Moore looked over and winked. Then he trilled the whistle, the snare

83

drums rolled and the whole band burst into "There'll Be a Hot Time in the Old Town Tonight!"

I waited until they were out of sight and the tune had faded in the distance. I felt suddenly weary, older and more grown up. It was too late to help Kitty with the chores, I thought, as I hurried home through the dusk.

8

The Great Fires

I t was April, 1896—always a whimsical month in Cripple Creek. Kitty likened it to a young girl trying to decide whether to get a new green dress or make her shabby white one do a while longer. A day might start with a raging blizzard and end in a downpour of rain, filling the streets with slush and washing out roads and bridges. Again, there would be a whole week of beguiling sunshine so warm and bright that little boys put away their sleds and played immies; and women began to talk about spring house cleaning.

Saturday, the twenty-fifth, came at the close of such a spell. No one would have thought of it as a day of catastrophe. Dr. Whiting had been quoted in the *Times* that morning describing Cripple Creek as "the ideal home where the chest expands and the pulse quickens, bringing a healthy flush to the cheeks and energy to the step." Down the page further, Mayor George Pierce stated in an interview that "Our splendid system of waterworks and well-disciplined firemen makes it possible to control and extinguish the most serious conflagrations; henceforth, our citizens can be free of this terror."

The atmosphere tingled with the general sense of well-being. Never before had the future looked so rosy. The population had jumped to 15,000 and predictions were that it would top 50,000 in another three years. The Midland Terminal, which finally arrived almost six months late, already monopolized the freight and shipping business and had an eye on all the passenger traffic. Its imposing red brick depot, erected at the upper end of Bennett Avenue, dominated the town; and two blocks down, the framework of the four-story National Hotel had begun to take shape. According to W. K. Gillett, one of the Midland officials, its "appointments would be the most elegant in Colorado, in a class with Denver's Brown Palace Hotel and catering to the same discriminating clientele."

Fortunes had been made in fields other than mining and railroading. Real-estate promoters such as Tutt & Penrose owned many of the lucrative brothels and dance halls on Myers Avenue as well as some of the residences with ell porches and bay windows on respectable Eaton Avenue. Frame structures with two floors had risen among the fifty gambling houses and saloons that lined Bennett Avenue between Second and Fifth streets. Zang's Brewery and the Masonic Hall, both of brick, distinguished West Myers from the red-light district. The underworld, too, was heady with prosperity. Beer parlors, sideshows and burlesques flourished, fattening the cash boxes of characters like Crapper Jack Crawford and saloonkeeper Millie Lavely. Negro and French prostitutes, snubbed by wenches of "pure American blood," crowded around the mines in upper Poverty Gulch.

The buoyant feel of good times was in the air, in the way people talked and carried themselves, in their easy promises and extravagant predictions. Only the Barbees, it seemed, hadn't been at home when good luck came to call. The bonanza at the Orizaba No. 2 had been as slippery as ever, yielding only small pockets of ore now and then to keep hope alive.

"You must be on the wrong track, Jonce," Kitty complained one day. "Others who came long after you did have struck it rich. Dear me," she sighed longingly, "if only you had taken Mr. Stratton's advice about prospecting on Battle Mountain!" He winced; Kitty was always throwing up "Mr. Stratton's advice" to him but for once he let it pass. "How do you know my turn ain't comin' next?" he said. "And when it does, all those big jack pots on Battle Mountain are goin' to look like chicken feed!"

Then the blow fell that reduced to ashes bitter fault finding as well as utopian dreams. It struck at one o'clock in the afternoon. My father had gone to work early and Kitty was hanging blankets on the line for airing. I had just finished raking the back yard and was about to set a match to the trash pile. Up and down the block neighbors were beating carpets and washing windows; the smell of boiling cabbage drifted from across the alley. Boys in the street were chasing wood wagons, hooking rides, hiding behind the coal shed of Molly and Jim Letts who had gone away for a couple of weeks. Over near the Midland depot an engine purred idly on the wye, waiting to switch the passenger train around, heading it back to Colorado Springs. Two locomotives chugged and gasped, pulling and pushing a half-dozen freight cars up the grade from Anaconda.

Suddenly there was the sharp crack of a pistol shot, followed quickly by another and another until I had counted six. It was the camp's dreaded fire alarm. "Fire . . . fire . . . fire!" I yelled, running to the porch to look for smoke. Kitty stood stock-still and one of the blankets dragged on the ground. "Can you see where it is?" she called anxiously. Her voice trembled and her face paled. Fire had always been an ever-present danger in Cripple Creek, despite the mayor's reassurance. The fateful warning never failed to strike the town with terror. The boasted waterworks consisted of a single reservoir not far above St. Peter's Church on the Golden Avenue Hill. It was primarily for fire protection—drinking water was still bought from carts—and depended on spring thaws for supplies. But in the struggle for moisture the dry air usually triumphed over the parched earth and the reservoir was seldom more than half full.

Kitty had barely spoken when billows of heavy smoke streaked with thin, purplish streamers, began to roll from the tenderloin toward Bennett Avenue. The crackling timber sounded so close that I thought for a second it was kindling in our kitchen stove. Now the big Percherons, Mandy and Bess, were galloping down the street, dragging the camp's fire engine. The bell clanged and the wheels screaked and wailed as they cut around the corner at Third. Brother began to scream for Kitty to hold him. "There, there, honey," she said, taking him up in her arms. "Don't be scared; the big fire engine'll put it out in a few minutes."

But the fire hose had no more effect than a lawn sprinkler; the fury and uproar grew worse instead of better and soon the whole sky was overcast with smoke, turning the golden sun to blood red. Miners from the night shift started running through the alley, yanking on their pants as if half awake, not stopping to lace their boots. Women called out to them:

"Where is it?"

"How'd it get started?"

"Will it catch up here?"

But no one stopped to listen; only the gluttonous flames and wind could answer. Long, searing tongues had begun to arch across blocks, licking roofs and dropping sparks. In another moment they had shifted eastward, only to coil back and drive in the opposite direction. No part of town seemed safe; there was no telling which way the terror would turn next. If the wind subsided momentarily, the fire created its own downdraft, and sucked at more fuel.

A boy came tearing by on a donkey shouting, "Topic's went, an' Crapper Jack's; nothin' left of Ol' Homestead an' Mikado . . . the whole town's goin' . . . beat it to Mineral Hill!"

"He's scared," Kitty said, "and doesn't realize what he's saying. Go down to the corner, Mabs, and find somebody we know who'll tell us what to do."

I ran all the way to Bennett Avenue without seeing a familiar face. Men were offering huge sums of money for wagons, carts, wheelbarrows—anything on wheels. Nobody paid any attention. They all were too busy saving their own possessions. Half-dressed, hysterical women from Myers Avenue ran around crazily, hugging a tiny dog or kitten. A magpie perched on one girl's shoulder kept squawking, "Hello sucker . . . hello sucker . . . go to hell!"

I was spellbound, and squeezed in closer among the on-lookers. The whole of Bennett Avenue beyond Third Street blazed like a roaring furnace. Fire fighters were falling exhausted and others, breathing through sponges, dashed in to take their places. Runaway horses and overturned wagons added to the chaos. Up by Gondolfo's fruit stand men worked frantically to mend the scorched firehose while the water diminished to a trickle. "Now they'll be after using giant powder," I heard a man say, "an' a fine job they'll make of it—'fore they get through, the whole goddamn camp'll be nothin' but kindlin' wood!" I flew back up the hill to tell Kitty.

"Well, we'll see about that," she said defiantly; "nobody's going to blow up my place so long as I can handle a shotgun!" I stood there staring at her, too astounded to speak, torn between admiration and fear. Kitty always faced up to desperate situations; nothing seemed to frighten her. But I recalled, too, that my father had forbidden either of us ever to touch his musket, and to make sure, he kept it on a rack of spikes well out of reach. For a moment his certain anger loomed as a greater threat than the giant powder.

Already the explosions were booming in widely scattered parts of camp. I could see timbers and furniture whirling through the dust. But the flames seemed to grow even bolder and more insolent. They played at will, heading north as if to devour the Sister's Hospital; then, with a quick twist, struck west toward Golden Avenue, and in another second shifted eastward as though eyeing the Midland Terminal depot. The dynamiters were moving up closer and closer to our block. Many of the houses along First Street had been blasted, and soon the old Roelofs place would be a shambles.

"Listen to me, Mabs," Kitty said calmly. "I want you to take Billie and go to the pond on Freeman's Placer. Wait for me there." I hesitated, not wanting to leave. She looked tinier than ever, holding the heavy musket all cocked and ready to shoot. "Quick," she grabbed my arm and gave me a shove. "There's no time to lose!"

But it was already too late. A huge fellow in a canvas coat lurched into the parlor, waving several sticks of dynamite. "Git out! Git to hell out, you an' your kids!" he ordered, "Git a move on or I'll make hash of you!" From his leering eyes and thick voice it was plain to see that he was crazy drunk.

"Who are you to be telling me to get out of my own house?" Kitty said, looking at him squarely. "We're not in the fire's path now—there's no need . . ."

"You heard me," he said, lunging toward her. "Git—you bast——" He stopped dead, as if paralyzed, and gazed at her in dumb amazement. She had raised the shotgun and was pointing it straight at him.

"Another move," she said deliberately, "and I'll kill you, so help me!"

A silly, baffled grin suddenly distorted his face. "Well, I'll be goddamned!" he muttered, and ran stumbling out of the door.

The explosions on Golden Avenue had come to an end and the fire, too, began to die with the setting sun. Neighbors who had fled when the dynamiters threatened drifted back and started to drag their household goods inside. They called out, thanking God for deliverance. Others strolled downtown to view the destruction. The fire had consumed eight blocks between Third and Fifth streets, stopping just short of the skeleton of the National Hotel. Everything, from Golden Avenue on the north to Poverty Flats in the south, was in smoldering ruins. Rhodes House and all the other rooming places on Carr Avenue had been demolished, together with four Protestant churches and most of Eaton Avenue's better homes. The heart of Cripple Creek lay seared and bleeding.

It was dark when my father reached home. He had lost his hat and coat; sweat streaked his haggard face. I helped him off with his boots and poured warm water in the basin, but he said he was too tuckered out for anything but rest. Little by little, while Kitty fixed supper, he told of his experiences. He had caught one of the first trains bringing dynamite from Victor. Immediately on reaching camp he was sworn in as a deputy sheriff and armed with a six-shooter.

Jailbirds had broken out and were looting stores and saloons. Hooligans and drunks carried off the powder unloaded at the depot and tossed the sticks around as if they were firecrackers, blasting everything in their way. "It's a miracle a lot of folks didn't get killed!" he went on. "Most of the crooks were rounded up and locked in the basement at the Midland. One of 'em got out somehow and made for West Golden Avenue, aimin' to finish up, I guess, but changed his mind." Kitty smiled and put her finger to her lips for me to keep still.

"When the worst seemed to be over," he continued, "I made my way up Church Hill, thinking I'd find you there. Looked like all the women in camp, hundreds of 'em, were crowded around the reservoir. Mothers crying for their lost children, dogs yelping and fighting, jackasses braying—I never heard anything like it! An' the junk they'd saved—busted wicker valises that had spilled God-knows-what over the hillside. Some hugged picture albums, chamber pots, looking glasses; others dragged washtubs piled with bedding. One old lady hung on to a kettle of beans!"

"Poor souls," Kitty said. "We might have been in their boots—or worse still—if the good Lord hadn't kept an eye on us!"

She sent me out to find anyone who was hungry and homeless, and that night our four rooms were crowded. People sat around on the floor until all hours telling stories of heroism and sacrifice, of children and old folks being taken to safety, of cripples rescued. A bartender had carried Blind Tom, the shoelace vendor, piggy-back all the way to Freeman's Placer. Someone told about French Mimi, who lived in Poverty Gulch. A lawyer who had once befriended her was dying of pneumonia in a Carr Avenue rooming house. She didn't stop to take any of her own belongings, but ran through the heat and suffocating smoke, cursing, threatening, bribing, until she found an expressman who would drive him to the Pike's Peak hospital.

Then my father spoke up. "Understand a woman turned a shotgun on a hoodlum who tried to blow up her house, somewheres in this neighborhood. That took innards . . ." He hesitated, as if suddenly suspicious, and looked up at the rack where the musket was kept and then down at the floor where it leaned in a corner. Kitty turned away her face as if to hide her blushing. "Well, I'll be damned!" he said. "So my Old Lady was the Annie Oakley!" Kitty made light of it and declared that any other Cripple Creek woman would have done the same thing if she'd had the chance. But I was convinced as I listened that my mother was one of the bravest persons in the whole District!

The plant of the *Morning Times* was among the first to burn, but enough machinery and type had been saved to issue a pint-sized edition the next day. The fire had started, it said, in an upstairs room at the Central dance hall when a denizen and her gambler friend got into a fight and knocked over a coal oil stove. Instantly the whole building was enveloped in flames and in the space of two hours eight blocks had gone up like tinder. The loss would run over a million dollars with very little of it insured. "But the spirit of our people was magnificent," the paper went on to say; "even while the fire raged out of control, George Holland rented the empty hall next to the Branch saloon and staged a burlesque last night; and Johnny Nolon, the popular saloonkeeper, put a force of men to work as soon as the ashes cooled and today he is open for business in a gospel tent at the same old corner."

Mayor George Pierce proclaimed that in spite of the suffering and destruction of property, the fire had doubtless been a blessing in disguise. It had wiped out forever many of the camp's worst dives and in the future, firetraps like the Central and Topic dance halls would be outlawed. He proudly refused the countless offers of help that poured in from all parts of the state, saying that the ravaged area would be rebuilt immediately, and that Cripple Creekers could meet present needs. "It will take more than a destructive conflagration to crush a city that is founded on gold," he added grandly, "for as everybody knows, gold is refined by fire!"

Four days later, on the twenty-ninth, at one forty-five in the afternoon, Cripple Creekers had occasion to ponder the irony of his words. Heavy clouds overcast the morning sky and a cutting wind drove the thermometer near zero; toward noon sleet began swirling against the woodpiles. Five hundred families had been packed into the houses and shacks of the unburned section and many others huddled in tents. Wagons loaded with green lumber skidded through the icy streets and the din of buzz saws and hammers filled the trembling air with urgency.

The Golden Avenue school escaped the fire but hadn't yet reopened. I was indoors because of a cold. Kitty had just taken a batch of lightbread from the oven and its steamy fragrance gave the house a warm, cozy feeling. "As soon as this pan cools," she said, covering it with a cloth, "you can bundle up good and take a couple of loaves over to——" She stopped abruptly and stamped her foot. "Listen, Brother; be quiet!" she stammered. "I think I heard a pistol shot. . . ."

I waited, almost paralyzed with dread. There could be no mistaking that direful sound. Again and again the desperate alarm was repeated until I could hardly hear the shots for the pounding of my heart. And once more I rushed to the back porch to look for the telltale sign but snow and fog obscured the view. Then a flash of crimson lit the sky above the Portland Hotel, at the corner of Second and Myers, and suddenly all that had been left of Bennett Avenue became a spiraling mass of smoke and flames.

The ferocity was far greater than that of Saturday's holocaust and its behavior even more erratic. In a matter of moments the main drive had shifted toward the northwest and Golden Avenue, and smothered us in soot and fumes. Behind the dark veil, mine whistles shrieked in vain from every hill and gulch in the District. The reservoir was only a sink of mud, and Mandy and Bess, the fine Percherons, were hauling loads of refugees to Mound City and Anaconda. Now we were truly at the mercy of dynamiters.

I looked to Kitty for assurance, wondering when she would again take down the musket. But she seemed bewildered, as if unable to meet this second ordeal. She moved aimlessly from room to room, picking up odds and ends to save and then putting them down. She brought overshoes and coats for Brother and me and threw her big plaid shawl around her shoulders. I ran into the kitchen for the pan of bread, and saw her standing in the middle of the floor, clutching the four volumes of the *Complete Works of Alexandre Dumas*, our only books. As we hurried through the parlor to the front door, she went back, all of a sudden, laid the books on the piano and grabbed my father's violin.

The thunderous explosions were so close that rocks and splintered wood fell on our roof. Outside in the street women were running toward Mineral Hill, half carrying, half dragging their young children. But they were not hysterical as they had been in the first fire, only strangely grim and silent. Few had tried to save any belongings. Kitty did not follow after them but hurried blindly up the street, with me at her heels pulling Brother along. I looked back once, just in time to see our house go up in a million pieces.

"Don't turn around, Mabs," Kitty said, giving me a yank. "It's better not to see. . ."

"But where are we going?" I sobbed.

"I don't know—to Freeman's Placer, I guess, to wait by the pond 'til Jonce finds us."

A stretch of sparsely settled land separated the placer from the rest of camp, and the shallow pond was used to store snow water for the miners' sluice boxes. Kitty had often mentioned it as the safest place to go in case the town should ever catch on fire. But it had never occurred to her evidently that dynamite is no respecter of firebreaks. For what seemed eternity we huddled there on the banks, dodging broken timbers, pieces of furniture and iron. Once I thought I saw a fat, round piano leg whizzing over our heads, but Kitty said that our place and everything in it had long since been in ruins.

No one had any idea what time it was until, unexpectedly, the clouds parted and we caught a glimpse of the waning sun. The fire, too, like the other one, began to abate as the sky grew dusky; and no more explosions shattered the heavens. At last my father came, as Kitty thought he would, to take us to the Masonic Hall which, together with Zang's Brewery, were the only buildings left standing in the downtown area. I couldn't believe my eyes when I saw the devastation. The forty acres where only the week before had stood a flourishing mining camp were now a vast dump of rubble and smoldering ashes. All that remained of Cripple Creek was Old Town and Poverty Gulch in the east and a fringe of scattered shanties toward Mound City and Pisgah graveyard.

The *Morning Times* had been wiped out completely and there was no news—only rumors and hearsay. Some declared that firebugs had started both fires, but others said that the second blaze was caused by a pot of grease flaming up the stovepipe in the kitchen of the Portland Hotel. The cook, a fellow named Angel, hadn't been found and it was believed that he had been killed. Reports of many other casualties turned out later to be false. But there was no question about property losses; they were beyond estimate.

The mayor no longer proclaimed that his proud city could meet its own needs. The two railroad depots had been saved, and now Cripple Creekers stood in line to get tents and allotments of bedding, food and clothing sent in by train from Colorado Springs and Denver. The fabulous tales of the gold field had encircled the world and money came from cities as far away as London, New York and San Francisco.

The day after the fire, as hundreds milled about, searching for remnants of their homes among the embers and broken heaps, word came that both the Midland Terminal and Florence & Cripple Creek had offered free transportation within an area of five hundred miles to any families wishing to leave the District. "Might be a good chance for you and the children to visit Silver Reef," my father said. "I'll send for you when the new house is ready."

She pulled absently at a loose thread in her dress as though recalling another promise he had made to send for us. "I'll wait 'til you can go too," she said at last. "I'd rather stay. This is where I belong."

9

The Brown Palace
of Cripple Creek

W E moved into one of the hundreds of tents W. S. Stratton
sent for the fire's victims. Kitty said she was thankful, too, for
the blankets from Colorado Springs and the generous supplies
of meat and vegetables contributed by farmers in the Arkansas
Valley. "The good thing about trouble," she told me, "is that it
makes you realize how much kindness there is in the world."
But I didn't agree with her about one thing—the ugly dresses
that had been donated for children. They were either too large
or too small for me and looked as if they had been designed for
orphans. I refused absolutely to wriggle into a long union
suit until Kitty cut it off at the knees.

My father sold one of his claims on Beacon Hill for enough
to build a new house on our lot. He did most of the carpentry
himself, and much to Kitty's embarrassment, it leaned slightly
toward Mount Pisgah. It was almost an exact copy of the
other except for the matched flooring. Before long our block
had been largely reconstructed with several newcomers oc-
cupying the better places. The only people still living in a tent,
months after the fire, were the Baltzells. It worried Kitty a

great deal and she often talked with Molly Letts about some way to help them. "If Jonce had any skill as a carpenter," she said, "I'd make him put up something for Mrs. Baltzell, but he can't drive a nail in straight."

"Jim's first-rate," Molly replied. "He could make a living building houses if he had a mind to. Maybe there are other men in the neighborhood who would lend a hand. I'll ask him tonight."

"You do that," Kitty said, "and I'll see if Jonce can't get Larry Maroney to donate the lumber."

Evidently everybody else in the block had been wondering too what could be done about the Baltzells. One day the Maroney Lumber Company pulled up with a load of planks and two-by-fours, and within a month a new six-room clapboard home, with an ell porch and wide front window, was ready for the family; and enough money was found to buy a sewing machine for Mrs. Baltzell. Alice, the serious, high-minded daughter, vowed to Kitty that when she got a position teaching, her first act would be to start repaying Larry Maroney. "But I guess there isn't enough money in the world," she added, "to wipe out the debt we owe our neighbors!"

The calamitous fires had truly been blessings in disguise. The *Morning Times,* now established in its modern plant, never seemed to tire of praising the reborn town. "The era of shacks has ended," an editorial read. "No longer can Cripple Creek be called a poor man's camp. In little more than a year after its ordeal it has become a city of handsome dwellings whose elegance and refinements are reflected in the brilliant social life. A throb beats through its every artery," the writer continued ecstatically, "giving the people a dash and drive that fascinates visitors. Nobody, once kindled by the romantic life of the District, ever fully recovers. Although he may travel far and look upon other scenes, his memory will revert with wistful longing to these hills and their treasures."

The population of Cripple Creek had reached 20,000, and the whole District claimed twice that number. Several reservoirs on the Pike's Peak watershed supplied abundant water for all purposes. Fifty-eight trains arrived and departed daily over the two railroads, and plans were under way for building another standard gauge to follow the old stage route from Colorado Springs, up behind Cheyenne Mountain.

Electric interurban cars already circled the hills, carrying passengers to and from the mines and camps between Cripple Creek and Victor. One line reached an elevation of 10,487 feet at a point near Midway on Bull Hill—a record altitude for any trolley in the land. The force behind these unbelievable developments was the zooming output of gold. In the four years since 1893, the start of the Golden Era, gross production had risen from $2,783,369 to $29,252,885; and shipping mines had increased from one hundred and fifty to over four hundred.

The "dash and drive" of the people showed up in the speed with which the camp had been rebuilt. Two- and three-story brick structures lined both sides of downtown Bennett Avenue, and each boasted of having a different trim. Plate-glass show windows of the dry goods stores drew flocks of women Saturday nights to gaze at displays of the latest fashions. Ragtime rhythms and laughter burst through a half-hundred saloon doors; and velveteen drapes subdued the whir of roulette wheels at Johnny Nolon's popular gambling emporium.

Brick walls hadn't made the brothels more palatable to the community, but now a slight flavor of respectability had been added to the area. A fine opera house towered above the cribs and dance halls on the south side of Myers Avenue, where prize fights and road shows competed with entertainments and graduation exercises of school children. New parlor palaces such as the Mikado and Laura-Belle's Golden Peacock flourished. But the Old Homestead in pink pressed brick, presided over by a shrewd beauty named Hazel Vernon, still catered to the select carriage trade—well-heeled playboys and millionaire prospectors.

The most impressive addition to the skyline was, by all odds, the National Hotel at the corner of Fourth and Bennett Avenue. It was said to be fireproof and the cost, "maybe as much as a hundred and fifty thousand dollars," was the talk of the town. My father criticized it as being too fancy for a mining camp. "It'll never pay," he commented. "Folks who can fly that high'll catch the afternoon train for the Antlers Hotel in the Springs. I'd be willing to lay a bet that the Midland backers'll be washing their hands of it inside of two years."

I often went down to watch the four-story building taking shape. It was of red pressed brick with a brown stone trim and topped by the gabled penthouse of W. K. Gillett. Many of the rooms were *en suite*, with private baths and service bells; telephones were to be installed on every floor, and an elevator, the first in the District, would operate twenty-fours hours a day. When word got around that W. S. Stratton had signed a fifty-year lease on the swankiest apartment in the building, "to show his faith in the District's future," townspeople nicknamed the hostelry "the Brown Palace of Cripple Creek."

Invitations to the inaugural banquet went out to the most prominent leaders in the town and state, but everybody in the District had been asked to come to the housewarming and inspect the elegant appointments. As the time approached, Kitty dropped hints to my father about taking us but he never noticed them. She did little extras such as cooking his favorite southern spoonbread for dinner, and put tidbits in his lunch bucket. But he paid no attention, not even when she complimented him on his young looks and suggested that he buy a becoming blue serge suit at Weinberg's sale.

One evening, after a week or two of softening, my father glanced over at me and winked. "Your mother is a card," he said, as if she weren't there, "but I can see through her. I know when she's buttering me, but it ain't goin' to do her a whit of good. She might as well give up!"

"But Jonce," she pleaded, "you never take me anywhere except once in a while to a Masonic banquet. It won't cost a cent and we needn't stay. Please, I only want to hear the music and see the flowers and watch the people dancing. . . ."

"No," he said emphatically. "I'd feel like a damn fool decked out in store clothes, staring at that society bunch. All Bert Carlton's freighters put together couldn't drag me to such a shindig. You and Mabs can go along with Jim and Molly Letts. I'll stay home with the boy."

She gave him a cold, piercing glance and flounced out the back door and ran across the yard to the Letts house. When her mind was made up she could be as determined as my father. Besides, she had made herself a pretty gray crepe de Chine dress to wear and I had no fear that we might miss the glittering event.

It was chilly that October evening, but the glow in the sky above the hotel made the surroundings seem warm and bright. Festoons of colored lights draped the front of the building clear up to the illuminated penthouse and flags billowed from all the windows. Strains of "The Sidewalks of New York" drifted through the transom of the barroom which opened on the street corner, and beyond, a large sign over the main entrance flashed WELCOME, in blinking electric bulbs.

The lobby hummed and buzzed with a clatter that almost drowned out Professor Schreiber's stringed orchestra. Everybody in the District, except my father, must have been there, hailing friends exclaiming over the luxurious furnishings. We strolled among huge pots of ferns and tall vases of American Beauty roses, sniffing their fragrance and touching the velvety petals. We edged closer to the wall to admire the polychromes of familiar scenes in large gilt frames—the Midland Terminal's powerful Mogul steaming from Tunnel 8, up Ute Pass; the Wild Flower Special from Colorado Springs, waiting on a siding in Upper Beaver Park while tourists gathered armfuls of columbine; the dramatic rainbow hues at sunset tinting the clouds above Pike's Peak.

Molly glanced around for Jim but he wasn't in sight. "Well, what do you know," she said, as if pleased. "He's given us the slip! I'll bet he's playing keno in that barroom. Suits me to a tee—now we won't have to go home so soon!"

The doors to the dining hall had just been opened and we hurried over with several others to watch the banquet which was in full swing. What a sight to feast the eyes! Immense bowls of bronze and yellow chrysanthemums alternated with twinkling crystal candelabra on the tables. Negro waiters in starched white jackets were deftly removing plates and filling glasses with sparkling wine. Two or three hundred men and women crowded the room.

Molly had a wider acquaintance in camp than Kitty and was up on much of the society gossip. She pointed out, importantly, some of the better-known guests. "The heavy-set, dark-complected fellow down at the end," she began, "is J. Maurice Finn, Stratton's lawyer. They say he's going to erect a mansion over on Crystal Street. Strikes me he's cockeyed." She stood on her toes and squinted. "That one with the black goatee, further this way, is Dr. Frank Hassenplug—surely you've seen him, Mabs, airing those funny, baloney-sausage dogs on Bennett Avenue—quite a sport! And of all things," she exclaimed, stretching her neck, "if there ain't T. P. Airheart, the furniture dealer. He's coming up in the world—must've made a pile of dough, somewheres. . . ."

"Who are those two just across—such lovely-looking folks?" Kitty asked. "Must be their daughter they're talking to. I haven't been able to take my eyes off her—she's so beautiful!"

"It's the William I. Howberts," Molly replied, "real quality, but the pretty girl ain't theirs. She's Ethel Frizzell from Colorado Springs. Her mother died not long ago and it's rumored that she's coming to the Creek to live with her father at the New Rhodes House, and take a job as Judge Stimson's stenographer. She won't last long at that," Molly chuckled, "not if Bert Carlton has his say!"

"Is he the one who owns all the freighters in camp?" I asked, remembering my father's remark.

Molly nodded. "The banks too; some folks say that before he's through he'll own most of the Cripple Creek District. That's him speaking to her now—some women have all the luck!"

"She's lovely in that blue chiffon," Kitty sighed. Then she gave me a quick, appraising glance as if wondering how such a color would become me. But I had the uncomfortable suspicion that she despaired of me, a freckle-nosed, long-legged girl of twelve, ever developing into a charmer like Ethel Frizzell, no matter what kind of clothes I wore.

"Come on," Molly said, "let's go upstairs now. We don't want to spend the whole night here, and if we hurry we'll be back in time to see the grand march." She slipped her arm through Kitty's and drew her away. "I'm simply dying to take a look at Stratton's hideout—everybody says it's swell-elegant!"

We got out of the jerky elevator at the fourth floor, together with a small group of other women heading for the Stratton apartment. Molly seemed to think that since she hadn't seen him at the banquet, he might be in his suite. But there was only a policeman standing guard. The sitting room resembled the lobby, on a very small scale, with its deep, red leather chairs, polychromes of the Independence, Washington and Abe Lincoln mines, and vases of flowers. The difference was in the roped-off fireplace which, according to a typed notation, had been constructed of sylvanite from Mr. Stratton's famous properties. But to me it looked exactly like the glistening, gray granite in Box Canyon.

The bedroom was far more exciting with its walls paneled in golden oak and mirrors. Molly, who never lacked something to say, stood speechless for once, in open-mouthed awe. "Well, I'll be darned," she muttered at last. "I'll bet this is a dead ringer for the madam's bedchamber at the Old Homestead!"

"Why would a white-haired old man want so many looking glasses?" Kitty muttered breathlessly. "All Jonce needs is the one over the wash basin in the kitchen!" Then, she began to prance up and down, admiring herself from all sides, smoothing her bangs, pulling at her basque and lifting her skirts slightly to glimpse her small feet. "This is the first chance I've had since I came to the Creek to see if my petticoat shows!" she added, and everybody laughed.

After marveling at ourselves in Mr. Stratton's mirrors, we strolled through the corridors, peeking into other suites, noting the shiny brass bedsteads, and even pulling the chain of the bathroom toilet. Kitty said she felt nervous about getting into the rickety elevator again, and we walked down the back stairs to the lobby. Jim had been waiting for us quite a while; he said it was time we started home. Molly's face dropped. "It's only the shank of the evening," she protested. "The fun's just beginning!" Just then the Cripple Creek Band, which had been hired for the ball, began to play "Sweet Bunch of Daisies," and she took him by the hand teasingly, and led him over to my mother. "Kitty loves to waltz," she said, "and hasn't had a fling in a coon's age. Come on, dearie, give her a a whirl. . . ."

I didn't know that she could dance and was amazed when she slipped into Jim's arms and glided gracefully out on the floor. Molly and I stood watching them and each time they passed us, it seemed as if more stars were shining in Kitty's dark eyes. "They make a nice-appearing couple," Molly said dreamily. "Kitty's feminine and dainty, the way Jim wants me to be. But I'm not built like that—I can't even do a two-step. I tried once, just to please him, and stumbled all over his corns. Never again. . . ."

A note of wistfulness crept into her voice and I turned unconsciously to see if she were serious. I had never associated her with sentiment; it seemed to have no place in her character. Sometimes I suspected that neither Kitty nor I really knew Molly Letts. She would talk freely about anybody else but never about herself. After five years of living next door to her, we had never heard her speak of her past—her family, where she came from and how she met Jim. Once, my curiosity almost got the better of me and I started to ask her if she ever went to school. But Kitty changed the subject quickly and later warned me against prying into other people's lives. "It's enough to know that Molly is a good woman and a fine neighbor," she said. "Anything more must come from her."

All at once there was the startling sound of scuffling and gasps of profanity coming from the barroom adjoining the lobby. "I'm going over and see what the commotion's about," Molly said. "You wait right here for the folks—remember now!"

But Jim and Kitty were at the far end of the hall, lost in a schottische, and I had no intention of standing alone, all by myself, until they came. Besides, I was as curious as any-

body about what was causing the excitement in the saloon.
I tiptoed over behind Molly, peering through the crowded
doorway. All at once I smothered a scream. A man and a
woman had ridden into the saloon, horseback, and everybody
shouted with laughter when they ordered "a couple of horse's
necks!" And how the people scrambled to get out of the way
as the bartender slid the drinks along the mahogany bar toward the rearing, snorting, champing animals!

"Who are those crazy loons?" a man asked, standing next
to Molly. "They're liable to trample somebody to death 'fore
they get through!"

"That's Spec Penrose," she replied, "and his new girl at the
Old Homestead, Grace Carlisle."

"Well, I'm a son of a gun!" the man said, grinning. "I been
knocking 'round most of my life an' I never seen shenanigans
to beat this, even up in the Yukon!" Then he happened to
notice me, all ears and eyes, and added, "Ain't it pretty strong
medicine for a kid?"

Molly turned, suddenly, and grabbed me by the hair until
I was sure she would scalp me. "Didn't I tell you to stay back
there and wait for your mother?" she scolded. "When Kitty
finds out she'll give you a sound thrashing, and I hope I'm
around to hear you yell!"

But Kitty was too flushed and happy to take in all that
Molly tried to tell her about the disturbance in the barroom
and how I had ignored her orders and seen the whole fracas.
It wasn't until we reached home that the incident struck her
with full force. My father had left the lamp turned low in
the kitchen and gone to bed. It was after one o'clock and I
could hardly keep myself awake long enough to get undressed,
but Kitty said she wanted me to listen to what she was going
to say.

"You are to go, first thing in the morning," she began, "and apologize to Molly for disobeying her. I wouldn't be surprised if she never wants you to go anywhere with us again. And another thing," she went on, lowing her voice, "you'd better let me tell Jonce whatever needs to be told—I mean about Mr. Stratton's bedroom and all those mirrors—and—me dancing with Jim Letts. We needn't bother about that disgraceful goings-on in the barroom—it'll be all over camp soon enough. But I don't want to hear of you ever looking into a saloon again. Do you understand?" My father stirred and coughed in the other room and she blew out the light.

I had scarcely been asleep, it seemed, when I heard her describing to my father, while she cooked his breakfast, the events of the night before, hardly omitting a detail. But she was strangely silent about the affair in the barroom and never once mentioned her dancing with Jim Letts. My father liked to read the mining news in the *Morning Times* while he ate his bacon and eggs and drank a second cup of coffee and he only grunted now and then as Kitty chattered.

"What does it say in the paper about it?" she asked, as if she might be glancing over his shoulder.

"Don't know—haven't looked," he mumbled. "But I see where Joe Winchester's dickering for a lease on the Doctor-Jack Pot, over on Raven Hill. He's crazy if he thinks he'll find ore in that abandoned shaft!"

"Here—give me the society page," she said, "if you aren't going to read it." I heard her pouring herself some more coffee and putting the pot back on the stove. After a few moments she exclaimed, "Just listen to this, Jonce!" And then she began to read rapidly, hesitating only at an unfamiliar word.

"Such a scene as was enacted last night at the National Hotel might have been witnessed in any eastern metropolis garnished with wealth and polished by age. That it could have taken place in a supposedly crude, uncultured mining camp in the West was, in this reporter's opinion, a matter of pride. The cream of Cripple Creek society was present. The exquisite gowns of the ladies were accentuated by the somber black swallow-tails of the gentlemen. The whole presented a veritable kaleidoscope of color and brilliance that is seldom seen anywhere. Perfect taste prevailed in the minutest details. It would have been difficult to find a single costume that would not have passed muster in any exclusive ballroom in the East. Altogether, the affair reflected distinction on Cripple Creek's elite. Among the fashionble dancers were Miss Claribel Levens, radiant in a toilette of cream lace garnitured with pink ribbons; Miss Ethel Frizzell, strikingly beautiful in turquoise blue chiffon . . ."

He pushed his chair abruptly from the table and moved about the kitchen, coughing and clearing his throat, putting coal in the stove, rattling the grate. "Stratton could have been kingpin at that banquet if he'd had a mind to but he don't give a tinker's dam for that kind of thing. I know 'im pretty well and I'd bet he'd rather sleep on his cabin floor over at the Independence than spend one night with all those mirrors at the National. He ain't a show-off and that cock-and-bull story about the fireplace was cooked up for gullible females." I could hear him pulling on his coat, getting ready to go to Beacon Hill. "It'd suit me better if you wouldn't put so much stock in what you call 'society,'" he added, opening the door. "Most of those folks're no better than the rest of us and some of 'em are a lot worse. I don't want you filling Mabs' head with crazy notions; soon as I can swing it, she's going somewheres for a decent education!"

"Was he put out with you about last night?" I asked Kitty later, as she braided my hair.

"A little, perhaps," she replied. "Your father's ideas and mine don't always jibe."

"Do you know what Molly said about you and Jim?" I ventured, aware of being on risky ground. "She thought you made a nice-appearing couple."

"Molly is a big-hearted woman," she said, flushing, "the salt of the earth."

The talk ended there, but I knew that although Kitty was thirty-two and well along in years, I could never again think of her as being old after that night at the National Hotel.

10

We Take in the Fight
of the Century

MY FATHER seemed to change in the months after the memorable affair at the National Hotel. It was as if he felt guilty about the way he had behaved toward Kitty and wanted to make up for it without admitting his mistake. He took her to the annual Masonic banquet and gave me a gold-plated watch with a long mesh chain for Christmas. I decided that he didn't really dislike women, as I once thought, but was merely baffled by them; and that Kitty in particular often mystified him to the point of exasperation. His distant manner and gruff voice might be just a protective wall, I figured, to hide his warm nature. But there was no getting around the fact that his interests and pleasures were peculiarly masculine. Now it seemed as though he were trying to share them with her.

One afternoon, the latter part of February, 1897, he came home from work in high spirits, saying that he had a rare treat in store for her. On March 17, Saint Patrick's Day, "the fight of the century" was going to come off in Carson City, Nevada. Gentleman Jim Corbett was scheduled to defend his five-year-old world's heavyweight crown against a Cornish-man from New Zealand named Bob Fitzsimmons. Kitty claimed she hadn't heard of it, although the papers had been full of little else for weeks. Even the young boys in camp had been in a lather, arguing on street corners, betting everything from immies to jew's-harps and sometimes demonstrating Corbett's famous uppercut to cinch a point. My father declared it would be the fiercest battle since Corbett's win over John L. Sullivan, after twenty-one of the goriest rounds on record, September, 1892, down in New Orleans.

Tom Howell, publisher of the *Morning Times*, and one of my father's best friends, had suggested that since the big event was to start at noon on Saturday, or one o'clock Cripple Creek time, perhaps Kitty would like to bring me and join his wife, "a great fan of Corbett's," and a few other womenfolks, to watch the bulletins as they were posted in his newspaper office. He described it as a history-making occasion not only on account of the importance of the contest, but because it would be the first time that any prize fight had ever been filmed for kinetograph, or moving pictures.

My father was carried away with enthusiasm, both for what the battle promised in excitement and because, it seemed, he had at last found a form of entertainment that the whole family could enjoy and talk about afterwards. So it was a jolt to him when Kitty stated flatly that she considered such spectacles cruel and vulgar; and that decent ladies never even read about them, much less dignified them with their presence.

"But this is different," he argued. "You'll not be at the ringside but in a newspaper office with other womenfolks. The bulletins are to be enlarged so that even a girl like Mabs could take them in at a glance. Fitzsimmons' old lady is going to be right down in front at the ringside. You're hundreds of miles away up in timber line—why're you so squeamish?" When she just sat there absently twiddling her thumbs, not answering him, he flared up, "Very well, then. Stay home! But don't ever squall again about me not wanting to take you anywheres!"

"Were you going with us?" she asked, her eyes brightening. "That might make a difference . . ."

"It's strictly a hen's party. I'll be with the boys just across the street, at Johnny Nolon's. Better make up your mind quick," he added coldly; "I have to let Tom know in a day or so—plenty of women would jump at the chance!"

Kitty might have saved herself the trouble of turning to Molly Letts for advice. She had often boasted about the time Otto Floto let her stand in the wings at the Topic to watch an Indian named Hightower wallop Tom Sharkey; and admitted that if she had been born a male she would have become a pugilist.

"Of course you're going!" she said. "Why, I'd give my eyeteeth to be asked. I've been thinking of dressing in one of my old man's suits an' sneaking in the back door at the Newport!"

"Oh, Molly, you *wouldn't!*" Kitty exclaimed, laughing.

"You don't know me. Some of the things I've done would shock you even worse. Maybe you'd quit speaking to me."

"How you talk!" Kitty said. "I only wish it was you going," she hesitated for an instant, "instead of me. I haven't a thing to wear. . . ."

"How about that blue cashmere with the tight-fitting bodice?" Molly suggested. "I'll come over and lace you up."

"I still have qualms about it," Kitty said later when we were alone, "as though I may be sorry. But I can't back out now that Jonce has told Mr. Howells."

It was to be expected that the coming fight would plunge the District into an orgy of gambling. Cripple Creek from the very beginning had been a magnet for speculators and gamblers. Taking a chance was in the blood of the early pioneers, in the air they breathed, in everything they did and said; and nowhere was it more pronounced than in their love of sports. They raced anything that could move, from Speed Wolff's gasoline buggy to Doc Hassenplug's pet turtles. The nation had been shocked in 1895 when Joe Wolfe—no relation to Speed—staged a notorious bullfight over in Gillett and afterward turned the ring into a racing course for jack rabbits and greyhounds. A baseball field got priority over sidewalks and every afternoon in summer, come rain, sleet or sun, rooters gathered on the flats below camp to cheer their favorite teams.

Sportsmen often strolled down Bennett Avenue with an English bulldog or a brace of mastiffs on leash, or a pack of dachshunds, the latest fad in canines, yipping at their heels. Highbred trotters, tailed by sulkies, could be seen almost any pleasant day kicking up the cinders on the track at the base of Mount Pisgah; and even women stared when J. Maurice Finn, the eminent lawyer, drove by in a phaeton drawn by Pearl, his blooded mare.

But such flashy exhibitions, thrilling as they were, failed to let off all the camp's excess steam. The one vent that took care of that was prize fighting. Every Friday night a bout at the Topic Theater followed any show that happened along. Once Fred Stone, a stranded hoofer, stayed in town several weeks training young hopefuls in the fine art of delivering the sneak punch. If no pros or hungry troopers were on hand to satisfy the thirst for blood, Otto Floto, bill poster for barnstorming carnivals, would raid the saloons for belligerent drunks and hire them to settle their differences on the stage at the Topic.

Thanks to Floto's enterprise, Cripple Creekers had cut their eyeteeth on the best in pugilistic muscle. He booked such redoubtables as Jack Dempsey, the "Nonpareil"; Mike Queenan and Dago Mike Mongone. In the summer of 1896 he arranged a match between Jim Corbett and Billy Woods; and brought Bob Fitzsimmons for four-round goes with Dan Hickey and Tom ("Sailor Boy") Sharkey. When opponents were hard to find and the season slackened, Floto billed the famous John L. in a tabloid called "Honest Hearts and Willing Hands," in which the great pugilist delivered a monologue highlighting his fistic style. A little later Corbett himself was not averse to flexing his tendons and displaying his handsome profile in an English melodrama, "After Dark Neither Maid, Wife Nor Widow!" But nothing ever turned the camp so completely topsy-turvy as the approaching "fight of the century," almost a thousand miles away in Carson City.

Long before midday miners began trailing in from the surrounding hills and gulches, some on burros, others in carts and many on foot. Hundreds jammed the trains that had been added for the occasion. Standing room was at a premium in the saloons, my father said, and dozens had stayed up all night to hang onto choice spots around the bulletin boards.

Tom Howell's large front office was crowded too, but with women who looked a bit self-conscious to be seen at such taboo doings. The wide, plate-glass window afforded no protection against gaping passers-by or grinning loiterers at the corner outside Johnny Nolon's. Several rows of chairs had been arranged in a semicircle facing the wall where the dispatches were to be posted. Kitty told me to take Brother and sit up in front where I could see better and hear the telegraph instrument ticking in the adjoining room. I prayed that he would go to sleep soon and not plague me with his endless questions.

Already news had begun to come in. Out at Cook's Ranch where Yarrum, Fitzsimmons' ferocious great Dane stood guard, the powerful John L., bellowing like a bull, made no bones of his hatred of the s. o. b. who had robbed him of his title. And Tom Sharkey, resplendent in boiled shirt, square topper and gorgeous green badge, was strutting about examining the ring with an air of authority, noisily challenging the winner and flashing a roll of seventy-seven grand that it would be the New Zealand kangaroo. The "Sailor Boy" was evidently unpopular in Cripple Creek where he had bankrupted the fans by his failures to deliver the punch. Now I could hear guffaws and heckling in Hanley's saloon next door. "Ah, shut up," they shouted, "get out, ya faker. Come up to the Creek—we'll show ya!"

As the zero hour approached, the atmosphere crackled with tension. I went over to the window, with Brother at my heels, to watch the anxious throng surging up and down, gathering in small betting rings, hurrying in and out of the Newport and Tom Lorimer's below Third Street, and clustering around Johnny Nolon's trying to push inside through the swinging doors. Brother wanted to know if it was the Fourth of July and why everybody wore green clovers instead of little red, white and blue flags. I told him it was Saint Patrick's Day and to keep still. Then he whined that he was thirsty and before I realized what would be the natural result, he had gulped two full glasses of water. "Now sit there," I said, yanking him up on the chair beside me, "and don't let me hear another squeak out of you!"

Now the staccato click of the telegraph had begun again and bulletins started to pour in; it was all the boy could do to post them fast enough and my unaccustomed eye skipped a line here and there. The Cornishman's red hair is slicked back, his step is buoyant . . . weighs in at one hundred sixty-six and a half . . . not quite six feet tall . . . shoulders broad, arms long and dangling like twisted cables . . . dark blue trunks embroidered with small American flags . . . pea-green gloves

... flanked by Martin Julian, Ernest Roeber and Dan Hickey. . .

Odds six and a half to ten on Corbett . . . weighs in at a hundred and eighty-five . . . handsome, confident . . . the crowd's favorite . . . sporting red, white and blue belt with green buckle and rosette . . . tan gloves . . . socks rolled down over shoe tops . . . in his corner . . . Charlie White, Jim Jeffries, Billy Woods, Al Hampton . . . thirty-five hundred spectators pack arena built for fifteen hundred . . . tickets five to twenty dollars . . . rush prevents gatekeeper from collecting all . . . purse fifteen thousand simoleons, side bet of five thousand. Mrs. Fitzsimmons escorted by Lou Housman enters her ringside box . . . first of her sex to witness husband's battle for pugilistic crown . . . loud applause from fans. . .

"How thrilling!" Mrs. Lucy Martin exclaimed, clapping loudly. "I admire her grit!"

"I'd call it brass," Mrs. Howell replied haughtily, "sheer, unadulterated brass!"

I looked around at Kitty to get her reaction but she was sitting grim and tight-lipped as if bracing herself against the first blow. Suddenly I became suspicious of Brother's stillness and found that he had taken the ten pennies from my red leather purse and thrown them on the floor, together with his unlaced shoes. I gave him a meaningful shove as I leaned over to pick them up. He started whimpering but stopped abruptly, unable to compete with the hubbub breaking through the wall from Hanley's saloon. "Throw out the wench —she's a hoodoo!" they yelled. "Get on with the fight!" And when Bob stooped to kiss his wife before climbing into the ring, the hoots and catcalls rumbled all the way over from Nolon's, reinforcing the boys at Hanley's who kept on pounding, stomping, hurling insults, and demanding that the referee cut out the mush and get down to business.

"Wasn't that mean of those men at Hanley's to talk that way?" Mrs. Martin said indignantly. "I think it was real sweet of Fitzsimmons. I hope he wins!"

"Tom told me once that sports don't like to see women at a prize fight," Mrs. Howell said. "They bring bad luck. Maybe the fans think he betrayed them by letting his wife come; and then, of all things, kissing her before everybody, right there at the ringside! I wouldn't be surprised if a lot of his backers switch their bets to Corbett!"

It was one o'clock by the bell in City Hall and noon in Carson City. An expectant hush settled over Bennett Avenue. Only the fitful tick-tickety-tick of the telegraph instrument dispelled the quiet within. A direct wire connected the newspaper with the arena but dispatches for saloons were sent out from the local telegraph office by frantic messengers. I sat forward eagerly in my chair trying to take in the sentences, puzzling over unfamiliar words, afraid of missing anything. . . .

The gong sounds. . . Corbett dances around the thirty-five-year-old challenger, nicking him, flipping an ear, taking his measure, easily outpointing him . . . Fitzsimmons' eyes grow uglier with each brush of Corbett's gloves . . . he swings from the waist, flat-footed, like a lean, sinuous gorilla . . . his long arm reaching for the hook . . . hitting with either hand from any position . . . both are sparring for time, feeling for holes. . .

It's the end of the fourth . . . fans are getting impatient, yelling for a show of blood. . . three-fingered Joe . . . a drunk crawls into the ring . . . starts to make a speech . . . police throw him out. Bell sounds for the fifth . . . Cornishman smiling, cocksure . . . he calls to his wife that it's in the bag

. . . Pretty Boy hasn't scratched him yet . . . it's the sixth . . . Corbett prances, swings, moves in . . . lets go a vicious upper-cut . . . Fitz is stunned . . . his knees wobble . . . boastful Bob goes down for a count of nine . . .

I glanced nervously at Kitty; she was chewing one of the fingers of her new kid gloves. Brother had unfastened his plaid kilt and whispered that he had to go. I told him to wait a min-ute—the fight was almost over. The avenue was in an uproar again and I grabbed him and ran to the window. The crowd outside thickened. Gamblers were pushing and shoving, form-ing betting pools, raising antes, arguing and brawling. Kitty called me to come back and sit down but I paid no attention. "Fitzsimmons' gang's running for cover," someone outside cried; "they've lost their shirts!" Another yelled, "Jim's got the kangaroo by the tail—it's all over but the pay-off!"

The bell of the seventh rang. I ran for my chair pulling Brother who kept muttering that he had to go; I pretended not to hear. The bulletins were tumbling in.

Corbett is aggressive, confident, a smile lights his handsome face . . . he springs from his corner anticipating a quick knockout . . . Fitz dodges cagily, feinting . . . on tenderhooks for the break . . . he lands a fast one on the mouth . . . knocks out one of Corbett's gold teeth . . . Bob swings a haymaker throwing him off balance . . . Mrs. Fitz, fearing the worst, climbs on the railing of her box . . . flashing her green dust ruffle . . . calls words of endearment to hubby . . . directing his blows . . . screaming curses at Gentleman Jim . . . chal-lenger takes heart . . . he's making headway . . . it's a come-back . . . crowd going crazy . . . Corbett winces under the blows . . . he's hurt . . . the Cornishman's punches strike home . . . he's a smashing, twisting typhoon . . . nothing can stop him . . . Mrs. Fitz dances up and down . . . almost falls off the rail . . . the mob howls . . .

Brother tugged at my sleeve, he whined and tugged again and said he couldn't wait. . . .

Corbett crouches. . . covering, fending. . . his arms quiver and blows go wild . . . dives for a clinch . . . rests on Bob's shoulder, his face lined and gray . . . red saliva drips from mouth . . . blood oozing from cut on forehead. The crowd is going crazy, booing, yelling, hurling invectives and tirades, cheering. . . referee elbows them apart as round ends. Challenger glides to corner, confident, self-assured . . . Corbett slumps on his bench . . . seconds work him over . . . massaging, sponging and staunching flow of blood from cut.

The eighth sounds . . . fans on tiptoe exhorting, pleading . . . Mrs. Fitz, hysterical, almost falls off railing again . . . Corbett perks up . . . a flash of his old style . . . backers in a frenzy . . . Mrs. Fitz goads the kangaroo, berates and directs him . . . Corbett's blows lose force . . . he's playing for wind . . . knees rock . . . Gentleman Jim teeters against the ropes . . . crowd's jeers stiffen will. He recovers and lands sharp uppercut on Fitzsimmons' jaw . . . bedlam let loose . . . fans throw gold pieces to favorite's corner . . . referee threatens penalty . . . kids wriggle under ropes reaching for loot . . . cops jerk them out. . . end of ninth.

Brother was slumped in the chair asleep. I glanced back at the women. They were staring at the bulletin board in silence, as if hypnotized. Kitty's face was drawn and white; she looked uncomfortable and sick at her stomach. Mrs. Howell, a rabid booster for Corbett, seemed to be thinking about the bets she was likely to lose; she had stopped smiling and her eyes were worried. The rooters at Hanley's, too, were strangely quiet, as though torn between loyalty to their hero and acclaim for a new champion who promised to retrieve their losses. The moment of decision was near. . . .

Now it's the tenth . . . the twelfth . . . the thirteenth!

Corbett never gives up but his punches are wild . . . his fans shake their heads and wipe their eyes . . . a few turn their pockets inside out and laugh gamely . . . it is clear that only a miracle can save Pretty Boy's crown. The fourteenth opens in a rain of blows from the New Zealander . . . his powerhouse punches never let up . . . he's swinging and swaying, moving in for the kill . . . a one-two on the jaw, like a cobra striking twice . . . a clean opening to the stomach with a left hand shift to his wind . . . without changing position of feet, the pug from down under shoots another left to the jaw . . . Corbett, mighty title holder and heart-smasher, drops to his knees, clings for an instant to the ropes and then wilts to the floor. His pompadour is soaked with blood . . . pain contorts his face . . . he makes a feeble effort to get up . . . sinks back, clutching his throat.

The mob waits, stunned, silent, while the referee counts . . . three . . . four . . . seven . . . nine . . . ten. Pandemonium breaks loose . . . fickle crowd cheers, roars, goes mad. It's a knockout! Mrs. Fitz is wringing her hands and crying for joy . . . band strikes up "There's Only One Girl in the World for Me!" as new world's heavyweight champion leans over ropes and smacks her on the kisser.

Shivers raced up my spine. I could almost see people crowding toward the ring and the victorious pugilist waving, acknowledging the ovation while the judges huddled to make a decision. I imagined I could hear the band striking up "El Capitan" while the bruised, gory form of Gentleman Jim lay prostrate on the mat. And my heart fluttered until I choked, thinking of that strong, brave world's heavyweight champion bussing his wife in his hour of triumph!

But new bulletins were flying in and glum-faced Cripple Creekers rushed back to the saloons. The fight's not over yet! Corbett is showing signs of life . . . he's regained con-

sciousness . . . doesn't know he went down for the count . . .
pulls himself up . . . thrashes the air like a lunatic . . . heads
for Fitzsimmons, who is still taking bows and smiling as vast
throng cheers . . . Corbett is on his feet . . . closing in on
his opponent . . . seconds try desperately to intercept him
. . . beats them off with the strength of a gored tiger . . .
bloody tears run down his face . . . he bawls . . . where is the
coward, the s. o. b. . . . I'll wring his neck . . . show me the
bastard . . .

The towering Cornishman is dazed . . . caught off guard
. . . fury steels his eyes . . . he lunges at Corbett and misses
. . . seconds jump in trying to restrain him . . . hold his arms
and hands . . . can't defend himself against maniac's thrusts
to face and neck . . . Mrs. Fitz throws shapely leg over ropes
. . . rips green dust ruffle . . . leaps into arena swinging fists
. . . screams let me at him—I'll batter his pretty mug . . . I'll
kill the dirty cur . . . vanquished fighter turns bleary eyes
on her . . . tumbles over ropes like scared pup . . . friends
carry the kicking, struggling, cursing ex-champ to dressing
room . . . keeps moaning . . . it ain't so . . . let me go . . .
I been robbed . . . the bastard . . .

I turned my eyes away and clutched the pit of my stomach.
For a moment I had lost my bearings and felt as though I were
waking from a nightmare. Suddenly there was a strange commotion behind me. Chairs were being pushed around in confusion and I could hear low, hurried mutterings, with Mrs.
Howell's voice rising above the others. "Get some water!" she
was saying. "Unlace her corset, Lucy! Somebody run to
Shockey's for smelling salts!" I stood up looking anxiously for
Kitty. Then, all at once, I saw her—stretched out on the floor in
a dead faint.

For several days little was said at our house about the "fight
of the century." Kitty seemed penitent, as if she felt ashamed·

of herself for being namby-pamby and bringing ridicule down on my father. But he reassured her finally by telling her that she got off easy. "The punch that knocked out Gentleman Jim," he declared, "had dealt the boys in camp a financial hook that laid them even flatter than she was when he picked her up off the floor in Tom Howell's place!" But I noticed that he never again said anything to Kitty about taking in another prize fight.

11

Windy Joe's Jack Pot

A FEW months after the Corbett-Fitzsimmons bout, a family named Winchester moved into the small house next to the Baltzells', four doors down from us. Susan, a pretty girl with taffy-colored hair and serious blue eyes, was about my age and the eldest of four children. We liked each other at first sight. But the main attraction for me was her father, Josiah, whom I came to know as Uncle Si. It wasn't unusual for me to attach myself to other families, especially where the parents seemed fond of stray youngsters. Before Susan it was Louisa Nevins, whose warmhearted father, Richard, always had orange juice ready for us after school; and before Louisa I was a steady boarder at the Baltzells'. Kitty's punishments and my father's scoldings were futile; the best they could do was to hope that I would soon wear out my welcome.

But there was an enduring quality in my attachment for the Winchesters that baffled Kitty. "I can't understand," she once said, "why you are so eager to scrub the floor and scour kettles for Susie's mother when it's all I can do to get you to wipe a plate for me!" I couldn't explain it either except that it gave me an excuse for being around when Uncle Si came home. "Now looka here," he would say to the younger children who were grabbing his hands and tugging at his coat, "get outta my pockets, you rascals. There ain't a thing in 'em for you—Daddy's ship ain't made port yet; she's due maybe tomorrow!" Then he would pat Susan's cheek and give my pigtail a twist and tell us all to skedaddle.

The sight of him hurrying up Golden Avenue always thrilled me. He was tall and erect and walked confidently. His gray eyes twinkled when he smiled and he spoke with a fascinating Mississippi drawl. But what especially impressed me was his long, slender hands and clean, polished fingernails. Molly Letts allowed that he must have smashed many a girl's heart when he was a gay blade down in Natchez and Kitty agreed that he had all the earmarks of a blue blood.

He had migrated west after the Civil War as my father had done, but there the similarity ended. Sometime in the early eighties he married the buxom daughter of a boardinghouse keeper up in Black Hawk, near Central City. My father always seemed cool when Kitty or I discussed Josiah Winchester. He referred to him as Windy Joe, a nickname acquired during his unsuccessful campaign for mayor. His chief complaint was that Winchester had set himself up as a mining man when, in fact, he was nothing more than "a promoter who had never worn a pair of overalls or dirtied his hands with muck."

"Is there some special virtue in calluses and black finger-nails," Kitty asked obliquely, "or in wearing grimy pants, day in and day out?"

"Well, at least I don't douse myself with stink-water," he replied weakly, "the way Winchester does." Then a frown clouded his face. "You let Mabs go down there too much," he went on. "Mrs. Winchester has enough to do with her own kids; yours has no business hanging around and getting under foot."

But even if Kitty had wanted to keep me away it would have taken stronger measures than she could muster; and Susan's mother apparently didn't mind adding another child to her noisy household. She never seemed ruffled or impatient, and appeared contented hours on end to wash, mend and cook. Pungent, mouth-watering food was usually boiling on the stove or baking in the oven, making it even harder for us to wait for Uncle Si to come home for supper.

As soon as the dishes were washed and the younger ones were in bed, Susan got out the parchesi board. "What're you up to now?" he'd say teasingly. "You an' Mabs aimin' to pull me into that tomfool game again?" Susan pretended not to hear. "I swear," he blustered, "a fellow can't find a minute's peace around this outfit. Put that thingumabob away. . . ."

"Please, Daddy, just this once," Susan begged. "I'll bet we can beat you tonight!"

"Uncle Si, *please*," I put in, "unless you want me to go home!"

Then the corners of his mouth would curl into a relenting smile and he'd reach over and tweak my ear. "Well, come on, guess there's no way out," he laughed, "but mind you, it's only for one game. Getta movin'. What's holdin' you up, Susie? Bring on your chips. You two ain't got a Chinaman's chance!"

Mrs. Winchester drew her chair closer to the lamp and began to sort the pile of stockings in her lap. We could count on her to settle the loud disputes that were always part of the game. Uncle Si made a great to-do of the preliminaries, rattling the dice, swinging the cup high and low and muttering a mumbo-jumbo before finally casting them on the table. He pushed the chips along the board with the air of a victor, even when he was momentarily losing; and he twitted us con-

The author as a freshman at Colorado College, 1902.
Photo by Emery

The Midland Terminal wye across Poverty Gulch, 1896.
Denver Public Library Western Collection

Rear guard militiamen at Midland transferring from train to stage,
bound for Cripple Creek during strike of 1894.
Denver Public Library Western Collection

The author, young girl in white, joins in welcoming Cripple Creek's
first passenger train, July 1, 1894.
Pioneers Museum Colorado Springs

Wreck of the Florence and Cripple Creek near Anaconda on its
return trip, July 2, 1894. *Pioneers Museum Colorado Springs*

A birthday party at The Towers, later known as "Finn's Folly,"
where Theodore Roosevelt was entertained in 1901.
Courtesy of Mrs. Eleanor Finn LaDuke

Basement servants' quarters, all that remains of The Towers today.
Courtesy of Mrs. Eleanor Finn La Duke

Favorite home of W. S. Stratton just below his Independence
Mine, in the mid-nineties.
Denver Public Library Western Collection

W. S. Stratton.
Denver Public Library Western Collection

Albert E. Carlton, financial wizard,
banker, and promoter, whose name
was linked with the district's growth
and development.

Courtesy of Mrs. A. E. Carlton

The Continental Hotel on Myers Avenue where the author and her
mother spent their first night in Cripple Creek. October, 1892.
Pioneers Museum Colorado Springs

Steam calliope and performer featured in all the
big holiday parades.
Denver Public Library Western Collection

The Crusher, Cripple Creek's first weekly newspaper, operated
in the rear of a laundry and lunch counter.
Pioneers Museum Colorado Springs

Teddy Roosevelt, Governor of New York, panning for
Cripple Creek gold, 1900.
Pioneers Museum Colorado Springs

Bennett Avenue in 1894.
Pioneers Museum Colorado Springs

Victor's disastrous fire, August, 1899.
Denver Public Library Western Collection

Dazed spectators stand by helplessly watching the fury of Cripple
Creek's first great fire, April, 1896.
Cripple Creek District Museum

Bennett Avenue looking toward the Midland Terminal Depot.
Poverty Gulch lies at upper right.
Pioneers Museum Colorado Springs

Pisgah Graveyard with its wild flowers, green grass, and colorful
funerals was a favorite playground for children in summer.
Collection of the Library of Congress

A barroom in early Cripple Creek around 1894.
Collection of Lowell Thomas

Theodore Roosevelt and group of prominent Cripple Creekers on
the seventh level of the Portland. Fourth from left is Clarence C.
Hamlin, fourth from the right is James F. Burns, host and owner
of the famous mine. Spring, 1901.
Pioneers Museum Colorado Springs

The discoverer of the Cresson bonanza, Richard Roelofs,
fifth from left, and his trusted crew, 1914.
Courtesy of Richard Roelofs, Jr.

The Independence Depot in June, 1904, after having been bombed
by Harry Orchard during the labor strike. Thirteen non-union
miners were killed.
Denver Public Library Western Collection

Anaconda in 1898. Many of the richest mines, Raven, Doctor-Jack Pot, Mary McKinney, among others, were discovered in the surrounding Gold and Raven hills. Camp burned down in 1904.
State Historical Society of Colorado

Heyday of the great mines on Battle Mountain. The Independence in foreground, Portland right, and Ajax upper left.
Collection of E. J. Haley

View of Cripple Creek from the summit of Globe hill, around 1900.
Collection of E. J. Haley McClure Photo

Cripple Creek in the spring of 1958. The Sangre de Cristo Range rises in the left distance, and to the right a glimpse of the Collegiate Range, near Leadville. In the foreground can be seen the once famous Molly Kathleen Mine, now a noted tourist attraction.
Photo by Mrs. Richard Roelofs, Jr.

A rare photo of Poverty Gulch in the early days. It was regarded as the slum of the tenderloin, and looked down upon by the denizens of Myers Avenue.
Collection of the Library of Congress

Housekeeping cottage for an elderly couple at the
Myron Stratton Home, built with gold from the
Independence Mine in Cripple Creek.
Courtesy of H. L. Stubbs, Trustee

Lowell Thomas as a boy in
Victor.

Collection of Lowell Thomas

Mrs. A. E. Carlton, Lowell
Thomas, and friend in the
Cripple Creek District for the
opening to the Carlton Cyanide
Mill, 1951.

Collection of Lowell Thomas

tinuously when luck was going his way. "Never say die, my darlin's, keep up your spirits, spend your last chip as if you had a million. That's Daddy's motto!"

Then he winked at Mrs. Winchester and tipped back and forth in his chair, roaring with laughter. "What a pair of scalawags for a man to waste his time with!" he grumbled. "Licked again, so help me, just as I coulda told 'em. What's ailin' you girls, anyhow?" We were on the verge of tears. "Well, you poor little devils, I'll give you one more try. But you gotta make it worth my while or I'll wash my hands of you—for keeps!"

One . . . two . . . three . . . four games and still Susan and I couldn't beat him. We might have kept it up until midnight if I hadn't heard Kitty's quick, aggravated steps on the front porch. "Mabs Barbee," she called, "don't you ever know enough to come home?" I looked at Mrs. Winchester appealingly, hoping that she would rescue me as she had done so often before. She laid aside her mending, went to open the door and asked her to come in, but Kitty said she couldn't stay, my father thought it was time for me to be in bed. "Why not let her spend the night with us?" Mrs. Winchester suggested. "She's no bother—there's plenty of room on the sofa with Susie."

I soon became a sort of fixture in the Winchester family, staying home only when the health officer tacked a quarantine notice on their front door. Sometimes a disease like scarlet fever or whooping cough attacked the children, one after the other, and Uncle Si would have to live for many weeks at the Palace Hotel. Nothing prevented me from talking with Susan through the window, however, and the moment the forbidding sign came down I was back inside again smelling strongly of asafetida and a little weak from numerous doses of castor oil.

Often Uncle Si had to go to Denver for a week or two, "to wind up a big deal." Without him the house seemed empty and forlorn and Mrs. Winchester would get so blue that tears would drop on her bosom when she sat in the lamplight patching clothes. But as soon as he returned, the rooms would ring once more with his bantering and laughter. His ship was about to drop anchor, he would announce grandly; it shouldn't be long 'til mother would be sporting diamonds as big as doorknobs. She protested that she didn't want to be rich or wear diamonds. She'd be happy enough if he came home to his family every day instead of spending his time in Denver, trying to make a million dollars.

I had never been in Denver. It was a sort of dream-place, like Heaven, where I hoped to go someday. But I read all about it in the *Denver Post,* and basked in the reflected glamour of the magnificent charity balls at the Brown Palace Hotel where ladies sparkled in Tiffany jewels and wore gowns imported from Paris. Molly Letts and Kitty gossiped about them with a kind of wistfulness. "If Jonce ever does make a big strike," Kitty said once, "I'm going to insist on having a nice brick home down in Denver!" Then she began to laugh in a mocking sort of way, as if the mere thought of ever leaving Cripple Creek were too fantastic for words. "Just listen to me!" she added, after a moment. "How I prattle! It's likely that we'll never get any farther from the District than Pisgah grave-yard!"

It was beginning to look as though the Winchesters, too, would end in that dismal burial ground. It was 1899; more than two years had passed since they moved to Golden Avenue and despite Uncle Si's rosy predictions, they were poorer than ever. Mrs. Winchester had taken in a boarder, a fat, crochety old man named Herbert Warne who, it was rumored, had loaned Uncle Si a lot of money and was getting it back in keep.

The gray thatched usurer lolled all day long in the best chair by the stove, letting Mrs. Winchester sweep around him while he read newspapers and magazines and munched gumdrops. We children would stand hopefully, lips moist, watching as he dipped furtively into his coat pocket, barely rattling the paper bag, and then his pudgy hand would slip a piece of candy into his mouth. He never so much as glanced at us as he chewed and smacked and swallowed; and reached again into his pocket.

My father had recently struck ore in his claim on Womack Hill, just behind the Midland Terminal depot, but it turned out to be another small pocket that brought in hardly enough to pay all his debts. He told Kitty that he was going back to the Orizaba No. 2 on Beacon Hill and try once more to locate the bonanza which his divining rod had once indicated. But progress was slow and lately his cough had got steadily worse. It was all he could do to climb even a little slope. He began to drink heavily again and Kitty, in her despair, quarreled and scolded and reminded him of his many failures.

But a ray of promise had unexpectedly brightened the outlook for Uncle Si. He finally secured the lease he'd been after on the Doctor-Jack Pot. It had been a fabulous producer for a few years but the vein pinched out and the owners spent their fortune trying to locate another lode. At last the mine was abandoned, the shaft covered over and the shops torn down and carted off. Cripple Creekers made fun of Windy Joe and his crazy notions about finding the lost Jack Pot vein. Nobody would risk a red cent in loaning him cash for machinery, tools and labor. He even offered my father a substantial interest in the property if he would do some development work on the twelfth level. "I'll guarantee that you won't be sorry," he said glowingly. "In a short while we'll both be on easy street." But my father put him off, saying that he couldn't spare the time from the Orizaba. Ore, there, might turn up any day.

A week or so later my father came home early, looking strange and agitated. He told us that Winchester had scraped up enough money to hire several miners to start crosscutting on the twelfth level. "With the first shot," he said, "they opened up a wide vein of sylvanite that looked like a thousand mirrors in the candlelight. It takes three shifts of ore sorters to keep up with the avalanche of gold." He went to the water bucket to get a drink and I saw his hand trembling so that he could hardly hold the dipper. "Joe stands to make a million or two in the first year alone," he added. "Quite a windfall!"

I didn't wait to hear more but went tearing down to the Winchesters', half expecting to find Uncle Si's ship anchored to the back porch. Instead, Mrs. Winchester was taking in washing from the line just as if nothing unusual had happened. I blurted out the astounding news thinking that she hadn't heard it yet. But she acted unimpressed, just put another clothespin in her mouth while she folded a sheet. Then she looked at me and smiled. "I been around mining camps too long," she said casually, "and fooled too many times to get stirred up now. If Josiah brings a sealskin coat from Daniels and Fisher's when he gets back from Denver, maybe I'll believe it."

Except for old man Warne who had left suddenly, we were all waiting on the front porch when he pulled up jubilantly in one of Welty Bros. smartest rigs. Packages of every size and shape filled the seats. A black Derby was cocked jauntily on his head, and his blue striped suit was of the latest cut. A white silk handkerchief fluttered from his lapel pocket and when he leaned down to kiss Susan and me, the delicious fragrance of Florida Water drenched the air. "Just keep the chicken feed, Jack," he said, dropping a gold piece in the driver's hand, "with my compliments to the missus!"

Susan and I had already begun to tear open the bundles. "Hey there, you young cayuses," he shouted, "just hold on. Stop throwin' paper all over the place! I declare, you all act like you never had a thing before in your lives!" When the floors and tables were piled high with packages he let us start opening them. What an astonishing sight! Toys of every sort littered the room, Klondike puzzles, sleight-of-hand tricks, magic lantern slides . . .

"Take a gander at this!" he was saying. "I'll bet you've never even heard of such a contraption. It's a Concert Grand Gramophone—plays two records with only one winding. Now listen, everybody—hey there, Spuds, stop beating that drum!" Then he slipped a wax cylinder into the machine and it began to play "Maple Leaf Rag" and "Mosquito's Parade." I could hardly believe my ears! "Here's another piece," he went on, "you all should remember." And we hung on every word of Elbert Hubbard's reading of his stirring "Message to Garcia."

But even more wonders were in store for us. There were clothes for everybody, a red crepe de Chine dress for me, a blue foulard silk for Susan. But I really caught my breath when I saw the high button, Julia Marlowe shoes, with opera heels and long, pointed toes—a pair for each of us! We tried them on at once, and were about to parade up and down Golden Avenue showing them off when Uncle Si called us back. "Wait a second, girls—you ain't seen anything yet!"

We watched, wide-eyed, while he opened the long shiny-gray cardboard box. Suddenly the odor of moth balls seeped through the room as he lifted out sheets of tissue paper and tossed them away. At last he held up an elegant black sealskin coat with Mrs. Winchester's initials embroidered on the brocaded lining. She stood for a second, just staring at it and twisting her hands as though she couldn't believe her eyes.

Then, all at once, she slumped over weeping and Uncle Si caught her up in his arms.

He lost no time moving his family to the brownstone mansion he had bought in the very shadow of the Capitol's gilded dome. He tried to persuade my parents to let me go with them "for a nice long visit." Kitty was pleased and anxious for me to have such an opportunity, but my father said he thought it was time I got acquainted with my own family and wouldn't give his permission.

My heart was broken the day they went away. I stood alone on the platform at the Midland depot, waving to them until the train disappeared. Then I ran home through the alley so that people would not see me crying and sat for a long time on the Winchesters' back steps. I looked around the deserted yard and listened for an echo of children's laughter, or the ring of Uncle Si's bantering inside the forlorn rooms. Over in the gulch above Anaconda heavy black smoke streamed from the big stack at the Doctor-Jack Pot and hung like mourning crepe against the sky. Only Kitty's voice broke the stillness. "I thought it was you I saw coming up the alley," she called, "and I couldn't imagine where you had gone. She cut cross through the Baltzell yard and sat with me on the steps. "Don't take it so hard, Mabs honey," she said, putting her arm around me. "You'll see them again but even if you don't, it's better not to cling to what's over and past—that's a lesson I had to learn after we left Silver Reef. Just be glad that Uncle Si and Susie meant so much, and look forward to all the other friends you're bound to make. Come now, child," she added, getting up, "dry your eyes. You don't want them to be so red when your father comes home."

It was a long time before I saw the Winchesters again, but there was no dearth of news about them from Cripple Creekers who made trips to Denver. They brought back fantastic stories of Josiah's extravagances and predicted that he would be flat broke within a year. Now, so the gossip ran, he sprinkled his bath with attar of roses instead of Florida Water; and Mrs. Winchester was wearing diamond earrings as big as four-bit pieces. A brougham driven by a coachman in green livery could be seen every day taking Susan to and from Miss Wolcott's exclusive school. And Joe was telling around that he'd had to send all the way to Natchez for a negro cook who could make *filet gumbo* exactly as he liked it.

Word of his good fortune traveled fast. In no time many of his high-born but impoverished relatives arrived, unexpectedly, for an indefinite stay with their "long lost Cousin Josiah." His reputation as an easy touch also spread rapidly and he seldom stepped out of his twenty-room home without being approached for handouts, loans or grubstakes. His large gifts to charity were the talk of Denver. Society leaders, it was reported, besieged him with invitations and select clubs eagerly extended him membership. But Mrs. Winchester remained in the background; it was understood that she had no interest in going to parties. Whenever occasion required it, Susan or one of the genteel kinfolks accompanied him.

Uncle Si made frequent trips to Cripple Creek to look after his mine but I saw him only once. It was the day he came to our house to try to persuade my parents to let me go east with Susan to attend a finishing school in Washington. "It won't cost you a cent, John," he said when my father refused, "and when they graduate I'll send them to the finest college in the land!" But the answer was still no. "I have other plans for her education," my father explained. "I want her to stay in the West."

Kitty was bitterly disappointed and accused Jonce of not wanting me to have advantages and even went so far as to say it was because he was jealous of Josiah Winchester. "That's poppycock," he said. "I'll be in a position to give her all the advantages she can take pretty soon, and I intend to put her in a school where she'll learn something besides how to use a finger bowl or dance a cotillion." He sat puffing slowly on his pipe. "By then," he went on, "Joe may have lost the Jack Pot and all his money. He's got a pardner now who's a lawyer and a politician. I wouldn't trust 'im any further than I can spit!"

Suspicion had apparently been left out of Uncle Si's make-up. I had often heard him boast that he was a man of his word and always gave the other fellow the benefit of the doubt. He wasn't likely to waste time pouring over intricate details of a contract. "My eyesight's worth too much," he once declared, "to strain it tryin' to read all that stuff in fine print. Signin' my name to a deal is just a mere formality."

To show his good will he set aside most of the tenth level, one of the Jack Pot's choice areas, to be held in trust for men who at various times had lent him encouragement as well as money. An eighth was to be given to an old fellow named Cronkhite, another slice to a couple of friends who had advanced him $250 to pay an overdue grocery bill. Joe Watson, for whom he had taken a liking, was also put down for an eighth. George Tabor was to have an eighth just because he said he wanted a chance to make an honest dollar. It seemed that Josiah couldn't do enough for his partner and legal consultant, Archie M. Stevenson of Denver, and when his daughter married, he made her a present of a generous slice of the Jack Pot's golden tenth level.

Still feeling magnanimous, he organized a company to take over his mining property, allotting to himself a million shares of stock. Out of this, 250,000 were to be put in his wife's name, another 100,000 were to go for his mother's needs, and 50,000 would be for his children. Herbert Warne, the aged skinflint

who ate Mrs. Winchester out of house and home, was to re-
ceive 100,000 shares for carrying out the arrangements of the
trust funds.

After setting his affairs in order, he announced plans to
take Mrs. Winchester and the family on a long-promised tour
through the East and South. He hadn't gone far when re-
porters caught up with him and tales of his prodigality were
played up wherever he went. Social barriers everywhere vanished in the warmth of his personality and free-flowing money.
His comings and goings were regularly noted in the Denver
papers: The Winchesters had arrived in Natchez to be feted by
prominent friends and relatives. The Josiah Winchesters were
to spend the Christmas holidays at the Waldorf-Astoria and
would leave later to stay several months at the Royal Poinci-
ana in Palm Beach. Miss Susan Winchester, their attractive
daughter, now attending school in Washington, was expected
to join her parents for the Easter vacation. The Henry M.
Flaglers entertained the Josiah Winchesters at their villa.
Dinner was followed by an evening of music with Russell
T. Joy at the pipe organ. Reports say that Josiah Winchester
has bought a yacht and will cruise the Caribbean before returning in April or May to his home in Denver.

But one March day the brief dispatches flared into headlines. Josiah Winchester had arrived unexpectedly in the capital city and stated that he had returned to file suit against his
partner, A. M. Stevenson. My father's dire prophecy had
come true, it seemed, and Uncle Si had been cleaned out of
the Doctor-Jack Pot with the thoroughness of a hurricane.

As he told his story in court, he had been forced to borrow
several thousand dollars from the First National Bank in Denver to meet the mine's payroll for the first month. The loan
was negotiated through his partner, Archibald M. Stevenson,
who had been authorized to put up Winchester's block of stock

as guaranty. According to agreement, if Winchester failed to repay the loan on the date stipulated, the stock held as security would go to Stevenson if or when he canceled the note. It was an intriguing deal at best and fraught with tempting possibilities.

Meanwhile, the Jack Pot was more than fulfilling its part of the bargain; production exceeded estimates and stock boomed. But Josiah Winchester was either riding too high in his new wealth and had forgotten the bank loan, or his order to repay it on the agreed date had miscarried. The first he knew of the delinquent note, he claimed, was the bank statement saying that because of his failure to repay the loan as scheduled, and its subsequent cancellation by his attorney, the stock put up as security had been turned over in compliance with his agreement to A. M. Stevenson.

When the case came up in court, Winchester's key witness, Herbert Warne, to whom he had sent the original instructions for repayment of the debt, was somewhere in Mexico and couldn't be reached, nor could any records of telegrams or letters be found. Josiah's story consisted of a straightforward recital of the facts, but without the support of other testimony the evidence was too slim to convince the jury and he lost the verdict.

Before appealing to a higher court, he added a further complaint accusing A. E. Carlton, Cripple Creek's rising young banker and freight overlord, once his close friend, of conspiring to get control of the Jack Pot. It was Carlton's money, Joe declared, that financed Stevenson's defense and sent Herbert Warne to an unknown destination in Mexico, thus depriving the complaintant of a vital witness. He went so far as to predict that if his suit failed, Bert Carlton would come into the open as the majority holder of Jack Pot stock.

Winchester became so obsessed with hatred of Carlton,

"the real skunk in the bushes," that he refused to speak to him. Bert sent word through a friend that he saw no reason why Joe shouldn't recognize him on the street. "Tell Bert Carlton," he said, "that I still have a few knickknacks in my pants pocket —a penknife, a couple of marbles and an old key ring. I'm kinda fond of 'em and if I spoke to him he'd get 'em away from me!"

The case ultimately reached the Colorado Supreme Court, with Winchester compelled to plead as a pauper. But again the verdict went against him. Now nothing was left, not even a specimen of sylvanite from the fabulous tenth level. The brownstone mansion had been sold; new-found friends had vanished and the relatives had returned to Mississippi, together with the specialist in *filet gumbo*. Newspapers made brief mention of him at the last, just a few words about Joe Winchester's having moved with his family to Arizona where he said he expected to take up a homestead and raise cotton.

A year later, shortly before Christmas 1900, the Cripple Creek *Morning Times* headlined the news that the Raven Hill property, known as the Doctor-Jack Pot, had been released from litigation through a consolidation with other adjoining properties. The officers of the new company were listed as A. E. Carlton, president; J. A. Hayes, vice-president; F. M. Woods, general manager; H. E. Woods, secretary; Irving Bonbright, A. M. Stevenson, directors. No mention was made of Josiah Winchester or his family.

12

The Second Greatest Day

MARCH 23, 1899, was a red-letter day in Cripple Creek, marred only by the usual prediction of snow toward nightfall. But nothing could have cooled the ardor of the people. They had been waiting two weeks for "the Shower of Gold," as the big celebration was called, and now they were pouring from every direction to swell the crowds milling up and down Bennett Avenue.

Kitty, Molly Letts and I took our stand in front of Neal's Assay office, across from the National Hotel. Here we could get a full view of the arrival of distinguished guests and later see the monster parade as it turned down Third to Myers Avenue, giving the denizens of the tenderloin a treat before circling back up Second Street and repeating the line of march. Much to my relief, Brother had been left with an elderly, rheumatic neighbor and, as might have been expected, my father and Jim Letts had box seats in the upstairs windows of Tom Lorimer's gambling parlors.

Kitty had fixed a lunch and we sat on the curbing, munching tongue sandwiches and watching the kaleidoscopic scene, looking for familiar faces passing by. Bennett Avenue was at its best, decorated from one end to the other with flags and golden streamers and jammed with good-natured spectators bent on having the time of their lives. The very sight gave me a thrill. I couldn't imagine a more fascinating street in all the world. It was the main artery through which the lifeblood of the camp pulsed, where the lights blazed night and day and the shuffle of feet was never stilled.

Everything happened on Bennett Avenue. It was the arena for fist fights and runaway teams; the setting for comedy, violence and death; the soundboard for laughter and sobbing. While drunken orators held forth in its saloons, Parson Holmes, the Negro preacher, exhorted sinners to repent, from his buggy hitched in front of Cohen's Thirst Parlor; and the Salvation Army with bugle and drum passed the tambourines among Johnny Nolon's free-spending customers. It was the glittering promenade, too, where good women like Kitty could take Brother and me on Saturday nights and stroll up one side and down the other, stopping to visit with friends or to admire the displays in store windows. Before going home we always went to the Palace Pharmacy for a lemon phosphate. Across the street at the Butte, a woman who was brazen enough could slip through the door marked *Ladies' Entrance* where beer was served at tables and a pianola banged out "Zizzy, Ze Zum, Zum" or "Sugar Baby."

Here it was only Friday afternoon and already Bennett Avenue was topsy-turvy with excitement. People were yelling "Hooray for Cripple Creek!" "Three cheers for Montgomery!" and "Long live Teller County!" It was deafening and even frightening. "Dear me," Kitty said, taking hold of my arm, "if folks're this wild now, what'll they be like by suppertime? There's something strange and foreboding about it."

"Don't let one of your foolish notions spoil your fun,"

Molly said, laughing. "Everybody's just wound up 'cause it's the most important day, I guess, since the first train came."

Two weeks before, on the eighth, the District had come of age when the State Legislature passed the bitterly contested measure creating a new county which would encompass the famous gold field. It was named Teller, after Colorado's distinguished senator; and Cripple Creek was destined to become the county seat. Up to that time, the area with its fabled riches lay in El Paso County, providing a well-traveled back-door entrance to Colorado Springs. The citizens of the Cripple Creek District had no say in what went on at the State Capitol, no share in spending the lush taxes and no political patronage. It was a humiliating situation for men who aspired after public office, as well as for the prestige of a camp whose mines had built most of the fine mansions on Little Lun'non's Cascade and Wood avenues.

The Ammons Bill, as it was called, might have had easier going if it hadn't involved the partitioning of other adjoining counties to form the new domain. The people of those shorn lands fought back with every resource of wealth that could be mustered. But the persistence and force of Colonel B. F. Montgomery, the District's leading attorney, was too much for them and the measure squeezed through to narrow victory. The following week, Governor C. S. Thomas signed it into law with a pen made of gold from the Independence mine.

Mayor Pierce immediately started wheels humming for a jubilation so spectacular that it would dwarf anything the people had ever witnessed, either on Labor Day or the Fourth of July. He announced that a holiday would be declared for schools and all places of business except the saloons; the monster parade would be headed by the governor, state legislators and other distinguished guests; and afterwards Bennett Avenue would be thrown open for dancing. Following a sumptuous banquet at the National Hotel, the visitors would attend masked balls at the Butte and Grand Opera houses. "Cripple Creek's inimitable cornetist and bandsman, Joe Moore," the mayor added, "will be in charge of music for the parade and street dancing; and he will lead the Elks Band for the grand march at the Opera House!"

The mention of Joe Moore gave me a reminiscent heart-flutter. He had married shortly after the great fires and moved away from our neighborhood, and I seldom saw him. But recently his name had been in the paper for having kicked Jim McVickers, "a gun-slinging drunk," from Lorimer's bar-room; and the fellow, "a well-known blowhard around town," had sworn revenge on Moore. I paid little attention to the item. The veneer of Joe's attraction for me had worn off with my advancing years; and he had long since been displaced as the hero of my daydreams. But now, on this auspicious March Friday, an unaccountable feeling of romantic excitement seized me and I could hardly contain myself at the thought of seeing Joe Moore, marching once again down Bennett Avenue in all his shining glory.

The throng had pushed in behind us so that it was all I could do to keep my footing on the sidewalk. It was getting late and glowering clouds hugged Bull Hill. "Stomp your feet, Mabs," Kitty mumbled, "so you won't get chilblains." Just then, two mounted policemen trotted by to clear the street, driving stray children and curious onlookers scrambling for room on the sidewalk. A sudden hush fell upon the air and everybody began to peer down the street. The next moment there was a ruffle of drums and before I realized it the Anaconda Drum Corps, in yellow uniforms, came strutting past, piping the "Mosquito's Parade" on their piccolos. And the crowd cheered and swayed in unison to the rollicking beat.

The chief of police on a prancing black mare followed next,

escorting the mayor and the governor, who rode in a smart victoria. How elegant they appeared in their cutaways and striped pants! And how graciously they smiled and touched their stovepipe hats to acknowledge the ovation! "Look, Mabs," Molly was saying, "there comes the Queen and her attendants—she's Frances Rose of Victor! She'd better have her winter coat on under them golden robes—quick—what's that fella with the megaphone tellin'—well, I'll be doggoned— the glass case in the Queen's lap holds the golden pen the governor used to record the birth of Teller County—that's what the fella said—darned if I can see it!"

Then came Colonel B. F. Montgomery, riding alone ahead of the legislators who had fathered the bill. Paper jonquils made by the ladies of the First Baptist Church were scattered in their paths as the carriages neared the National Hotel. "Gosh, wasn't that thrilling!" Molly exclaimed. "I swear, I never seen so many big-guns at once in all my life!"

"See there," Kitty nudged me. "It's the new hook-and-ladder wagon! Don't Mandy and Bess look proud, all decked out in rosettes and with their tails braided in yellow satin ribbon!"

But at that instant a loud blare of trumpets caught my ear and I almost fell off the sidewalk, leaning over, trying to see if it was Joe Moore at last about to swing his musicians up the avenue. But it was only the Portland Miners Band from Victor —our deadly rival. This band always tried to make a big splash in Cripple Creek parades, flaunting signs about VICTOR—CITY OF MINES! and BATTLE—MOUNTAIN OF BONANZAS! The players wore blue denim overalls for uniforms, and miners' candlesticks flickered in their caps. But it had to be admitted—they were clever. Now, when they broke into "Mister Johnson, Turn Me Loose!" I stomped and sang and swayed my shoulders along with all the other syncopating onlookers.

"When it comes to playin' the band," Molly said, "I guess there ain't any rivalry between Victor and the Creek." Then, with a wink at me, "Joe Moore'll have to go some to beat them fellas!"

Somebody had said that there were six bands and two drum corps in the long procession in addition to the steam calliope, and I had begun to despair of seeing Joe Moore's aggregation before dark. Many elaborate floats had passed by, tossing out samples of Pears soap and Malt Nutrine and tiny envelopes of Pozzoni's face powder. By far the most popular of these was an enormous whisky barrel mounted on wheels. On top, dimpled, roguish Jack Dewar, sporting his Scotch kilties, intermittently played the bagpipes and pelted the scrambling hangers-on with small bottles of Dewar's Whisky. Then members of thirty-four fraternal lodges, all arrayed in their particular uniforms, limped, hop-skipped and sauntered past, trying to keep step with Cook's Drum Corps. I was tired and disappointed and wanted to weep. Then I saw the familiar purple banner with the white letters B.P.O.E. inscribed. "It's the Elks," I screamed, giving Kitty a hug. "The Elks are coming!" And in a moment Joe Moore, leading the band, burst into sight.

What a dashing figure he cut, in his royal-purple bandsman's outfit, adorned with brass buttons, gold fringe and epaulettes! I strained my eyes for every detail. He marched like a thoroughbred, as if knowing that all eyes were on him, that the crowds were waiting breathlessly for his downbeat. Then he gave the signal, lifted the glistening cornet to his lips and the band broke into "Ta-ra-ra-boom-der-é!" Shivers raced through my body as people up and down the block started cheering and singing,

"Not too young and not too old
Not too timid, not too bold

143

Just the kind for sport I'm told
Ta-ra-ra-boom-der-é!"

A drunk had stumbled into the street, cursing and shaking his fists at Joe Moore. A policeman ran over and yanked the fellow back. The crowd laughed and made fun of him and hurled epithets. Joe Moore paid no attention but continued as if nothing unusual had happened, high-stepping with the band ringing out "Ta-ra-ra-boom-der-é!" until the last note faded somewhere on Myers Avenue. The parade was over, so far as it concerned me, and I was grateful when the arc lights began to sputter at six o'clock and Speed Wolff, having just caught up with the tail end of the line, pulled his gasoline buggy to a stop in front of the National Hotel.

Molly suggested that we go to the Saddle Rock Café for a bite to eat before the street dancing started. "Lots of folks'll likely go home after supper," she said, "and the mob'll thin out. If Jim shows up, maybe him and Kitty can have another waltz together. They'd take the cake, I'll bet!"

"Not me," Kitty said, as if she had been waiting to leave for some time. "It's after six and I must go for Billie."

The threat of storm had passed when we came outside, and a sharp wind was sweeping the last wispy clouds from the sky and whipping the bunting to shreds. Above the cone of Mount Pisgah the moon arched a curious eyebrow before rising quickly to a full view. I pulled my coat closer around me. The warming smell of buttered popcorn and hot tamales steamed from tinkling pushcarts. If anything, the crush seemed greater than ever and Kitty looked anxiously for my father, but neither he nor Jim Letts was in sight. "I think we'd better work our way toward home," she said. "It's getting rough—already too many folks're feeling their oats. . . ."

All at once I heard the unmistable quaver of Joe Moore's

cornet. "Please wait—just a minute," I begged. "See, it's Joe Moore—he's marching again—coming up the avenue!"

"Not here, by Tom Lorimer's!" she objected. But now the converging throng made it impossible for us to move in any direction.

Joe and his musicians were cakewalking up the middle of Bennett Avenue. He beckoned everybody to fall in behind and soon a long line of revelers began to weave in a serpentine, back and forth across the street, dancing grotesquely and singing,

> "When you hear dem bells go dinga linga ling
> All join in an' sweetly you must sing,
> An' when de verse am through
> In de chorus all join in,
> Der'll be a hot time in old town tonight
> Ma Ba—aby!"

In and out they wound, past the Salvation Army pounding drums and shaking tambourines, by Parson Holmes trying to outdo them, barely missing the hawker and his long telescope near Gondolfo's fruit stand, past Jim Hanley's place, the Newport, the Branch. Now Joe was leading them directly toward Tom Lorimer's. Even Molly Letts seemed worried and nervous. "I wish we could beat it from here," she said. "They must all be soused. It don't look good to me."

She had scarcely spoken, it seemed, when a shot rang out and only a few feet from us a tight knot of twisting, brawling, cursing men rolled and tussled on the sidewalk. Then another shot! Someone was groaning and choking for breath; and I saw a thin trickle of blood on the cement. A policeman ran up and began to push through the mob, yelling for someone to get a doctor, ordering people to move on. Kitty, Molly and I were shoved into the open doorway that led to Lorimer's upstairs rooms—an unthinkable escape. We were trapped!

Other officers rushed in and helped pull the fighters apart. One of them started to run but was caught and handcuffed; another leaned weakly against the telephone pole. A gun in his hand was still smoking. Somebody said he was Jim McVickers. . . .

I felt Kitty's arm around me. She was telling me something about not looking—covering my face. But I stood paralyzed with horror as I caught a glimpse of Joe Moore lying crumpled on the sidewalk, gasping for air. Blood had matted his dark hair and dripped on his gold epaulettes. Dr. Hanford had come and was kneeling down, feeling his pulse. Then he nodded solemnly; the struggle for life had ended. All of a sudden an eerie stillness of awe and grief hovered over Bennett Avenue.

The story of the tragedy filled the front page of the *Times* next morning, leaving scarcely any space for a description of Teller County's great celebration. Boxed in the center, and bordered with black, was a poem that tore at my heartstrings.

> Farewell, Joe Moore, we wish you well
> In that mysterious land to which you go.
> We loved you well and knew you as you were,
> A staunch and trusted friend in weal or woe.
>
> Farewell, Joe Moore, we'll meet you presently
> In that great lodge room up in the skies,
> Where once again with warm fraternal clasp
> You'll welcome us within that paradise.
>
> Farewell, Joe Moore, we grieve to see you go
> And leave us here upon this earthly plane.
> We hope to know that we shall meet again
> In that bright land where parting comes no more.

His body was shipped to Denver for burial but that didn't prevent Cripple Creekers from giving him a fine funeral. The Elks Band, in deep mourning, led the cortege, playing "Saul's Death March." Three express wagons full of flower bouquets and set-pieces followed behind the hearse. Every union and fraternal order in camp sent representatives; and all the saloons and gambling houses on Bennett Avenue were closed between the hours of one and three o'clock.

Except for the funereal music and muted drum beats, I thought it was every bit as spectacular as the parade two days before. Not since Pearl De Vere committed suicide had there been such a turnout on Bennett Avenue. Joe would have been mighty pleased. When the saloons were open again crowds of thirsty customers made up for lost time. I had intended to cross over before reaching Tom Lorimer's, fearing to see black crepe on the locked door and the stain of Joe Moore's lifeblood on the sidewalk. But I needn't have worried. The cement walk had been scoured clean; the doors were swinging busily and somewhere inside a gramophone was screeching "Goo Goo Eyes" above the guffaws.

Only a string of yellow bunting, torn and raveled by the wind, hung limply from the telephone pole in front of Lorimer's bar, a melancholy memento of "the Shower of Gold" and the birthday celebration of Teller County.

13

Finn's Folly

CRIPPLE CREEK reached her majority when she acquired a county of her own and became the county seat. But no town, even with a fine red-brick courthouse, could consider itself grown up without a single mansion to point to with pride. It remained for J. Maurice Finn, a prominent attorney, to remedy the situation. He had been boasting about the great house he planned to erect in camp ever since he came in with the gold rush. But here it was, nearing the end of the century, and The Towers, as he called it, was still only a figment of his imagination. It might never have materialized if, in an expansive moment, he hadn't invited Teddy Roosevelt to visit him when he was elected Vice-President of the United States.

My father liked Finn; they had been friends since the early days and had much in common. Both were Democrats and backsliding Baptists, strongly individualistic and cursed with an equal capacity for Kentucky bourbon. Finn hailed from Upper Michigan where he practiced law when he wasn't campaigning for political office. He emulated his idol, William Jennings Bryan, in bearing, and except for his pudgy, smooth-shaven face and a tendency to paunchiness, might have been considered handsome. He was loquacious, affable and ambitious for a career in politics but although he had been a perennial nominee in his native state, he had never won an election. The highest distinction he ever received from his party was that of making the seconding speech nominating Grover Cleveland for another term as President. At the time, Finn was running for Congress against Republican Sam Stephenson.

Cleveland won—and so did Stephenson. Victory had again slipped through his fingers in spite of his brilliant electioneering. Defeated and broke, he was said to be washed up and through with politics. As a last feeble effort to save face, he claimed that his opponent had won by fraud; and threatened a lawsuit. But just then news of the fabulous gold field behind Pike's Peak was beginning to fill the newspapers, and diverted him. He knew nothing about mining except that rich strikes inevitably led to legal snarls. A sudden impulse moved him to pull up stakes and without even saying good-by to his partner, he joined the stampede to Cripple Creek.

When he came to our house he often talked about his bitter years in Michigan politics. "Well, J.M.," my father once commented, "I guess there ain't a man in this goddamn camp who didn't run away from something he couldn't swallow back where he came from—all of us up here have got a streak of rebel in our make-up." J. Maurice found it tough getting a start in Cripple Creek, largely for that reason. He was too outspoken, especially regarding taxes. "Taxation's a steal from the poor to make the rich even richer," he declared. "Let 'em brand me as a delinquent! I'll rot in jail before I'll ever pay a cent!"

His father, a Baptist minister, had instilled in the son a genuine sympathy for outcasts, who often imposed on his generosity. All the camp's rogues, felons and miscreants fled to him in time of danger. His good intentions were never questioned but he had been known to skirt the rules. When he strode into court, dressed in his Prince Albert, all eyes were on him, waiting to see what magic he could pull out of his sleeve to free his client. He was at his forensic best in murder trials, using every ingenious device to play on the heartstrings of a jury. The reports of these subterfuges in the *Times* were as gripping as anything I had ever read on the sly in the *Police Gazette*.

How he gloated over a cleverly won verdict! One of his murder cases would keep me on tenterhooks for weeks and rob me of many a night's sleep. I shuddered every time I thought afterwards of the way he once outwitted a corps of prosecuting attorneys by finagling a doctor into sawing off the murdered man's skull, and getting it presented as exhibit number one. Then he proved to the satisfaction of the jury that if the cranium had been thicker the pistol blows that killed the victim would have glanced off with no damage done. Therefore, the unusual thinness of his skull was really responsible for his death.

After two days and nights of deliberation the jury agreed with Finn and a verdict of "Not guilty" set the alleged murderer free. The community called it a travesty on justice and a mob of two hundred miners formed a lynching party. But the sheriff got wind of it and railroaded the fellow out of camp. J. Maurice Finn, likewise, had urgent business elsewhere. His second wife had died not so long before and he hurried to Michigan to persuade her younger sister, Elsie Belle, a widow, to marry him.

Tempers had cooled by the time he returned with his attractive bride and the future looked bright. W. S. Stratton, impressed by Finn's resourcefulness and knowledge of the law, engaged him as legal counsel for all his mining interests, including the Independence. The attorney immediately took advantage and began to acquire properties of his own and money rolled into his pockets. Elsie Belle's taste in tapestries and oriental rugs was excellent and her husband encouraged her to lay in a supply to be stored in readiness for their new mansion. For his part, the time had come to enlarge his already extensive law library with rare and costly volumes, and to add to his collection of marble and bronze busts of great American patriots. Nobody seemed surprised when it was rumored, finally, that Finn was broke and about to go bankrupt. "He spent too much on tomfoolery," my father commented. "The only sensible thing he's got to show for his money is a couple dozen cases of Kentucky bourbon."

To make matters worse, the unpredictable Stratton began to complain that J. Maurice was using him for his own purposes, and wasn't worth a hoot in hell as company lawyer; and he was fired without notice. The loss of that lush connection left him poorer than ever and he sought forgetfulness in his ample supplies of bonded whisky. But early in the winter of 1901, a news report jolted him back to consciousness. Teddy Roosevelt, the story said, had announced his intention to visit Colorado in April and expected to include a trip to the Cripple Creek District to renew his friendship with Danny Sullivan and "that distinguished Democrat, J. Maurice Finn."

To be singled out as a future host to the Vice-President of the United States was a heady elixir for a man whose world had just crashed about him, but it also posed a serious problem that stemmed back to Roosevelt's first trip to the famous mining camp as nominee of the Republican Party for the nation's second highest office. He was Governor of New York, at the time, and made the blunder of publicly sympathizing with the antilabor stand of Colorado's Governor Peabody. To add oil to the fire, he took Coloradans to task for their stand against adopting the gold standard as opposed to bimetalism, or the double monetary standard, so strongly favored by people of the Cripple Creek District whom he labeled as "crackpots and impractical visionaries."

Cripple Creekers resented the slur but at the same time they were flattered at the prospect of entertaining such a notable person, one who someday might easily become President of the United States. They went ahead with plans for a banquet in his honor, at the National Hotel, and a big meeting at the Lyric Theater where it was announced that he would make an address.

The City of Mines over on Battle Mountain, however, couldn't swallow its fury. The stronghold of the miners' union was there and its members were resolved to make Roosevelt's presence in camp as tough as possible. His special train was due around three o'clock. After a brief speech at the Armory he was to go on to Cripple Creek, attend the banquet, make his address, and return later that night to Colorado Springs. The big crowd waiting at the Victor depot was plainly in a nasty mood. The miners made no effort to conceal their intention of giving the unwanted politician such a hot reception that he would hightail it back to the Springs at once, and leave Cripple Creek, their two-faced rival, with a lot of cold chicken to pay for at the National Hotel.

Teddy stepped down from his special car looking radiant in his tall hat, Prince Albert and striped trousers. But before Mayor Franklin could shake hands with him, the throng let out a roar of boos and jeers loud enough to be heard all over camp. Aside from two or three policemen who were clearly in cahoots with the demonstrators, no one was on hand to preserve order. Cripple Creekers had got wind that there might be trouble for the Colonel and had sent two bodyguards to accompany him from Victor. One of them was Danny Sulli-

van, the formidable Irish postmaster. It was decided, however, that the tension had reached such a pitch that it would
be wiser for the bodyguards to wait at the station while Teddy
went to the Armory, so as not to appear to be invading Victor's
sacred precincts.

No one, least of all the doughty Rough Rider, was prepared
for what happened next. As he and the mayor started the
two-block walk down the hill to the Armory, the hecklers began trailing after them, displaying placards warning him to get
out and threatening to tar and feather him if he failed to heed.
But he seemed to take it all in the spirit of fun, flashing his
toothy smile and tipping his stovepipe hat as though he were
hailing friends. Once inside the hall, however, the situation
couldn't be smiled off; it was unmistakably ominous. The
mayor pounded the gavel in vain, shouting for order, but his
voice couldn't penetrate the deafening noise.

At last Teddy evidently saw the futility of trying to make his
speech and beckoning to the mayor, whispered something in
his ear. Suddenly he and his party disappeared through a side
door. They had almost reached the depot before the outwitted
mobsters caught up with them and began throwing rocks,
bottles and tin cans; and then closed in on him. His hat was
knocked off and his thick-lensed nose glasses dangled from
their ribbons, leaving him half blind. Again and again the
thugs were fought off but it was becoming apparent that
unless help came, Teddy's life would be in danger.

Danny Sullivan was around in front of the depot talking
with the locomotive engineer when he heard the commotion
and hurried to see what was up. Instantly he tore down the
hill like an enraged beast, just in time to deflect a length of
two-by-four which was hurtling toward Teddy's head. Sullivan, a man of enormous build and utterly fearless, grabbed
the heavy beam and flailed a path through the attackers, scat-

tering them in all directions. A person less valiant than the heroic Rough Rider might have been unnerved by this close brush with death. But after he had wiped the dust from his hat and adjusted his glasses, he turned to thank Danny. "Now," he said, shaking the Irishman's hand vigorously, "I'm ready to pull out any time—for Cripple Creek!"

Cripple Creekers were quick to recognize good sportsmanship, especially in a political foe, and that night the Lyric Theater couldn't hold all the people who wanted to hear Roosevelt speak. When J. Maurice Finn, the dauntless Democrat, stepped forward on the stage to make a few introductory remarks, the audience howled him down, shouting again and again, "We want Teddy!" My father said that he had never heard a more stirring speech. The people applauded even when he berated them for fighting the government's adoption of the gold standard. Although they were mostly Democrats, they stomped their feet until the lights trembled as he finished expounding the principles of the Republican party. And how everybody laughed and clapped when he lit into a scornful tirade against "that silver-tongued orator, the Great Commoner, William Jennings Bryan!" My father said that the ovation was not for the Governor of New York, nor for the famous hero of the Spanish War; not even for the Republican nominee for Vice-President—it was for the character of a first-rate American.

Roosevelt made no mention of what had happened a few hours before, in Victor, until he neared the end of his speech. Then his voice lowered and took on a personal tone. "My friends," he began, "I hope you will excuse this digression but I feel impelled to pay tribute to one of your most courageous and loyal citizens. This afternoon, as you doubtless know, an unprovoked bodily attack was made on me by a few misguided people who, I am confident, in no way represent the spirit of your fabulous mining camp. Today my life was saved by a man to whom I shall always owe a debt of deepest gratitude. His name is Danny Sullivan!"

"It looked like the house would bust open with the applause," my father went on, "and at last, when it died down, J. Maurice Finn made a stab at saying a few words. He declared that at heart Governor Roosevelt was a good Democrat and as such, Finn himself might even cast his vote for him in the coming elections. Then he turned to Teddy and said, 'Someday, Colonel, I hope you will revisit this great District and give Mrs. Finn and me the honor of entertaining the Vice-President of the United States at our home, The Towers!' Roosevelt was obviously touched and delighted," my father concluded, "and promised that J. Maurice could expect him in the spring of next year."

It was a magnanimous gesture on Finn's part and the approval given him by the crowd was almost as hearty as that of the guest. But there was one hitch which probably hadn't occurred to him in the flush of excitement. The Towers hadn't yet been built. Indeed, the lot hadn't even been selected. But that was a simple matter, soon remedied. He and Elsie Belle set out the very next morning to decide on a location. They found what was described as "the most perfect site in the entire Pike's Peak region," at the head of Placer Street, on the west slope of Church Hill. No spot around offered such an inspiring panorama. It swept majestically from Bull Cliff above Victor to the white, faraway teeth of the Sangre de Cristo range. Unfortunately the city owned the land and had set its price at $3,000—an impossible amount for the Finns to pay.

But J. Maurice's resourceful brain began to work overtime figuring ways and means and as usual he came up with a bold solution. It was nothing less than a proposal to the city council that the property be donated to him, free of taxes. He argued that the kind of mansion he planned to erect would be an asset to the town as well as an adornment—a fitting home for the entertainment of the District's most distinguished guests. Surprisingly the City Fathers saw the point, and knowing his aversion to paying taxes, approved his request. They even went a step further and appropriated $2,000 to cover the cost of grading the foundation. Citizens were indignant over the deal but on second thought they too saw the advantages in the camp's having a mansion to point to with pride.

As a rule, it didn't take long to build a house in Cripple Creek, but the construction of The Towers dragged on and on and it began to look as if it would never be finished. Elsie Belle had sacrificed her $8,000 in savings to pay for lumber shipped from Michigan "because no other was sturdy enough." Already the original estimates of $25,000 had doubled and Finn was hopelessly in debt. Other troubles had piled up on him. Besides losing his lucrative job and W. S. Stratton's friendship, his mine, Mountain Beauty, had petered out and no longer paid royalties; his law practice had dwindled because of long neglect; and finally, he had become a confirmed alcoholic. Only the gaunt framework of his dream house stood on the hillside, a ghostly reminder of his past hopes.

It was likely that deep in his heart he had regarded Roosevelt's promise to visit him as a sort of political byplay made in the warmth of a pleasant occasion. The realization that the great man had spoken in earnest and actually planned to call on him at The Towers in a few months shocked J. Maurice into immediate activity. He hurried to the First National Bank to explain his dilemma to Bert Carlton, the hardheaded and tightfisted president, who, to everybody's amazement, consented to advance the several thousand dollars necessary to finish the mansion in time for the Vice-President's arrival.

The memory of Teddy's previous trip was still fresh, and soon Cripple Creekers were in a fever of preparation. Bennett Avenue was scraped and many houses all over town were given a coat of paint. Even Victor, where the Hero of San Juan had been so shabbily treated, caught the spirit and couldn't do enough, it seemed, to show her change of heart. An impressive tour of Battle Mountain's most famous bonanzas was arranged, ending with a trip through the mile-long Economic Tunnel with lunch afterwards at the Gold Coin Club. If there were any disgruntled miners in the crowd that gathered at Victor's depot for a second time to greet the Vice-President, they kept respectfully silent.

The camp had put on its gayest Fourth of July garb of flags and red, white and blue bunting. The Portland Miners Band played the national anthem as the great man alighted from his special car; and cheers of welcome resounded in the brisk air. He stood back for a moment, looking puzzled, as if not quite sure that he had landed in the right town. Instantly Mayor Franklin and James F. Burns of the Portland came forward to greet him with a token of good will—a golden key to the City of Mines.

"Well, bless my soul!" Teddy sputtered. "What's this all about?"

"We're delighted, sir, that you have honored us as our guest," the mayor said. "The musicians here, all underground miners from the Portland, can say it more eloquently." And with that, the band struck up "El Capitan!"

"I declare—that's bully!" Teddy exclaimed, scrutinizing the faces of the players as though they were the most unusual performers he had ever seen. "All miners, you say—it's remarkable! On my word! Sousa himself couldn't have done better!"

Carriages were on hand to drive him and his party through

the hilly camp. He spoke in wonder of the big mines with their smokestacks towering into the sky, of the scenery, with the Sangre de Cristos in the far background, of the healthy children and fine homes. He seemed to think it a delightful lark when Mrs. Harry Woods, wife of one of the owners of the Gold Coin Mine, still dressed up in her luncheon finery, climbed into the cage with him and all the others and went sliding down to the eighth level of the Gold Coin Shaft. When her husband handed him a pick with an invitation to help himself to the rich ore lining the stope, he tackled it with characteristic vigor. In a few moments he had dug out five hundred dollars' worth of high grade which was later shipped to Washington.

He'd had such a bully time in Victor that he was well behind schedule when his train, stopping at some of the smaller camps between, finally pulled into Cripple Creek. Hundreds of people were crowded around the depot, waiting, and the sidewalks along Bennett Avenue were lined with enthusiastic greeters. Some of them must have wondered how the Creek could possibly outdo the spectacular entertainment Victor had provided for the noted visitor. Of course, he would go first to the National Hotel to meet Republicans and other prominent leaders in town. Then he would ride in a carriage with Mayor Crane, Danny Sullivan and J. Maurice Finn, heading a long procession up and down Bennett Avenue. That sort of public homage had become commonplace as more and more world-wide celebrities stopped over on their way to New York or San Francisco.

But Cripple Creek could offer one distinct feature which Victor lacked. Theodore Roosevelt, the Vice-President of the United States, whose coming had inspired the completion of J. Maurice Finn's fifty-thousand-dollar mansion, had consented to christen it "The Towers" at the magnificent reception

the Finns were giving in his honor. Engraved invitations were
sent to almost everybody in the District, including the Barbees. But such an affair would never draw my father, "not even
if Almighty God was going to be on hand!" So Kitty took me
in his place. I begged her to hire a carriage as many others
would do, but she called that putting on airs. We could easily
walk the two blocks to Placer Street. Her practical streak
often exasperated me. "If you don't want to go on foot," she
said with finality, "Molly Letts would jump at the chance."
And that settled it.

What a stately sight the mansion was, standing aloof near
the crest of Church Hill! Its three stories made the surrounding cabins and houses look shabby in comparison. Four towers
surmounted the corners of the twenty-six-room building; and
each was topped by an enormous American flag, waving from
a still taller pole. The plate-glass windows sparkled like mirrors in the afternoon sun. The gray paint was still damp, and
carpenters' tools, scraps of lumber and other debris had been
thrown hastily under the front steps. A fresh smell of newness
pervaded the atmosphere.

There was the hum of women's voices as the wide doors
were opened and the next moment we were in the rotunda,
being greeted warmly by Mrs. Finn and her daughter, Eleanor. The myriad lights and flowers seemed to dance to the
music of a stringed orchestra concealed behind a screen of
potted palms. Filling the wall near the broad, semicircular
stairway was a giant fresco of the Mount of the Holy Cross and
a real brook tinkled down through one of the snowy gulches
in the picture to splash into an aquarium below filled with
mountain trout. Everyone gazed at it in amusement. Kitty,
who had been speechless up to then, leaned over and whispered, "Who else but J. Maurice Finn would ever have
thought of such a stunt!"

So far no men had arrived at the party and Mrs. Finn explained that everything had been thrown out of kilter because of the lateness of the Vice-President's train. She suggested that some of us make a tour of the house with Eleanor. Altogether there were fourteen bedrooms and each one opened on a balcony encircling the rotunda. Kitty said it was just like the Brown Palace in Denver. It made me dizzy to look down on all the women flitting around and chatting. We returned to the main floor to see the library and trophy room; and were drinking punch in the dining room when suddenly there was a flurry outside and in a moment J. Maurice Finn entered with Teddy Roosevelt, followed by Mayor Crane and Danny Sullivan. I hurried over near the door just in time to hear Teddy turn to the mayor and mumble, "This is worse than San Juan Hill!" and the mayor replied, "Fire and fall back!" I had no idea what they meant but suspected that the Vice-President intended to slip out a side door, just as he had done the year before at the Armory in Victor.

J. Maurice Finn acted as though he could hardly wait to show his celebrated guest around the mansion, but so far as I could see, Teddy was too captivated by his host's remarkable library of law books to go further. He examined the exquisite tapestries on the wall which were evidently well known to him, and exclaimed over the collection of sculptured busts of America's great patriots. "You may be interested to hear," J. Maurice said, "that every main room in the house is named after one of my favorite characters in history. The library, for instance, is the Abraham Lincoln Room. Over there where you can glimpse my trophies is the Thomas Jefferson Room."

"What a bully idea!" Teddy said, moving gradually toward the door. "Extraordinary—really fantastical!" Finn was trying to steer him into the trophy room, but just then Teddy caught sight of the painting of the Mount of the Holy Cross with the actual miniature stream cascading over a cliff into the large fish pool. For a moment he just stood gazing at it open-mouthed, as if struck speechless, or perhaps trying to decide if it were real or merely an illusion. Then he reached over and let the water ripple through his fingers. "I say, Maurice, this is phenomenal. You deserve a Congressional medal for your ingenuity!" And they both threw back their heads and roared with laughter. It was hard to tell which was having a better time, the genial host or the ebullient Teddy Roosevelt.

Danny Sullivan had kept in the background as though fearful of some crank harming his idol. Now he went over to touch Teddy's arm and, opening his big, silver biscuit watch, reminded him that it was past time for the special to leave. He would have to hurry or he'd miss the banquet to be given in his honor at the El Paso Club down in Colorado Springs. "Bless me! How short the day has been!" Teddy said regretfully. "It's been bully—every minute!" He turned around unexpectedly, asking for Mrs. Finn, but instead he bumped squarely into me. He looked embarrassed for an instant, begged my pardon, and then gave me one of his famous, toothy smiles. "Upon my word," he said heartily; "this must be a fine, healthy place for young girls, to give you such rosy cheeks and pretty blue eyes!"

I couldn't remember whether I ran or flew to the depot, following the crowd, to watch the train pull out. J. Maurice Finn, who was also going to the El Paso Club banquet, beamed happily as he saw Teddy clasping hands jovially with all the important Cripple Creekers who had come to see him off. Then Teddy called out, "Where's my friend Danny Sullivan? Don't tell me he's not in this crowd!" Danny pushed his way up to the car and Teddy grasped his hand and gave him a star sapphire ring from his own finger. "I hope you'll accept this small token, Danny," he said, so that everybody nearby could hear, "as a souvenir of that day a year ago when you saved my life. I trust you will wear it a long, long time."

A few weeks later, William McKinley was assassinated and Theodore Roosevelt became the twenty-sixth President of the United States. But he still remembered one proud Cripple Creeker. The following Christmas a small registered package, addressed to the postmaster, arrived. It bore the mark of Tiffany's in New York and contained a beautiful, slim gold watch. On the inside of the lid was the inscription,

> To fighting Danny Sullivan
> The only one of his kind in America
> From his grateful friend,
>> Theodore Roosevelt.

Teddy never got around to christening The Towers, and perhaps it was just as well. J. Maurice Finn became so hounded by creditors, before long, that he moved his law practice to Denver, returning to camp only occasionally to see his family. Mrs. Finn managed to stay on in the great house by renting the once luxurious rooms to school teachers. Among the townspeople Cripple Creek's only mansion, mortgaged to the flagpoles, came to be known as Finn's Folly.

14

The Divining Rod
Makes Good

I WAS seventeen, the summer of 1901, and had finished the third year of high school. It began to look as though my father's hopes of sending me away to study would never be realized. Kitty said that it was probably for the best. Already I had more education than most girls she knew; it was time I began to consider marrying and having a home of my own. Jonce's health had taken a serious turn for the worse, and he looked almost too frail to weather another winter in Cripple Creek. Kitty worried continuously about what would become of us if he should die. "It would relieve my mind," she said one day, "if you were settled with a good husband to take care of you."

I had been going for quite a while to parties and picnics with boys but they always struck me as being unromantic and callow. The fascinating image of Joe Moore still haunted me vaguely, and my infatuations were of brief flowering. Then a hoist engineer at one of the mines started courting me. At first Kitty seemed far more attracted to him than I was and couldn't say enough to promote the match. She pointed out his maturity, his ability to earn top wages and become a good provider. Furthermore, she said, he was rather handsome and had refined manners—not rough like so many miners.

But my father, who knew much more concerning the men in camp than either Kitty or I, had decidedly different opinions about the hoist engineer. In fact, he was opposed to my getting married to anybody until I'd had more schooling. "I've not given up yet; my claim is looking better every day. I'm still aiming to send her to that college they tell about down in the Springs. They'll fit her there to be a teacher like Alice Baltzell, and her taste in fellows will improve too."

He was full of strange contradictions which never failed to baffle me, but this time it struck me that his judgment was better than my mother's. She persisted, however, in her determination to do what she regarded as best for me. She reminded me that my father had a streak of jealousy in him and that, although he never paid much attention to me himself, he rebelled against sharing his daughter with another man. "Remember," she once said to me, "how he acted toward Josiah Winchester and all the fine advantages he deprived you of. I'm surprised that he doesn't want to lock you up someplace, in a convent!" When my father forbade me ever to see the hoist engineer again, she connived secret meetings, and soon she began to hint of our elopement.

One afternoon in late July my father came home in high spirits. He had struck the bonanza which had been playing hide-and-seek with him all these years! The assay values indicated that he had uncovered a lode far richer than even he had expected. Kitty appeared incredulous, as though she suspected him of trying to get ahead of her through deception; and she plied him with questions. "Why didn't you strike it before—how did it happen just now?" She almost seemed sorry at his stroke of fortune.

"You'll probably swear that I'm pulling your leg," he

chuckled, too elated to catch the undertones in her voice, "but it's the God's truth—I outwitted the tommy-knockers!"

I had always known that my father was very superstitious. He had been steeped in black art by Lutie, his childhood nurse in Kentucky, and had never outgrown it. Before Nina was drowned in Silver Reef, he had spoken of seeing a little white dog following him in the drifts and stopes of his mine. He had often declared his belief that evil pixies lived in the dark recesses underground to torment humans who laid waste their hide-outs; and blamed them for his continued bad luck. But I was dumbfounded when he told how he had managed, at last, to confuse and throw them off the track. Kitty, too, sat listening in amazement.

"I guess I'd grown desperate," he went on, "knowing the ore was there, almost hitting it time and time again, and then losing the scent. I couldn't figure it out to save my life. Then it occurred to me about a week ago that maybe if I changed the name of the mine to something patriotic, on the order of Stratton's Independence, Abe Lincoln, or George Washington, my luck would change too, and the little stinkers tormenting me would get lost." He wiped the beads of sweat from his forehead and told me to bring him a dipper full of water. "I chose to call it the Cripple Creek Columbia," he said, "and swore myself to secrecy lest the imps get on to it. And as sure as I'm sitting here, the next day I ran into the most beautiful lode of sylvanite I'd ever seen. Today's assays bore me out." Then he turned directly to me with an air of triumph. "It was in a drift I'd just started, about three hundred feet below the surface in the exact spot where the forked stick did a flip-flop the day you were there, Mabs, and made me out a liar!"

News of the strike on the Columbia created quite a sensation in the District. The *Times* wrote, "John Barbee, who has found more ore on Beacon Hill than any other operator in camp has

made a phenomenal find on the Columbia. On Monday an unexpected vein was encountered on the west side of the shaft.
Samples run $720 to the ton and the ore resembles the high
grade of Barbee's first Orizaba, the adjoining property." But
experts still belittled the discovery. The big deposits all lay
to the northeast, in the vicinity of Bull Cliff and Battle Mountain. Barbee, they asserted, had merely run into another rich
pocket which would soon peter out as the others had done.

Such skepticism on the part of mining authorities made
it difficult to raise any cash for development. Finally, Clint
Tillery put up several hundred dollars for a half interest. But
it was my father who did the back-breaking labor of mining,
sorting and then shipping the ore to the chlorination plant in
Florence. Instead of narrowing, the vein widened into a main
artery with tentacles branching off in the same general direction. Before long, other prospectors began to scrape the surface of Beacon Hill for locations and still others leased
abandoned claims. Potential investors, evidently aware of my
father's financial pressures as well as his precarious physical
condition, began to make him meager propositions which he
steadfastly refused as if mindful of his promise to Kitty, long
ago, to hang on to his next jack pot.

One day as he was about to leave the shaft, two brothers,
former Missourians whom he knew well, dropped around to
congratulate him, they said, and to get an idea as to the extent
of the vein. He was only too glad to take them down the ladder
and show off the glistening ore body. The casual visitors were
Sam and George Bernard, two grocers from the little
town of Monument near Denver whose acquisition of the
Elkton mine for a bad debt of some thirty-seven dollars had
transmuted them over night into millionaires. They were living
now in palatial homes in Colorado Springs but returned to the
District often to keep a wary eye on new developments.

They showed interest in what they saw of the mine but surmised that it would take a pile of dough to work it into a paying concern. Even so, it might be worth a small gamble, George said, and out of a blue sky offered my father $10,000 for his share of the property. It was a lot of money for a man who was poor and had one foot in the grave, but he had given his assurance to Kitty and he'd always taken pride in being a man of his word. Then Sam, who apparently anticipated a turn-down, jumped into the breach and raised the sum to $12,000 spot cash. "And in addition," he said, reaching in his pocket for his checkbook, "I'll agree to wipe your slate clean of debts. Tomorrow morning you'll be able to look the whole goddamn world in the eye—a free man!"

My father still intended to refuse, he told me later, dreading what Kitty would say. Then it occurred to him that he'd never been one to discuss his business affairs with her or seek her advice. After all, he was the man of the house, the one who paid the bills and made the decisions; and furthermore, it was his mine to dispose of as he saw fit. Almost involuntarily he took the check and said, "It's a deal!"

Kitty was heartbroken and made a terrible scene the night he told her. She swore that she wouldn't ever believe him again, "not on a stack of Bibles!" He had never given his family a thought, she declared, but let chance after chance slip through his fingers only to make others rich. "Think of it," she went on bitterly, "selling your first bonanza to a couple of grocers for $12,000 when it could have been $12,000,000!" She began to clear the kitchen table rapidly, as if trying to hold back the flood of words tumbling through her mind. "At least you could have held out a share for yourself," she continued, "something for me and the children to fall back on when——" Her voice broke suddenly and she wept into her kitchen apron.

So far, my father had kept silent. Always before, when Kitty turned her fury on him he had slammed out the door and stayed downtown drunk until it seemed likely she'd cooled off. There was something frightening, now, about his stillness. "You've got me wrong," he said slowly. "I won't live long, you think, and maybe you're right. But this ready cash will enable me to do two things before I cross over. There'll be enough to send Mabs away to school this fall; and we'll have plenty for you and Billie and me to go back to Silver Reef and get out of this climate for a year. I've been thinking about it quite a while; all that southern Utah warmth and sun might be good for my cough. We could even live in our old house, like as not, and see how things have gone with Nina, out in the graveyard—you know, plant some new grass and flowers . . ."

"Look, Jonce," she pleaded, drying her eyes as though she hadn't been listening, "go to those Bernard boys. Give them back their money. Say you've thought it over and don't want to sell. Say that you are a sick man, not young any more. Tell them you must provide for your family. Maybe they will at least let you keep a small interest. Do this for me, Jonce, say that you can't tramp over these steep mountains much longer, that the chances of your making another stake are slim. Please—I beg of you!"

He turned on her fiercely and his voice was hard. "What're you trying to do—make me out a simpering fool?" he flared. "A deal's a deal—I gave my word—it's different when you give your word to another man—not the same as to a woman. You can make it up to her in different ways. I said they could have the mine and they gave me the money for it. We made a deal in good faith and I'll never go back on it!" He pulled his pipe from his coat pocket, shook tobacco into it and asked me to get him a match. "I guess the time's come to tell you something else," he went on in a calmer tone. "I'm not finished, not by a long shot. I'm on to the game now and when we get back from the Reef I'll find another bonanza that'll make the Columbia look like a beat-up gopher hole!"

Kitty slumped in her chair, crushed and dejected. "Waiting —waiting," she mumbled. "It seems as though I'd spent my whole life just waiting." Then, with tight lips, she went into the parlor, sat down by the lamp, and reached for her sewing basket. She had given in to him as she had done so often in the past.

I searched my heart for something to say. As I watched her, so troubled and unhappy, it came to me that it wasn't the loss of the Columbia, or my father's failure to keep his promise to her that had caused her rebellion. It was all the circumstances of her life—the bare, ugly camp, so alien to her nature; the wide gap between her dream of a home and the drab reality of the house on Golden Avenue; her never-ending loneliness. A gulf seemed to separate her, even from Molly Letts, her neighbor and one close friend. But worse than all else was the mortifying disease with which mine dust had stricken my father, laying upon his family a blight she couldn't mention to others, or acknowledge to herself. While I stood there, leaning against the door, thinking, it struck me that I too was becoming infected with these insidious poisons. I vowed never to marry a man of the mines and once I escaped, I'd never live again in a mining camp.

My father was disappointed to hear from Colorado College that a high school diploma was required for admission. It was suggested that he send me to Cutler Academy, instead, which also provided residence for students. But on second thought, he guessed that an extra year might help me grow up more and manage myself to a better advantage; and he gave Kitty money and told her to fix me up with everything a girl should have.

Our house was soon in a turmoil of activity getting me ready for the great adventure. Molly Letts was as excited as though I were her own daughter and she went along with Kitty and me in an orgy of clothes-buying. The two women seldom agreed on what was suitable or becoming for a girl of my age and they rarely consulted me. Molly seemed to confuse my going away to school with getting married and favored the frippery that could "do double duty as a wedding outfit." Kitty gave in to her insistence that I have a black satin corset "to show off that nice figure." It was Molly, too, who persuaded her to let me wear my skirts floor-length, with even a short train on my best suit, a black mohair lined with sage green taffeta. It was Kitty's idea, however, to arrange for Mlle. Watchke to marcel my hair and do it up in a pompadour and puffs on top of my head. How much taller and more sophisticated it made me look! I stumbled and almost fell off the sidewalk trying to catch glimpes of myself in the barbershop mirrors and store windows along Bennett Avenue!

My father had promised to take me to Colorado Springs over the new Short Line Railroad whose magnificent scenery had already added to Cripple Creek's fame. Even Teddy Roosevelt was said to have exclaimed, a few months before, that "its grandeur bankrupts the English language!" I had often watched the train climbing up Gold Hill, zigzagging back and forth ever higher and higher to the top and then disappearing over Hoosier Pass.

It might have been harder to say good-by to Kitty, Molly Letts and Brother if my father hadn't been in such a gay humor. He laughed and joked like a person who was at last basking in the warm, rosy glow of a dream come true. All during the three-hour trip I was conscious of his glancing shyly at me from the corner of his eye as if to reassure himself that I was really his daughter. He hardly seemed like the stern parent who had kept me at a cool distance so many years. He had on a dark blue business suit—the first I had ever seen him wear. His face had been freshly shaved and his blond mustache neatly trimmed. Only one thing set him apart from other well-dressed men—his soft-collared shirt was unbuttoned at the neck without even a tie to hold it in place. Kitty had done her best to make him wear one but he accused her of wanting to turn him into a "fashion plate," and besides, a tight collar with a necktie would cut off his wind and he'd choke to death before he ever got out of camp.

We went directly from the depot to Cutler Academy to look up the principal. He was a tall, distinguished-appearing man with genial blue eyes and a blond goatee. He introduced himself as Clement Gile. His pleasant, friendly manner immediately put my father at ease and brought out a kind of charm in him that surprised me. He said simply that he had come to enter me in the academy. "I'll appreciate it," he added, reaching for his fat billfold, "if you'll tell me what the cost will be."

"Have you decided what subjects you want your daughter to take?" the principal asked. "Possibly you'd like to discuss it. We offer two courses—the college preparatory and then a general program which is terminal." He reached for a catalog and I noticed his clean, slender hands and trimmed fingernails, just like Josiah Winchester's used to be, and I half expected to get a whiff of Florida Water.

For an instant my father looked baffled but quickly recovered his composure. "I'm not up on the lingo of you school folks," he said, smiling self-consciously, "but for one thing, I'd like her to study music. You see I play the fiddle a bit myself and I want her to learn enough to be able to accompany me on the piano."

"I understand," Professor Gile said. "Music doesn't happen to be in our curriculum. However, we can arrange for her to take private lessons. The fees are rather high and, of course, would be extra. . . ."

"That's all right," my father broke in. "It makes no difference. I'm anxious for her to have the best—money's no object. Certainly she's going on to college when she finishes your academy. I wouldn't consider any terminal business—whatever it is—so that's settled." He cleared his throat and fumbled with a pencil on the desk. Then he narrowed his eyes as if an idea had just struck him. "Come to think of it," he began, "there's one study in particular I'd like to have her take—something I've been mulling over myself for a long time. Is there any course listed in the book there under the heading of 'magnetism'?"

"Magnetism?" Professor Gile repeated in astonishment. "No, we have no such subject." And he leaned far back in his chair with a puzzled expression on his face. "Tell me—I'm curious to know why you want her to study magnetism."

I dreaded what was coming. My father was on the verge of making himself a laughingstock and I wondered frantically how I could head him off. But already he had a good start and there was no way I could stop him. "Well, it's like this," he was saying. "I'm a prospector up in the District," he squared his shoulders with a show of pride, "and without bragging, I've discovered a few deposits of ore that developed into some of the richest mines around there—the most recent being the Cripple Creek Columbia over on Beacon Hill. Some folks call me the 'Father of Beacon Hill,' but I don't go much for that sort of ballyhoo. But what I started to tell you—and you may not believe me—was that all my discoveries have been made with a divining rod."

"You don't say!" Professor Gile exclaimed, seemingly impressed. "That's remarkable! Have you any idea how it works?"

My father took an old envelope from his pocket, reached for the pencil and began to make a simple design. "It's my theory," he said, "that the force I call magnetism pours from me into the rod and on down to the gold in the ground. When that happens, the wire rod is slowly pulled to the earth, like a hooked fish." He glanced sharply at the principal. "Maybe you don't get what I'm driving at," he said. "Miners talk a different language from you school fellows."

"Of course, I do get it," Professor Gile hastened to say. "Please go on."

"Well, there's not much more. All I know is that if I dig long enough I'm pretty sure to hit a rich lode, right where the rod indicated!" Then he turned unexpectedly toward me. "Mabs, here, scoffs at the whole business—calls me superstitious." He uncrossed his legs and rested an arm on the desk. "Professor, I'd like her to learn the facts about magnetism— what it is; where it comes from and how it operates. If I'm wrong, I want to know it, but if I'm right, damn it, she's got to admit it!"

I felt embarrassed, afraid that the principal had been shocked or worse, amused by my father's credulity. But he seemed intensely interested. "There may be some basis of truth in what you've told me," he said earnestly. "At least it is a fascinating supposition. I've often speculated about it myself and it's my guess that magnetism is a force that pervades all creation. But exactly what it is—that's a matter which even scientists haven't yet discovered."

"Is that so?" I had never seen my father so carried away.

"There's one thing, especially, I'd like to know. A university graduate—Dick Roelofs," he said in an aside to me—"told me not long ago that the divining rods were among mankind's earliest tools for outwitting nature, that the Chinese in centuries past made them of hazel twigs and called them 'witching sticks.' Did you ever come across this in your studies?"

"Indeed I did!" the professor said. "The Hindus used the device as far back as 1500 B.C. and I understand that even primitives such as the Maoris of New Zealand and the Zulus of South Africa practiced the magic of the forked stick. I might add," he went on, "that many farmers in my own New England still rely on the dowser, as we call it, for locating underground water."

"Well, I'll be da——" he caught himself in the nick of time. "Did you hear what Professor Gile said, Mabs?" He gave me a quick, penetrating glance as if to make sure that I had been listening. Not a word had escaped me but at the same time I was absorbed in discovering a new aspect of my father who had always been such an enigma to me. He was warm, affable and had lost every trace of self-consciousness; even his speech with its slight southern accent was less harsh and ungrammatical. In a few brief moments his true nature had broken through its shell of defense; and I was moved with pride.

It wasn't until we were outside on the steps of the gray-stone building that I realized we were saying good-bye; and suddenly I couldn't bear to let him go. It struck me with anguish that nothing would ever be the same again, neither my father and mother, nor the house on Golden Avenue, nor the mining camp of my childhood. I longed to live it over, to tramp the hills with him once more, to hear Kitty sing "In the Gloaming." But now it was too late—there could never be any turning back.

I reached for my father's hand and for the first time in

years he put his arm around me and kissed me on the forehead. "Be a good girl," he said hoarsely, as he started down the path, "and write your mother often. She'll be anxious to know how you are making out—and tell me if you run low in cash—don't forget!"

I watched his stooped figure disappear down the street and all at once it seemed as if I were going to faint. Hot tears blinded me and I crumpled on the Academy steps, torn with uncontrolled sobbing. Then the door opened and I heard Professor Gile's voice. "Come, my dear," he said, helping me to my feet, "try not to take it so hard. We are all your friends here; you'll soon feel at home." I wiped my eyes and smiled weakly, sorry that I had been such a baby. "I am taking you home with me. Mrs. Gile is expecting you tonight," he said, slipping his arm through mine. "They'll be waiting dinner for us."

As we walked together in the late afternoon twilight, thoughts of my father and Kitty again drifted through my mind. Soon their long cherished dream would be realized; they were going back to Silver Reef. But I had no wish to be with them. Even the name had grown tarnished and the little town which Kitty had described as "paradise on earth" had become a faded memory. I was setting out on a different journey, not into the past but to some undetermined destination far away in the strange, beckoning future. And suddenly the lonely ache in my heart gave way to eagerness.

15

A Fruitless Pilgrimage

K I T T Y sent a note or post card every time the train stopped, it seemed. When they reached Salt Lake City, Jonce had decided that it would be a good idea to lay over a while and rest up at the Knutsford Hotel, which he said was "every bit as luxurious as the Brown Palace in Denver." They had gone out to Saltair but the season was closed and they couldn't show Billie how to float on the briny water without sinking. They saw Amelia's Palace where one of Brigham Young's favorite wives had lived, and visited the Tabernacle to hear music played on the "biggest pipe organ in the whole world!" But the most wonderful thing of all, she wrote, was the present Jonce had given her as a souvenir of the trip—a pair of flaw-less, solitaire diamond earrings. "I didn't want him to be so extravagant," she said, "but he claimed he'd got them at a bargain not only for me to wear but for an investment; and as nice heirlooms some day, for you and Billie."

Many weeks passed before word came from her again. I thought little of it until the mail I had sent to Silver Reef was returned with the stamp, "No Such Address." Then at last a bulky letter arrived, penciled in Kitty's fine Spencerian writing. It was postmarked Saint George, the small Morman village some twenty miles east of Silver Reef. I hadn't heard from her, she said, because there'd been only bad news to tell. But finally she realized that, sooner or later, I would have to know and it was better not to put it off any longer.

"We expected to take the stage from Saint George to the Reef, just as we had always done," she wrote, "but there are no stages any more and no such place as Silver Reef except in the recollections of old-timers. Now it is just a deserted ghost town." She went on to say that my father looked up the Lund family, neighbors who had moved to Saint George. "They remembered us," she said, "and offered to take us to the Reef in their surrey to see what was left of the camp."

"Words fail me!" she continued. "I could never picture to you the desolation that met our eyes. Jonce said it almost seemed as though imps of hell had wreaked vengeance on the little town for having dared to beautify the desert. The sandstone buildings are mostly piles of rubble. Only one wall remains of what was once the leading drugstore. The roof of the Wells-Fargo Bank has tumbled in," she wrote. "The shutters of the broken windows sagged and banged in the wind and pack rats scurried beneath the rubbish as we tried to enter. It made me heartsick and I wanted to cover my eyes and run away, but Jonce persisted in searching for some familiar relic."

They might never have come upon the spot where our house had stood except for the honey locust tree that grew in a corner of the front yard. "Now it is stunted and dying," she said, "and there are no moss roses, no peach trees, no wisteria vines, not even a street—just a vast waste of stones, weeds and ruins." The day was wearing on, the letter read, and she felt that it was time to start back. The road was too bad to drive after dark. But Jonce seemed bent on trying to find the graveyard. He said that it would be easy to see the large head-stone on which he had chiseled Nina's name. But he and Mr. Lund searched in vain through the matted thistles and sage-brush. Huge ant heaps filled the clearings, and gophers had burrowed into sunken graves. "It was all I could do to bear up," Kitty added, "but I had to—for Jonce's sake. He looked so pale and dejected. No trace is left of our beloved Nina—only the memory of her laughter."

The letter ended abruptly near the bottom of the lined paper and a full month passed before she touched it again, with no explanation. My father's health had improved in the warm climate, she began, and the Lunds had helped them find a small house. She hoped that Jonce could be persuaded to stay a year so that he would be entirely well before return-ing to the Creek. "But you know him," she said, "he was never one to sit around and twiddle his thumbs. If he should get too restless, like as not he would pull out any day. He talks about the camp much of the time, even now, and declares that he is strong enough to hit another pay streak on Beacon hill. He claims that the surface hasn't been scratched yet. I asked him one night," she went on, "if he thought Cripple Creek, too, would become a ghost town some day. He looked at me as though I had lost my mind even to ask such a question, and said that the District's mines would be pouring out gold long after the last Barbee had crossed the range. But," she concluded, "I'd be happy never to see that camp again!"

Although the doctor had advised against my father's leaving Silver Reef before a year was up, they returned the following August. I had stayed on in the Springs to make up credits in Latin which I needed for college admission. The camp was in the throes of a periodic epidemic; this time it was the dreaded typhoid fever. The first news Kitty heard on arrival was that Molly Letts had died of the disease only the week before, and that Jim had gone to live at one of the Carr Avenue rooming houses. Her second blow was the discovery that my father had sold our home on Golden Avenue without telling her, and had rented the large two-story house that had been built after the fires on the corner lot where the Roelofs place once stood. Out of her forlornness she wrote me several times a week, often enclosing clippings from the *Times* which she said might interest or amuse me, such as:

Lew Dockstader's Minstrels met the late train after last night's show at the Grand Opera House, to welcome the returning honeymooners, Bert Carlton and his beautiful bride, the former Ethel Frizzell. They responded by inviting Lew and his black-faced singers to the luxurious Carlton apartment over the First National Bank. According to reports, the champagne flowed freely and merrymaking lasted until dawn.

The Vanderbilt party arrived yesterday in a private car, eighty-two feet long. After being taken through the Portland Mine by host James F. Burns, the distinguished guests had luncheon at the mansion of J. Maurice Finn. Members of the party recalled how only a few years before, their syndicate turned down the chance to purchase the Portland for $250,000, because experts had estimated deposits of not more than $85,000 in value, and in addition the property was hopelessly involved in litigation. But Jimmie Burns extricated the mine and later took $7,000,000 out of the ground. The Vanderbilt party travels in a city on wheels, consisting of five cars. One of them is fitted up as a stable so that the eminent visitors may go horse or buggy riding whenever it strikes their fancy to stop the train.

The Gaikwar of Baroda arrives on a sightseeing trip. Before leaving the region he will kneel on the summit of Pike's Peak for a half hour of prayer on a magnificent golden rug. He is accompanied by his wife and a retinue of servants. Many Cripple Creekers went to the Midland depot to look at the elegant private cars. Gaikwar, which means keeper of the sacred cows, is the title given the ruler of Baroda, a province in Western India. He is also the Maharaja, or Great Raja. He has come to the United States to observe our educational and industrial institutions.

But Kitty's favorites were the little items culled from the "City Briefs" column, saying:

Miss Cunningham was shot in the thigh last night by the explosion of a revolver in the hands of a gentleman caller. The wound is not very serious.

Miss Della Benton horsewhips Mr. E. J. Johnson for wronging her.

Miss Allie Opie, winsome little Victor girl, drew the largest audience that ever packed Eagles' hall. The program consisted of a drama called "The Burglar's Guest."

Once she sent an interview with my father, cut from the mining page. "Keep this in your memory book," she wrote, "it sounds so like Jonce, always praising the Creek, seeing only the best side." It read:

"There isn't another mining camp in the West that would make me turn my back on Cripple Creek." These were the words of John Barbee, recently returned from an

extensive stay in Southern Utah. He needs no intro-
duction to the people of the District. His friends are
legion. All mining men know what his record has been
in discovering some of the richest ore bodies in camp.
Such words from him are worthy of note and should en-
courage other prospectors to rustle the hills. "I think Cripple Creek presents as many opportunities today as it ever
did in the past. I tell you," Mr. Barbee said, enthusi-
astically, "every time I come back from the outside I
am more impressed with the future possibilities of the
District. Fact is, no other place can compare with it or
has so much to offer as a home town. Take Mineral hill
over there, which prospectors abandoned long ago on
advice of so-called experts; someday that mountain is going to come into its own and start another wild boom.
Pin your faith on Cripple Creek and you'll never regret
it." Mr. Barbee is better known as the Father of Beacon
Hill. It was his confidence and persistence that led to the
discovery of Columbia lode, now the fabulous El Paso
mine.

Evidently my father's paean to Cripple Creek's future
deafened him to the ominous troubles corroding the
present. He had been out of touch with events for almost a
year—a long time in the life of a mining camp. A desperate
showdown had been rumbling behind the scenes between
the mine owners and the Western Federation of Miners which
dominated the local unions. Charles Moyer and Big Bill Haywood had stated that the Federation's aim was to secure a
larger share of the wealth for the laborers who produced
it. Mine owners resolved to rid the District of organized labor
by employing more and more nonunion miners. The opposing
groups were becoming increasingly arrogant; it was only a

question of time when one or the other would openly throw down the gauntlet; and the District would again be plunged into a bloody strike.

But the battle that was already under way had nothing to do with labor grievances; it concerned the railroads. Oddly enough, it worked to the advantage of travel-happy citizens. The Florence & Cripple Creek, the camp's first-born rail line, had prospered greatly during the year before and just after the Midland Terminal arrived. But what with continuous cloudbursts or blizzards washing out trestles and roadbeds, piling debris in tunnels and snowdrifts on tracks, the little narrow gauge was no match for its mighty competitor. Before long it became a subsidiary of the Midland Terminal, doing menial jobs mostly, such as switching ore cars from shafts on its own lines to the standard-gauge interchange points. Only one train, a passenger coach attached to a long string of freight cars, made the daily round trip to Florence.

All might have been well if the Midland's absentee directors, drunk with success, hadn't raised freight rates so high that it had become profitless for mines to ship their low-grade ores to the mills. A group of financiers and Cripple Creek millionaires living in Colorado Springs decided to remedy the situation by building the Colorado Springs and Cripple Creek District Railroad, known generally as the Short Line, into the District. Its route would cut the distance by following much of the old stage road, up behind Cheyenne Mountain. The first train reached camp the latter part of March, 1901.

The new line not only lowered freight rates but soon became known for its scenic beauty and developed into a popular tourist attraction. The Midland people fought back by reducing passenger fares between Colorado Springs and the District.

In normal times the cost of a one-way ticket was $2.75 but now the round trip went as low as twenty-five cents; and passes were handed out liberally to anyone who had the slightest pull. For a while it seemed as though most of the population was living on wheels, riding merrily back and forth between the two cities.

Of course, it was too wonderful to last and the end came abruptly when the holding company for the Midland Terminal and its step-child, the Florence & Cripple Creek, failed to pay interest on the bonds and went bankrupt. Control then passed to a new board of directors made up of local capitalists such as Spencer Penrose, A. E. Carlton and Charles M. MacNeill. Usually the Carlton brothers, Bert and Leslie, worked quietly in the background but now Bert's name was appearing often as a member of boards of trustees and on interlocking directorates of important firms. He had come to be regarded as the shrewdest, most acquisitive and powerful business genius in Cripple Creek, and it was confidently predicted that some day he would own every rich mine, and run all the banks and railroads in the District. Owing to his talent for manipulation a new holding company, the Cripple Creek Central, was set up to control and operate all of the camp's rail systems.

The free rides were over for Cripple Creekers. They'd had a fine time and were ready, apparently, to settle down and attend to their jobs. My father said he'd had enough traveling to last him the rest of his days. He was as excited as a schoolboy to see Bennett Avenue again. It seemed as if he could hardly wait, Kitty said, to visit the familiar haunts and tell his old cronies about his experiences. He still had a promising claim on Rosebud hill, in the vicinity of Beacon, and talked about getting to work on it with all the zest and vitality he'd shown in the early days. He was absolutely certain, he declared, that the Columbia vein apexed on the Little Rosebud and he'd have no trouble uncovering it.

I had come up for a visit with them and to buy new clothes before entering college as a freshman. My ideas were rather extravagant and I was conscious of Kitty trying to curb my spending. Finally she said, "Be careful about money, Mabs. I don't know how much Jonce has left from the Columbia sale but I'm certain it's not enough for you to buy too many expensive dresses."

"But he says he's likely to strike it rich again soon." I somehow overlooked his many similar predictions in the past.

"I wouldn't bank on it," Kitty replied. "You know how he always tried to put his best foot forward. The question of his health, for instance, he's not as well as he pretends—it's just a brave front he's putting up. He still has bad coughing spells and some mornings he's so weak he can hardly get out of bed. But he drags himself off every day, packing his lunch, stuffing his coat pockets with hand tools and sample sacks and carrying the divining rod tucked under his arm. It's better for you to know this," she added, "so that you can do your part and not buy things you don't need."

Then something happened a day or two after I reached college that cast a shadow over the whole mining world. W. S. Stratton, the District's famous multimillionaire, died at his modest home on North Weber Street in Colorado Springs. Although he had moved away from Cripple Creek shortly before the great fires, and few people saw him when he came back on business trips, he had never lost reality as a symbol—the living fulfillment of every prospector's dream. Stratton's comings and goings, the things he said and did, his solitary ways, were fresh on every man's tongue. My father had not seen him for several years but he often quoted him and repeated over and over the little anecdotes "W. S." had once told him. "It has been a terrible shock to Jonce," my mother wrote. "For the first time I can remember, he broke down and sobbed like a baby. To folks up here Mr. Stratton seemed to be Cripple Creek itself and his dying was almost as if the camp too had begun to die."

16

Pity the Poor Millionaire

CRIPPLE CREEK, by 1902, had produced a total of $111,361,633 and between thirty-five or forty bonanza kings. But many who had stumbled into fortunes, in spite of themselves, had a faculty for shedding them. One was murdered in a saloon brawl, which doubtless saved him from reaching ultimate penury. Most of the others left camp immediately to make futile attempts at crashing society in Colorado Springs or Denver; and still others, dead broke, had gone to Alaska or Canada's Porcupine country, hoping vainly to hit the jack pot again. With one or two exceptions, both the rich and ex-rich shared a trait in common—neither wanted to build so much as a watering trough for mules in the Cripple Creek District.

W. S. Stratton, the multimillionaire, was never known to have spent a night in the magnificent suite which he leased a year later at the National Hotel. The garish mirrors eventually found their way to the more exclusive parlor houses in Cripple Creek and Victor. On his frequent trips to camp he preferred to stay at his small frame house a few steps from the Independence mine.

My father and many others like him seemed to look up to Stratton as the embodiment of things hoped for, and living proof of Cripple Creek's vast riches. But to me, as a young girl, he personified the mining camp in a more telling aspect. There was no place in his scheme of life for the so-called "good women" like Kitty; and he seemed to regard children as necessary afflictions to be endured.

This did not mean that he scorned feminine companionship. His exploits among the denizens of the tenderloins in Cripple Creek and Victor added spice to camp gossip. It was often said that some of his adventures were so violent that they seemed to come from a man bent on revenge rather than the gratification of his desire for pleasure. He was never without a current favorite at the Old Homestead and few rivals dared to poach on his domain.

Jimmie Burns tried it once. He stole off to a dance hall in Victor with one of Stratton's best girls and bribed the manager to lock the doors. Stratton's face turned white when he discovered the trick. He went immediately to the owner and asked how much he wanted for the place "right now just as it is." The price suddenly hit the ceiling but Stratton never batted an eyelash. After he had doled out the cash and taken over the keys, his first act was to kick Jimmie Burns into the street, minus the girl.

It wasn't the last time he resorted to such tactics. The story was told about how he happened to acquire ownership of Denver's Brown Palace Hotel. He tried to register there one night with Lola Livingston, madam of Cripple Creek's Mikado parlor house. The desk clerk, evidently new on the job, said it was against the rules. Stratton walked out in a huff, and early the next morning bought the hotel for some $750,000, the amount of the mortgage. Needless to say, the clerk got his walking papers, "just to teach him to mind his manners." This incident was afterwards refuted but it gained credence because it was characteristic, and also because Stratton had really purchased the hotel at about that time.

Several of his beautiful paramours ended by taking over-doses of morphine because, it was said, they wanted more than he was willing to give—love and marriage shored up by his millions. He admitted that when he was poor he had taken on a wife in a moment of weakness, and because of his bitter disillusionment decided that there'd be no more wedding bells for him; henceforth he would limit himself to professionals who didn't have one eye on getting hitched. Kitty was horrified when she heard it. "Mr. Stratton may know a lot about mines," she said scoffingly, "but he's awfully dumb about women. I'll bet there's not one poor unfortunate on Myers Avenue who doesn't hope to get married some day!"

It wasn't Stratton's ignorance that blinded him as much as his deep-rooted antagonism toward females like his mother and sisters. He was born in Jeffersonville, Indiana, in 1848, and named Winfield Scott after the famous general in the Mexican War. He was the first boy and the last-born in a family of nine children. "What with my mother and all those simpering girls hovering over me," he told a friend, "it was enough to hog-tie any red-blooded kid. I was in a constant pet and ready to pull the trigger on the next one who tried to boss me around." The unlucky fellow happened to be his father, Myron, who swore and called him a lazy lout when the boy showed little zest for learning his own trade of carpentry and boat building. The son went into the house, took down the shot gun and fired, barely missing his father's head. He brooded so much over this near-tragedy that he left home, and after spending some time with relatives in Iowa and Nebraska, arrived in Colorado Springs in 1872.

He had learned more about carpentry than his father suspected, and was fortunate to have this means of earning a living. He worked steadily and managed to save almost $3,000. But he didn't like carpentry. He told another Colorado Springs carpenter, D. K. Lee, that he might take a fling at prospecting. Lee replied that he himself had been thinking of striking out for the hills and they agreed to make a trip together the coming summer.

Colorado's great silver mines around Leadville and down in the rugged San Juan Mountains had already produced millions of dollars. The two carpenters decided to explore around Lake County in that area. Lee bought an interest in a development called the Golden Fleece which later brought him a modest fortune. But Stratton found nothing of promise. He took a course in assaying from Professor Lamb at Colorado College, and read all the books he could find on Colorado's geological formations. Summer after summer he went prospecting, occasionally with Lee but more often alone, until he had rustled most of the mountains in the state, and was still without any leads.

His marriage in July, 1876, threatened to interrupt his usual routine. He said he was tired of prospecting and wanted to settle down and raise a family like other men. The girl, Zeurah Stewart, was his junior by eleven years. She had come from Illinois, and worked at the boardinghouse where he lived. But no sooner was the ceremony over than she made the disastrous confession that she was three months' pregnant and claimed that he was the father. Stratton flew into a violent rage, denying the accusation; and shortly afterwards Zeurah left for her home in Illinois. Six months later a baby boy was born. Although the divorce was delayed for three years,

Stratton and Zeurah never met after the fateful night of their marriage.

Every June for seventeen long, wearying years he locked his carpenter's chest, packed a mule with grub, bedding and tools, and headed into the wild country. He might have given up, he once said, if the life hadn't suited him. It offered freedom to do as he pleased without people arguing and meddling in his business. The wilderness was meant for him. His needs were simple; it didn't take much to keep him contented.

He had known Bob Womack, who first discovered gold in the District, since the early days; they had reached Colorado Springs at about the same time. Stratton said he regarded Bob as being weak in the head, and never listened seriously to his talk about finding gold up in Poverty Gulch. But in June, 1891, he decided to investigate and do a little prospecting in the Cripple Creek District. He had studied the land beforehand and was convinced that the lip of the Cripple Creek basin dipped toward Battle Mountain in the southeast, spilling whatever rich ore deposits there might be into that area. With this in mind, he pitched his tent on Wilson Creek which skirted Battle Mountain, and set out to examine every foot of the region. Within a few weeks he located two claims, about halfway to the top of the slope, and since it was the Fourth of July, he named one the Independence and the other the George Washington.

Then he ambled north over Raven Hill, cast a hasty glance at Beacon, and moved up Gold Hill to Poverty Gulch. A small rush seemed to be in the making in that section. But he wasn't impressed and returned to work on his Battle Mountain location. One day when he came back to his tent after touring the District, he found that he had company. Three acquaintances from the Springs, Jimmie Doyle, a ditch digger; Jimmie Burns, a plumber; and Sam Strong, a butcher and Jack-of-all-trades, had come up to see what all the talk was about. Apparently they planned to stay for a while; they had pitched their tents not far from Stratton's and unpacked supplies of food. Not one of them knew anything about mining but they said perhaps Stratton wouldn't mind giving them a few tips. His advice to them was not to waste time in Poverty Gulch but to stick to Battle Mountain.

He labored for three years keeping up the assessment work on the George Washington and digging an eighty-five-foot shaft on the Independence. It was beginning to look as if people were right when they called him a fool to turn his back on Gold Hill and Poverty Gulch and he was about to give up. Then a San Francisco gambler named Sam Pearlman happened along and offered $5,000 for a thirty-day option on the Independence. If the deal went through he'd pay $150,000 for the mine. Stratton jumped at the chance. In the course of gathering up his tools he snooped into an abandoned crosscut at the fifty-foot level which he had used as a sort of dump ground for trash and waste. While poking through the rubble he noticed some peculiarly colored rock fallen from the wall of the drift and recognized it at once as sylvanite, or Cripple Creek gold. He slipped a few samples into his pocket. He was careful to leave the waste just as he had found it and covered his tracks as he tiptoed out of the drift. The extent of the vein and the assay results indicated that some $3,000,000 in ore lay waiting for somebody to mine it.

I remembered well the evening he told my father the exciting story. "I hadn't been to church for a coon's age," he said, "but I'm telling you, I got down on my knees and prayed for three solid weeks that Pearlman would overlook that hot crosscut even though it seemed mighty unlikely." To make matters worse, Sam Strong had just come into a rich streak down the mountian, and up the slope a bit further west the two Jimmies had hit a jack pot. "If Pearlman ever uses his noodle, I says to myself, or sees beyond his nose, old man Stratton'll be a dead gopher without a hole to his name!"

But Jimmie Doyle and Jimmie Burns were equally anxious to keep their discovery secret. The vein didn't surface on their ground, and according to Colorado mining law a vein belonged to the property on which it apexed. For months they sacked the golden treasure and carried it on their backs at night to the mill in Pueblo, saving the cash against the inevitable day when the news would leak out and they'd find themselves in a mesh of legal entanglements. It would be bad for Stratton, too, if word of this strike at the very door of the Independence ever reached the public. It would mean that he'd have to go back to carpentry, his bonanza thrown away for a few paltry thousands.

Pearlman evidently neither saw nor heard anything unusual in Stratton's shaft. He made no effort to conceal his low opinion of the Cripple Creek District and in his desire to get back to San Francisco gave the Independence only a cursory examination and by-passed the pile of waste in the abandoned crosscut. At the end of thirty days the option expired and Pearlman left on the first train. In a matter of hours the wily ex-carpenter had three shifts of miners on the fifty-foot level, scooping the rich harvest of gold into buckets. One stope called the Bull Pen ran so high that the ore wasn't even sorted but shipped directly to the mill.

Stratton built a small frame house not far from the mine where he lived for a year or two while supervising operations. No visitors were allowed and miners were warned not to talk about their jobs when off the property. It wasn't long until he had more money than he knew what to do with. Now he could relax and indulge his taste for Kentucky bourbon and other pleasures. No more cheap harlots for him! He would have nothing less than the Old Homestead's beautiful madam, Pearl De Vere. She was a costly toy with her craving for Paris gowns, diamond lavalieres and imported wines. But what was money to him? There would always be more where it came from. Too much, in fact, for his peace of mind. Every time he stepped out, beggers hounded him, old prospectors pleaded for grubstakes, promoters buttonholed him with crackpot schemes and inventions. So many wanted handouts of food that he kept several restaurants supplied with free meal tickets.

His generosity and inability to refuse even the boldest spongers finally led him to move to Colorado Springs. But mail followed, sometimes four or five hundred letters a day. Strangers waylaid him as he walked the three blocks to his office. Hack drivers shouted through megaphones and pointed him out to sight-seeing tourists. To avoid their stares and gapes he would sneak out the back door to the alley and jump into a waiting rig. When this proved futile, he began to seclude himself at home and to nurse a festering resentment against mankind. He tormented his servants by brushing his fingers over the furniture continuously, looking for dust. He would order a meal prepared to his liking and when it was set on the table, fly into a rage over some trifle, send it back to the cook and stalk out of the dining room.

Meanwhile the ever-rising stream of gold threatened to engulf him and in order to keep ahead of it, he gave away thousands of dollars to churches of all denominations, the Salvation Army, Colorado College, the Colorado School of Mines and many individuals. Although he owned the municipal railway system he bought bicycles for all the laundry girls in the city so that they wouldn't have to walk to work or pay car fare. He gave $15,000 to his old Leadville friend Haw Tabor, who had lost his own fortune and was trying to make a comeback on his old Matchless Mine. He even recognized his son to the extent of sending a hundred dollars a month for his expenses at the University of Illinois, but only on condition that he stay away from him. A talented lad named Louis Persinger happened to make his way into Stratton's parlor one evening and played such beautiful violin music for him that he decided to send this young prodigy to Germany for study under some of Europe's finest teachers.

His bounty was often impulsive and eccentric, and as surprising as it was welcome. He might send a load of coal at Christmas to a man whom he scarcely knew, or make out checks for $50,000 for each of his mine foremen. But it was the city of Colorado Springs that really blossomed under his philanthrophy. He bought the old county courthouse and paid for a new one; gave the ground for a fine city hall and purchased the post office block and turned it over to the government at half-cost. He built a five-story brick and stone building for the Mining Exchange and purchased and brought up to date the city's streetcar system. And out where North and South Cheyenne canyons met to form a tangled glen of scrub oaks and cottonwoods, he developed a beautiful park with a playground, picnic tables and grills, and a bandstand where concerts were given on Sunday afternoons in summer.

Cripple Creek and Victor, in the District that had been the source of his millions, stood by empty-handed, hoping for the library, playground or opera house that would have made life in their communities less rugged and more enjoyable. But they never materialized. "Just wait," some people said, "he'll most likely remember us handsomely in his will!" Perhaps it was this prospect that gave Cripple Creekers a charitable attitude; or possibly they realized dimly that no man with any hope of immortality would want to build his memorials in a transitory mining camp.

People of Colorado Springs tried to show their appreciation by granting him the social recognition that had been denied other Cripple Creek millionaires. They went out of their way to send him invitations to elaborate dinners, which he tore up and burned in the fireplace. Then the Mining Exchange had the temerity to honor him with a banquet at the Antlers Hotel. The guest list bristled with the names of celebrities. Eulogies were to be given by the governor, the mayor, President Slocum of Colorado College and President Alderson of the School of Mines. Stratton had agreed to be on hand, but when he found out at the last moment that he was expected to wear a tuxedo, he unlocked the hand-carved cabinet where his supply of liquor was kept, got out a bottle of his favorite bourbon and proceeded to forget the entire affair.

There was one young man in Little Lun'non's upper crust who managed to get close to Stratton. His name was Verner Z. Reed. In most respects he was the direct opposite of the withdrawn, embittered, lonely millionaire. He had knocked around the world a lot, winning friends with his outgoing personality, impressing them with his versatility and brilliance. He had tried his hand at writing novels, selling real estate and at one time had been engaged by Stratton to effect a consolidation that finally untied the legal knots of the Portland Mine and led to the formation of the Portland Gold Mining Company, one of the most successful ventures in the District.

Best of all Reed's attributes was his ability to tell amusing stories. Stratton enjoyed having him drop around evenings, and before long began to talk freely with young Verner, telling him some of his ideas and plans. Reed, however, was too restive to settle down in Colorado Springs, and the next thing the home town knew, he had opened offices as a broker of stocks and mines in London's financial district. He came to know John Hays Hammond, who had achieved world fame as Cecil Rhodes' consulting engineer, and was now associated with the Venture Corporation of London.

It was Verner Reed who finally manipulated the sale of the Independence to the Venture people for $11,000,000, one million of which paid Reed's commission. It hadn't been easy. Stratton, a lone operator, had proved to be as recalcitrant with the English as he had been with the elite of Colorado Springs. Even after the deal had been practically closed, he was tight-lipped about the matter and went so far as to deny it. But in 1899 he and his personal physician journeyed to London where he signed the papers. He was sick with a serious kidney ailment at the time and went on to Carlsbad for treatments.

When he returned home in late summer he was in very bad physical condition and seldom left his house. My father managed to see him briefly the day he took me to Cutler Academy. I never knew what passed between him and Stratton in their last moments together. Kitty wrote from southern Utah that "Jonce was shocked by the change in him; he was barely conscious and his sick eyes were hollower than ever. Poor fellow! I used to think how wonderful it would be if Jonce were that rich but I'd be grateful now if he could just get back his health. Most of Cripple Creek's millionaires seem to come to an unhappy end; and Mr. Stratton who had more millions than any of them was the most solitary too, and pathetic. I have only pity for him."

Few people in Colorado Springs or Cripple Creek were close enough to Stratton to grieve over his passing as a personal loss. He had long since become a story-book character. It was almost impossible to think of the carpenter and prospector of long ago as the multimillionaire of today, breathing his last in an alcoholic coma. His legend would live on but the miraculous decade of "the greatest gold-mining camp on earth" in which he had played a vital role had come to an end; and somehow its luster had begun to fade.

He was hardly in his grave when everybody began to speculate about the will. There was no telling how a man of Stratton's singular, erratic nature would dispose of his millions. Colorado College and the State School of Mines expected substantial additions to their endowments; and the churches which had received other bounties from him had reason to feel certain of generous sums. Who knew, perhaps Cripple Creek would soon have that much-needed library, and the children of Victor would be frolicking in a new Stratton playground!

When the will was opened, the rumble of disappointment and indignation shook the foundations of homes and institutions all over Colorado. A half million went to his relatives, including $50,000 each to Zeurah Stewart's son and a few friends and servants. The remaining $6,000,000 was to be used for the establishment and maintenance of a home for the poor children and old people of El Paso County, as a memorial to his father, Myron Stratton. In explanation, the will stated,

> It is my special desire and command that the inmates of said home shall not be clothed and fed as paupers usually are at public expense, but that they shall be decently and comfortably clothed and amply provided with good wholesome food and necessary medical attendance, care and nursing to protect their health and insure their comfort.

Those will qualify for admission who are by reason of

youth, age, sickness or other infirmity unable to earn a livelihood, and who are not, by reason of insanity or gross indecency, unfit to associate with worthy persons of the condition in life above named.

The will further provided that applicants should be actual residents of Colorado at the time of their application and that those from El Paso County should have preference over applicants from any other part of the state. The Testament was dated August 5, 1901. Friends of Stratton said that he had made an earlier one in 1898 when the Cripple Creek District was still in El Paso County and that for some reason he failed to amend the later will, which was almost identical with the first, to include applicants from Teller County. Some were bitter in their denouncement of the District's richest and most famous man. But most Cripple Creekers passed it off with a shrug. "What's the difference?" they said. "Who expects to grow old here anyhow?" They all agreed that not much would be left, even for the indigents of El Paso County, once the lawyers got through fighting all the court battles that were certain to follow.

Sure enough, the contents of the will had no sooner been published than a thousand and one claimants began to buzz and swoop down like bees in a field of clover. Zeurah Stewart's son was the first to try to break the provisions and succeeded in getting his inheritance increased from $50,000 to more than $300,000. But by the time he had paid court costs and attorneys' fees he would have been better off if he had accepted the original amount.

His success inspired a motley crowd of petitioners to try their luck, men claiming that they had loaned him money that had never been repaid, or had grubstaked him for an interest in all his future discoveries. Women eagerly debased them-

selves, swearing that they were illegitimate daughters or com-
mon-law wives. Twelve of them attempted to prove that they
were his widows and one had developed such a convincing
list of forgeries and introduced so many seemingly credible
witnesses that she almost won her case. It took long months
of patient investigation by an attorney for the estate, David
P. Strickler, to show that the claimant was an imposter and
forger. But in spite of long-drawn-out, costly litigation, the
$6,000,000 for the Myron Stratton Home remained intact.
The tragic carpenter, prospector and "Midas of the Rockies"
turned out to be as canny in making his will as he had once
been in negotiating the sale of the Independence.

17

The Fateful Year

IN THE midsummer of 1902, at about the time my family returned from southern Utah, two men arrived in the District who were destined to play diabolical roles in the imminent showdown between the Mine Owners' Association and the Western Federation of Miners. Their names were Jim Lambert, alias Jim Warford; and Albert E. Horsley, alias Harry Orchard. They were about the same age, thirty-six, and although Jim was born in Kentucky and Harry in Ontario, Canada, their lives followed the same general direction. Both struck out for themselves in early youth and drifted to the wild, lawless mining camps of the West. They seemed to have an affinity for trouble spots and were available, at a price, for wholesale killing, strikebreaking and pillage. There was never any evidence, however, that the two had met. They worked opposite sides of the street and chose different weapons.

Harry favored the homemade infernal machine which could blot out a dozen lives as easily as one. He had learned his trade up in Coeur d'Alene, Idaho, during the violent strike of 1899. His most dastardly accomplishment was the blowing up of the Gem Mine under orders of the Western Federation of Miners. Idaho's Governor Frank Steunenberg, outraged by the crime, sent in troops, declared martial law and ordered the strikers deported. Orchard fled in such haste that he forfeited his stake of a tenth interest in a promising mine named the Hercules. The property soon developed into a bonanza and Harry brooded about his loss so bitterly that he resolved to return to Idaho before long and get revenge on the governor.

He finally landed in Cripple Creek after his escape from Coeur d'Alene, and settled in Independence, a thriving little camp that had sprung up around Stratton's mine. He was especially liked by his neighbors, who described him as a domestic fellow who kept his cabin as clean as that of the most careful housewife. At first he worked as a mucker at the Vindicator Mine and became familiar with various underground exits. This enabled him to do considerable high grading and accumulate money on the side. His outstanding trait seemed to be his fondness for children. Almost any day after work he could be seen playing baseball with young boys; and he was always encouraging little tots to rummage in his coat pockets for candy and gum. Naturally it came as a terrible shock when he confessed later that all the while he was figuring on how he could kidnap one of the youngsters and hold him for ransom.

His public spirit was especially notable. Mrs. Clara Rogers, the postmistress, commented on how he came to the office every Saturday morning to collect contributions made by the saloonkeepers toward the preacher's salary and not so much as a dime was ever missing. "He was very nice-looking too," Mrs. Rogers said with a touch of wistfulness. "I often glanced up at him as he stood waiting at the mail window. His sandy hair was neatly brushed and parted in the middle, and he had

the most honest expression in his blue eyes. When he turned
to go he never forgot to give me the friendliest smile." Widows
were unusually strongly attracted to him and one day he
married one of the comeliest in camp. The fact that he still
had a wife and two small daughters up in Ontario didn't seem
to bother him in the least.

Jim Warford was of another stripe. He stayed in the District just long enough on his first trip to get the lay of the land
and make a few important contacts. He returned in August,
1903, a little before the Western Federation of Miners called
the strike. Oddly enough, he too decided to make Independence his headquarters. Located in the heart of the District's
richest mining area, it offered an excellent listening post. Soon
Jim was sporting a shiny deputy sheriff's badge and hob-
nobbing with mine owners and prominent members of the
Citizens' Alliance. It was clear that he had become their
trouble shooter and chief agent for ridding the District of
hated unionism.

People in Independence didn't think much of him but knowing his reputation as a bad man, they kept their mouths shut.
Although he was tall and handsome and far more virile and
aggressive than Harry Orchard, widows and young women
never chased after him. He boasted too loudly about his
sharp-shooting prowess and seemed proud of the fact that
both his father and grandfather had barely escaped lynching
because of their gun scrapes. Only a few years before, Jim
himself, who had been Tom Horn's chief triggerman during
the Wyoming range wars, had fled to Colorado when Tom was
finally caught and strung up. He hid out in the mining camps
over in the San Juans, which at the time were involved in
bloody labor battles. But Jim Warford couldn't keep his presence secret for long. Two pistols which he could fire simul-
taneously from the hips always hung from his cartridge belt;

and he never missed his target whether it was the heart of a man or the beady eye of a blue jay. Few mortals, aware of the notches on his guns, had the temerity to start arguing with Jim Warford!

The Western Federation of Miners had been a powerful force in the Cripple Creek District ever since it had won a minimum wage of three dollars for an eight-hour shift in the strike of 1894. The unions controlled important elective offices and influenced industrial employment policy. Miners who failed to join a union were often intimidated and compelled to get out of town. Mine owners had persistently refused to recognize the principle of the closed shop, fearing, it was claimed, that the unions would try next to confiscate the mines.

Frustrated in its attempt to gain even more strength in Cripple Creek, the Federation began to look for other means of attaining its end. It was decided to unionize the miserably paid millworkers at the U. S. Refining and Reduction plant in Colorado City where much of the District's ore was shipped. About a fourth of the workers agreed to form a union. It was enough to cripple the mill as well as the District's mines if they should go on strike, which they proposed to do if their demands for minimum pay and hours were not met. When the Reduction heads stood their ground without compromise, the Western Federation ordered its union members to quit work.

On August 10, 1903, Cripple Creek unions struck in sympathy. It marked the start of the most disastrous labor war in the history of Colorado. The sheriff of Teller County was a union man and mine owners did not trust him to preserve order. They engaged their own guards for the vital El Paso drainage tunnel, then nearing completion. Only one of the largest mines, the Golden Cycle, was independent enough to attempt operating with nonunion miners, but before long it too was forced to shut down.

My father's lingering sickness had exacted a heavy toll of his strength but even if he had been well, it wasn't likely that he would have taken sides and joined either the Citizens' Alliance or the union. Both parties were in the wrong, he claimed, and no genuine attempt had been made at arbitration. Each was determined to destroy the other and didn't give a damn if, in the struggle, they also wrecked the Cripple Creek District. He considered Jim Warford a blackguard and a ruffian who had been hired as a tool of the Mine Owners' Association; and Harry Orchard, he declared, was in the pay of the Western Federation of Miners and so low down in the scale of thuggery that even Jesse James would have scorned him. "Conditions in camp are mighty dangerous," he said when I was leaving for college after Christmas, "and I don't want you coming home again until this strike's settled. Nobody's safe on the streets, night or day, and having you here would only mean extra worry in case of trouble."

But I read full accounts of the frightful events as they were published in the Colorado Springs papers. Governor James F. Peabody had sent in state troops at the urgent request of the Mine Owners' Association, with arrogant Sherman Bell in charge. This action was taken as the result of an explosion, caused by an infernal machine, on the seventh level of the Vindicator Mine. The superintendent and a shift boss, both widely respected in the District, had been killed; as a result a large segment of public support turned against the unions. The Citizens' Alliance, emboldened by the influx of new members and spurred on by the Mine Owners' Association, determined that every union miner and sympathizer should be driven from the District and never allowed to return. In order to distinguish the sheep from the wolves, all Alliance men were expected to wear a white enamel button on their lapels which bore the warning, "You Can Never Come Back!"

As the line of deportations lengthened, Sheriff Ed Bell and his deputy, Jim Warford, grew so ruthless that women trembled at the mere mention of their names. Then the commander of the troops said that something should be done to put a stop to the pro-labor editorials in the Victor *Daily Record*. "They are likely to incite riots," he asserted, "and lead to the destruction of life and property. A raid on the plant some night might teach the radicals a lesson or two." The job went to triggerman Jim Warford. As he herded the editor and four members of the staff toward the door, Jim stopped and looked back at the wreckage. Only the big clock on the wall was running as usual. It angered the deputy sheriff and, letting out a string of oaths, he shot off the clock's minute hand. "There, by God," he shouted, booting the editor, "that'll learn you to mark time an' get in step!"

The foray on the *Daily Record* proved to be so heady that Warford and his outfit began to attack other individuals who had spoken out of turn or looked as if they might have offensive opinions. When Goldfield's "bull pen" began to overflow with prisoners waiting to be processed, it was decided to take direct action and run suspects out of camp without further ado. The Reverend Mr. Leland was forced to join the endless procession down Long Hungry Gulch because his sermons were "obnoxious." He begged to stay a few more hours with his wife and children but moved fast when Warford told him that twenty rifles were trained on his cabin. "Git agoin', " he yelled, "or I'll give orders to shoot!"

Harry Orchard himself almost got caught in the deportation net. Jim had heard about his little hobby of contriving infernal machines and suspected him of having perpetrated the Vindicator crime, but luck happened to be with Orchard. It seemed that once when he was peeved at his Federation bosses he had double-crossed them by leaking important information to one of the officials of the Florence & Cripple Creek Railroad. They had paid him a small fee and somehow his name was put on the payroll. Word of this connection reached the deputy sheriff just in the nick of time. Orchard apparently never knew of his close shave with the law and, having made up with the Federation chiefs, he continued tinkering in peace with his homemade bombs, working on the biggest assignment of his whole career. Townspeople never saw him anymore playing ball with schoolboys or tempting little tots with pockets full of candy. But he still managed to go to the post office on Saturdays to collect contributions for the minister's salary; and he never forgot to smile pleasantly at Mrs. Rogers when he turned and went out.

Meanwhile Jim Warford had become the man of the hour. His very strut on Victor Avenue sent children screaming to their mothers; and a sudden knock on a cabin door at midnight panicked the whole neighborhood. Even the mine owners seemed afraid to question his wild acts of terrorism and some of the steadier members of the Citizens' Alliance spoke openly of their concern over the unholy partnership with a fellow of Warford's caliber. One day, they predicted, he would demand his pound of flesh. But nobody actually advocated breaking with him so long as a single card-carrying union member remained in the District.

Jim evidently got wind of the criticism and to show that he was still indispensable, he began to create new crises. The *Daily Record*, for instance, was alive and kicking again and the editor was urging such treacherous ideas as the recall of the militia and the return of the strikers to their former jobs. Warford concluded that another, more thorough, raid on the plant was due. This time he so completely demolished the presses that the paper couldn't resume publication for more than a year. Only the circumstance of the editor's switching his loyalty to the mine owners saved him from the ignominy of being tarred and feathered and forced to get out of camp.

The long-drawn-out struggle for power was beginning to look as though Warford's outlaw methods were winning victory for the Mine Owners' Association. Governor Peabody had recalled the militia. Some of the big mines were cleaning up debris as if preparing for full-time operation by nonunion miners. A few stubborn holdouts of organized labor, in camps such as Goldfield and Independence, still caused some trouble. But it was only a question of time until they too would be rubbed out of the District. A feeling of hope was in the air. The last days of May had come and the quaking aspens were in leaf over in Pinnacle Park, the other side of Bull Hill. Men had begun to get out their rods and flies and talk about the best fishing streams.

But the Western Federation of Miners had no notion yet of throwing in the sponge. Too much was at stake for defeat to be so easily accepted. In spite of the dark outlook, Moyer and Haywood still had a trump card under the table. They had expected to play it some weeks before, but Harry Orchard dallied along and kept raising the ante. Finally they sent for him and threatened that if he didn't come through with the goods at once, they'd turn him over to Sheriff Ed Bell of Teller County as a double-dealing crook. That was enough to put the fear of hell-fire into Orchard; and he assured his overlords that in a few days he'd set off an explosion that would be heard around the world.

Early on June fifth he casually mentioned to several neighbors that he and John Neville, a bartender, had hired a wagon and team and were going fishing down in the meadow brooks around Love. They might be away quite a while, he said, but he was taking along an extra cayuse just in case he got fed up and wanted to come home. Nobody thought anything further about it. Even when the explosion occurred, less than twenty-four hours later, no one had the slightest suspicion that it had been sparked by mild-mannered, kindly Harry Orchard. Some townsfolk refused to believe it possible, although Harry admitted it later at his trial in Idaho for the assassination of Governor Steunenberg.

Under the spell of religious conversion, it seemed, he had made a full confession of all his sinful deeds. Among them was the blasting of the Florence & Cripple Creek depot in Independence at two o'clock in the morning of June 6, 1904, which killed thirteen nonunion miners and crippled six others. According to his story, he and an accomplice, Steve Adams, had placed a heavy charge of dynamite earler in the night under the depot platform. Then they attached a three-hundred-foot roll of wire to an open bottle of sulphuric acid which hung from a beam above the giant powder; and they crept along the ground, unwinding the wire cautiously until they reached the abandoned Delmonico Shaft. Here they sat on the dump and waited for the miners at the Findley to come off the graveyard shift and hurry down the slope to catch the owl train home.

The night was clear, with a waning moon, he went on, and in a little while they saw lanterns flashing and knew that the men had started down the hill. "The headlight of a switch engine at the Portland and Strong mines glared at us once and we flattened against the dump like old timbers until it turned away." Here and there lamps flickered in the sleeping town of Victor on the lower slope of Battle Mountain and somewhere a dog was yelping. A few of the scabs had already reached the depot and were milling about on the platform. Shortly there'd be more; if lucky, they'd net at least forty from the Shurtleff, fifty yards further up on Bull Hill. "Steve and I was tense," he related, "scarcely daring to take a breath, not even letting out a whisper. There was only ten or fifteen more minutes to wait."

Then, all of a sudden, the train whistled. It was coming around the curve ahead of time, not more than six hundred feet from the depot. He felt jittery and confused and his hand shook so that he could hardly pick up the wire. "Don't pull yet, you goddamned fool!" Steve was saying; "another second and we'll wipe out the train and every bastard scab on the hill!" But it was too late; his fingers had already jerked the wire. The explosion was deafening; splintered boards and rocks were crashing all around them; they stumbled and fell when they tried to run for their cayuses hitched a couple of hundred feet away. "It seemed like I could hear men groaning and women screaming," Orchard said, "all the way to the cutoff where Neville waited with the wagon."

The camp of Victor, where numerous windows had been shattered by the force of the depot explosion, was crazed by fury. Citizens demanded immediate retaliation against the Federation by searching every tent, cabin and house for union members and routing them forever from the District. A mass meeting was called the afternoon of the disaster and a huge crowd gathered in the vacant corner lot at Victor Avenue and Fourth Street, just across from Union Hall. Clarence C. Hamlin, the fiery-tempered attorney for the Mine Owners' Association, was chosen to harangue the throng. He had profited handsomely from his connections with such rich, powerful men as Bert Carlton, Charlie MacNeill and Spencer Penrose, and had his eye on a political career. His strong, resonant voice belied his slight stature and his gift of oratory almost equaled that of J. Maurice Finn. His besetting sin was intemperance both in habit and speech; and on the day of the great mass meeting he pulled out all the forensic stops.

The spectacle of hundreds of incensed, determined listeners

drinking in his every word seemed to inspire him to new heights of invective. He teetered back and forth unsteadily on his toes, often dangerously near the edge of the improvised platform, shouting, gesticulating, pleading to men of guts to revenge the tragedy of the camp's orphaned children and desolated homes. The faces in the crowd were tense; blood was in their eyes. Applause and calls of approval almost drowned out the speaker's tirade. Then, all of a sudden, a defiant shot zipped through the air from Union Hall. Only quick action by a deputy sheriff named Jim Warford saved Hamlin's life.

The line of battle had been drawn; bullets began flying in every direction. Two innocent bystanders were killed. The state troops, which had arrived only an hour before, surrounded union headquarters. Mobs of citizens raided union stores in all parts of the District where supplies of food and clothing were kept for the strikers, and scattered the damaged goods in the streets. The dreaded deportations began again, creating a terrorism worse than anything the Western Federation might have conceived. Homes were broken into in broad daylight and families torn asunder. Now, a man had only to be a friend of a union member to be classed as an undesirable.

A board of appeals was finally set up by General Sherman Bell to still the indignant protests pouring in from all over the state. But its members included C. C. Hamlin and top officials of the Mine Owners' Association, and the board became more of a travesty than an instrument of justice. Innocent victims along with the guilty were lined up, crowded into freight cars and dumped like garbage on the plains of Kansas or in the scrubby hills of New Mexico, several hundred miles away. Some were sick, others barely clothed, and all were ill-fed. Their families back in the District were not much better off; they huddled in their houses afraid to light the lamps at night, shuddering with fear at the slightest sound outside the windows. Even those women who might have felt safe, the wives of members of the Citizens' Alliance, kept behind their locked doors, not sure whether the raiders scuffling through the streets were friends or enemies.

Then one day after almost a week of horrors a sudden calmness settled over the District. Children ventured to play in the streets once more and clothes lines sagged with accumulated washings. Mine whistles blew again and the trails bustled with miners hurrying to work. And Jim Warford patrolled the streets of Independence with an air of assurance, as if knowing that one of the key higher-ups, C. C. Hamlin, owed him a debt of gratitude, and that he would have to sing when Jim Warford saw fit to call the tune.

Although Orchard had tried to murder Governor Peabody and one or two other prominent Coloradans before leaving the state, neither he nor Adams was ever caught or charged with the Independence crime. Steve soon dropped out of sight and Harry continued his roundabout journey back to Idaho. There he had another little job to get out of the way before heading for the Klondike where, according to reports, trouble was brewing. But the time was running low for Harry. He was arrested and held for murder after he had assassinated Governor Steunenberg by putting a bomb under his front gate. It was while he moped in jail that he was led to confess all his past crimes and pray for God's mercy. The Almighty may have listened and eased his conscience, but few in Colorado believed in Orchard's repentance. People in the Cripple Creek District claimed that even if he had told the truth he had merely been a stupid dolt taking orders from the Western Federation of Miners.

Harry Orchard got off with life imprisonment for the murder of Governor Steunenberg; and escaped indictment for his atrocious deeds in Colorado. The explosion he set off in the early hours of June 6, 1904, had blown the last remnants of the Western Federation of Miners from the Cripple Creek District. But it was doubtful whether his warped brain ever realized that when he triggered that fatal blast it left a wound in the heart and spirit of the great mining camp from which it would never recover.

18

No Minimum Hours for Death

D U R I N G the first days of April, when a brief lull brought hope that the strike would soon end, another killer far more deadly than an infernal machine crept stealthily into the scene. It was the season of pneumonia and this year the dreaded disease promised to be more virulent than usual. Cripple Creek was never entirely free of it and now the few scattered cases suddenly flared into a widespread epidemic. Hardly a family escaped its ravages.

Then Kitty wrote me one day that Jim Letts had died. "There was no room for him in the hospital," she said, "and nurses couldn't be hired for love nor money. When I thought of the poor fellow sick and alone in that Carr Avenue rooming house I went every day with food for him and rubbed hot turpentine and sweet oil on his chest. I don't think he knew me," she went on; "most of the time he was out of his head and kept mumbling the strangest things about Molly, how he had taken her from one of those disgraceful places up in Salida and wanted to marry her but she refused; said he should be free to love a good woman some day. It was crazy talk," the letter continued, "out of his delirium, but maybe there was some truth in it. When I leaned over, putting cold applications on his fevered head," she wrote, "I thought of all the things I had said about those poor unfortunates and prayed for Molly's forgiveness—she was a good woman if there ever was one. And while I stood there, crowding back my tears, Jim opened his eyes a moment and seemed to recognize me. Then he reached for my hand and whispered my name—the next instant he was gone."

It was only a few days later when the telegram came from my father saying that Kitty was sick and to come. I caught the first train, but pneumonia worked fast in Cripple Creek; my mother was dead by the time I arrived. The funeral was on May Day and three feet of snow lay on the ground. Plows were kept busy hour after hour clearing the road to Pisgah for the many burials, and the gravediggers built fires to keep warm. My father was too weak and crushed to go with us; Brother and I rode in the carriage with the minister. We huddled there alone while he stood on some planks and read a few passages from the Bible. Then the casket with its spray of white roses was lowered quickly into the ground. I put my arm around Brother to comfort him but no words would come. My heart was heavy with anguish and my eyes smarted but I couldn't weep.

The world seemed strange and empty without Kitty. She and I had often talked together about how we would manage when my father died. I was prepared, in a way, to face that likelihood, but now, without her, I felt confused, unable to see beyond the fact that I was needed at home and must withdraw from college at once. My father would object, that much was certain; but I was twenty and grown up. I resolved not to let him silence me as he had done so often with Kitty.

He listened quietly when I told him of my decision. "We

don't have to live in such a large house," I said finally, "and as soon as I return from the Springs I'll look for another."

"You seem to have settled some mighty important matters without consulting me," he said seriously. "I'll grant that I'm a weak reed to lean on. The Almighty should have taken me instead of your mother, but it was willed otherwise." He got up to put coal in the stove and shook the grate. "I'm good for quite a spell yet," he went on, sitting down again, "and I I don't aim to take orders from you. Is that understood?"

"Perhaps my judgment is better in some things," I replied. "I'm not a child any more."

"You've had your say," he interrupted. "Now it's my turn. Cripple Creek's no place for you right now with the strike likely to get worse before it ends."

"But there's Brother—he's only nine."

"Kitty's folks over in Salt Lake have offered to keep him until I can get on my feet again. One of the boys downtown is leaving for Park City next week; he'll be glad to take Billie along."

"Surely you're not planning to live here alone—in this big house!"

"I could if it seemed best," he said assuredly. "But as soon as I can get rid of what little stuff there is, I aim to rent one of old lady Barry's rooms over the hardware store on Bennett Avenue. It's only a step from there to the interurban car that passes close to my Rosebud claim." Then, as if realizing my concern, he smiled and said, "Don't worry about me, girl. I'll be downtown in the thick of things with no chance to get lonesome. The boys at Burnside's across the street'll keep an eye on me. If I run into trouble one of 'em will get in touch with you. But I don't reckon that'll be necessary. Pretty soon, when I strike it again, maybe I'll do like the other nabobs and buy us a fine mansion down on Wood Avenue in the Springs."

I felt my props weakening, but there was another crucial matter that had to be settled before admitting defeat. "What about my college expenses?" I ventured. "I can get jobs tutoring children this summer but it would be impossible for me to earn enough after school starts. Can you afford this cost?"

"Have I asked you to pay your own way?" he said indignantly. "It's all right for you to pick up a little pin money down there in your vacations—it'll keep you out of mischief." He cleared his throat importantly. "But when classes start, you're to put all your time on studies. Maybe before you're a senior the Rosebud will be bringing in fat royalties."

The echo of his many other predictions floated through my memory. "But just in case the Rosebud doesn't—what then? I am young and strong. Isn't it better for me to work now so that your money can be saved for a rainier day?"

"I swear," he said, "you're as bad a worrier as your mother—always shaking hands with the devil before she'd meet him! Well, if it will make you feel better, I have enough to see you through and if worse comes to worst, there are still Kitty's diamonds to tide you over."

Then I flung a question at him that had been in my mind a long time. "Tell me," I said, "why is it so important to you for me to finish college?"

He reached over and emptied the ashes from his pipe into the coal scuttle. "It's a long story," he said. "I can't go into it now. To put it in a nut shell, I wanted you to get training as a teacher so that you could live where you chose and take care of yourself. Kitty tried to make the best of Cripple Creek but I knew she was never happy here. It takes a lot of love to stick with a fellow who mines for a living. He's apt to work in harsh climates and rough, barren country and pull up stakes at the drop of a hat. But womenfolks are different, it seems; they want to settle down in a pretty house and raise flowers and a few youngsters." He coughed and ran his sleeve across his mouth. "Kitty was loyal and sometimes that takes the place of love. It accounts for her not leaving me often when I had it coming. I want you to have it better."

He was silent for a few moments, just gazing at the blue flames licking the isinglass of the stove.

"Ever since you were a little tike," he went on, "and I saw that you were quicker and smarter than most, I've had it in mind to see that you got a good education so that you could be independent in your own way and someday marry well. I've never been one to show my feelings; afraid, I guess, of looking foolish. But this idea—giving you a better chance than either your mother or I ever had—has been with me for a long, long time." He looked at me searchingly for a moment and said, "I reckon you don't get what I'm driving at; I'm not worth a goddamn at this kind of talk."

"I understand." I had suddenly glimpsed a surprising, new side of his character.

During the summer I made frequent trips to Cripple Creek and found him miraculously improved. He had given up drinking and rarely missed a day's work on the Rosebud. The camp, too, seemed to be making recovery from its long ordeal. The mines were running full force and production was climbing to its old-time peak. The population, however, had dropped more than a third of its high of 50,000 in 1900, and many houses were for sale or rent. Even so, the former spirit of optimism had returned, and people were claiming that the Cripple Creek District's greatest bonanzas would yet be discovered. But the fact was never mentioned that there were two hundred and fifty fewer mines shipping than there had been before the strike.

Many new faces were seen on Bennett Avenue, mostly younger men, recent college graduates, getting their first mine experience. Only one remnant of the camp's terrorism remained. Jim Warford, still wearing the badge of deputy sheriff, stalked through the streets with his mighty six-shooters flapping against his corduroys, searching the dark alleys and hide-outs for "union thugs" who might have sneaked back to see their families. "The District'll never get rid of him," my father said, "so long as folks keep voting for Ed Bell as sheriff."

But as it happened, Jim overplayed his hand one morning in November and started a series of events that finally ended his career as an officer of the law. It was election day, the first since the finish of the labor war. Ed Bell was up again for sheriff and Clarence C. Hamlin was running for district attorney of Teller County. Warford and Brown, another deputy, had gone to Goldfield, a small town across the gulch from Independence, which had always been regarded as a stronghold of organized labor.

The crisp, sunny air had brought out a large number of voters who were lined up to cast their ballots. The two deputies were looking for trouble, and as they approached the polling place they saw Isaac Leibo and Chris Miller, Goldfield constables, leaning against a fence, with their hands thrust in their overcoat pockets. Warford let out a curse and ordered them down the hill, claiming that they were out of bounds. The constables refused to budge and without another word, Jim Warford, aiming from the hips, shot both men and severed their spinal cords at identical spots. Ed Bell rushed over from Cripple Creek and went through the formality of putting his deputy in jail and relieving him of his ivory-handled six-shooters. The next day election results showed that Bell and Hamlin had won by a narrow margin. Their first case was that of prosecuting Jim Warford for murder.

Warford pleaded justifiable homicide in self-defense at the trial in January. The result was a hung jury. Then several months of new trials, appeals, and reversals followed, with Jim in and out of jail and Hamlin resorting to every legal device to avoid prosecuting the man who had once saved his own life. At times it must have seemed to the indomitable district attorney that it would have been better to die that day of the Victor riot than to be endlessly debt-bound to a scoundrel like Jim Warford.

As the time passed, with the accused languishing in prison waiting a new trial, I lost interest in his fate. Other, more pressing matters consumed my attention and energy. A variety of jobs came my way—delivering invitations to formal receptions at the President's House for twenty cents an hour, starting a children's dancing class with one of my classmates who played the piano, darning and mending for faculty wives, tutoring freshmen who were failing in Spanish, and helping to correct test papers.

The year passed quickly and left me with a feeling of accomplishment. I went to see my father before starting my summer job clerking in a candy store. I could hardly wait to tell him about all the excitement of the past weeks—the good times and many friends, of my improved grades and the tuition scholarship I had won. "And what do you think!" I chattered on. "I was chosen to be head of my boarding club and for the small responsibility it involves I'll get all my meals free next year!"

Suddenly I noticed how frail he had grown. He sat watching me intently, with a pleased smile in his eyes, puffing his pipe slowly and shifting his thin legs now and then for greater comfort. "Now tell me about yourself," I asked eagerly. "How are you feeling?"

"Fine!" he said, straightening up in the chair. "Couldn't be better. Old lady Barry takes good care of me and friends drop in evenings to keep me company."

"And the Rosebud?" I ventured. "Struck it rich yet?"

"I ain't been able to work it for a few weeks, what with May blizzards and all. But I expect to begin going over there every day now that the snow's melted. I should run into ore shortly."

"How would you like it if I gave up that candy store job and spent the summer here with you?" I suggested. "I could easily find a little house. It would be fun!"

"We've had that out before," he said firmly. "I'm doing first-rate as it is. I still don't think a mining camp's any place for a girl without her mother. You can come Sundays once in a while, but not to stay. I don't want you bringing that question up any more, do you hear?"

I knew better than to argue further. But I couldn't shake off my depression during the months that followed, and I lived in dread of hearing the telephone ring, or a messenger boy's knock at the door. The frequent trips to camp only increased my concern. It became obvious that he was stubbornly maintaining a brave front. I thought once of talking with some of his friends but with one or two exceptions I didn't know exactly who they were; he had always kept his downtown affairs in a separate compartment from his family life. There was also the possibility that he would discover my prying into his private matters and think it an unforgivable betrayal.

Then one day in August the message came; he had died in his sleep the night before. The long funeral procession moved slowly down Bennett Avenue, out the dusty, wind-swept road to Pisgah graveyard. Hundreds of men lined the street, with bared heads and grave, reflective eyes.

I went to his room after the services to gather up his belongings. There wasn't much—his fiddle in its scuffed leather case leaned against the wall by the window; his pipe was on the table by the bed together with a tablespoon and a half-used bottle of cough medicine. I searched through the dresser drawers for the wallet where he kept Kitty's diamond earrings, but found only a broken pencil and a few of my old letters. Perhaps Mrs. Barry had taken the money or valuables to her room, I thought, and I was about to start down the hall to look for her when she appeared at the door, in bedroom slippers and old calico wrapper. She was a plump, unkempt woman, with straggling gray hair, but her manner was motherly and kind.

"It sounded like somebody was in here," she said, narrowing her eyes. "Are you Mabs, his girl? I broke my glasses this morning and I'm blind as a bat—that's why I didn't get the place cleaned up before you come."

"Yes, I'm Mabs," I replied. "I was just looking around but there's nothing of much value. I wonder if you may have taken his wallet, by chance, for safekeeping. It contained my mother's diamond earrings."

"Bless you, child," she said, putting a sympathetic hand on my shoulder. "He didn't have no use for a wallet after he sold them pretty diamonds—that was quite a while back." She delved into her deep wrapper pocket. "This was all he had—his Masonic watch charm and a twenty-dollar gold piece. He must've had a premonition that he might go soon," she added, holding them out to me. "It was only a day or two ago that he ast me to give 'em to you if anything happened."

"What of his room rent—did he owe you . . . ?"

She hesitated an instant as if wondering what to tell me. "No—oh no, he didn't owe me nothin'. He always paid in advance. Your pa was a fine, upright man; you can be proud

of him. And my, how he worshiped you! Poor fellow, he used
to say that all he ast of the Almighty was to let him live long
enough to see you graduate from that there college."

I suspected her of not being altogether truthful about the
rent; and I recalled, too, my father's telling me that she often
asked him to eat supper with her when it was blizzardy and
bitter cold outside. "You keep the gold piece, Mrs. Barry," I
said, "and give me the watch charm. I'd rather have it than
the money."

"You mustn't do that," she protested. "You need it yourself.
It'd be enough if you felt that you could give me the fiddle.
My grandson might learn to play on it some day."

"Of course—take it," I said, relieved to have the sad duty
over with.

She began to sniffle and tug at the handkerchief stuffed in
the depths of her ample pocket and as she pulled it out, a
folded paper fell to the floor. "Dear sakes," she said, reaching
down hurriedly. "I almost forgot to give you this; it was in the
Times yesterday."

It was a long article about my father. I put it in my purse to
read later when I was alone on the train. For some reason, I
dreaded seeing his story in cold print. I sat by the car window,
hardly noticing the familiar hills with their famous mines
as they disappeared from sight. At last I took out the clipping
and unfolded it in my lap. The article filled several columns of
the first page. But even the black, boldface headline, JOHN-
SON BARBEE, PIONEER PROSPECTOR, CROSSES
THE RANGE, seemed with unreal, as if it referred to someone else unrelated to me. I read on,

In the death yesterday of Johnson R. Barbee, Cripple
Creek lost a pioneer citizen, a mining man of long experience and sagacity; a man who bore the respect and esteem

of every person with whom he came in contact. His most pronounced trait was an almost Puritanical sense of honor and an unswerving allegiance to what he deemed right. Few men in the District had a wider acquaintance and all feel saddened by his demise.

Then followed a sketch of his past, the Civil War days, the years of mining and prospecting in Nevada, Utah and finally his arrival in the District in 1892:

. . . he explored every foot of ground in the region and it is universally conceded that his work has meant much to the development of the great camp . . . the peculiarity of his operations was his partiality to the use of the forked stick in searching for ore and instances are numerous where his divination proved absolutely and often unexpectedly correct. The existence of the El Paso mine is due to his discoveries on his claim, the Columbia. The astute men who purchased this claim from him secured what soon proved to be one of the greatest ore bodies yet uncovered in the District . . . up to his last hours he manifested a cheerfulness and courage that set him apart during the years when he plodded incessantly over the mountain slopes, prospecting for the yellow metal with a faith and perseverance seldom equalled. . . .

He began to emerge from the page all at once, and I saw him that day long ago on Beacon Hill, walking slowly back and forth over the ground. He called me to come quick, to see for myself how the forked stick curved downward toward the gold "singing under the grassroots." I heard again his hurt reply when I said that there was no magic in a rusty baling wire and accused him of being superstitious. "You'll see; sooner or later I'll uncover a jack pot on this claim, below the very spot where I'm standing—just mark my words!" The prediction had come true after many years of discouraging work and declining health, but others reaped the fortune.

To his many friends who visited him at his rooms, Mr. Barbee expressed a willingness to take the long trail that leads to the unknown . . . his last thoughts were not of himself but of his daughter in whom his whole life was wrapped up . . . he dreamed only of seeing her graduation from College. . . .

An aching lump choked my throat and I looked out at the cathedral rocks, pink granite spires rising from a bed of spruce and aspen. The train was pulling into Summit. Off to the right the great dragon of Cheyenne Mountain slumbered, and to the north, snuggling against the foothills of Pike's Peak, lay Colorado Springs, with its white steeples among leafy elms and maples; eastward, the scorched August plains stretched endlessly to the far horizion. And suddenly I was blinded by tears.

19

For John's Girl

I T was with a heavy heart that I went to the college, a day
or so before the opening, to withdraw and pack my mementos, books and pictures. As I sat on the floor, fondly con-
templating my possessions, thinking of all the college friends
I might not see again, and of the studies I had come to enjoy,
it seemed that I would never have the courage to leave. Once
more I began to figure ways and means, over and over, but the
results always came out the same. There was no alternative,
I concluded; it was clear that I would have to give up and say
good-bye as quickly as possible.

My eyes grew misty and I was on the verge of weeping
when all of a sudden I heard footsteps hurrying down the
corridor. It was Jessie, the pretty, pink-cheeked maid who
looked after us as though we were her own sisters. "It's a
lucky thing you came back early," she said. "This special delivery letter arrived for you last night and I had no idea
where to reach you—it looks important."

I tore it open nervously, afraid that it might be bad news
about Brother, who was still with relatives in Salt Lake. But

it was from Griff Lewis, the Cripple Creek druggist and one of my father's good friends. I recalled him as a rather stocky man with a pleasant face, who never got out of sorts when a lot of giggling schoolgirls cluttered up his store to gaze at the fascinating atomizers, celluloid toilet sets and boxes of complexion powder that stood temptingly on the showcases. He must have known all of us by name, but I had never given him a second thought. Why under the sun was he sending me a letter by special delivery!

It had come back to Cripple Creek, he wrote, that I was going to give up college and my father's friends were disturbed about it. They knew how much he had banked on my completing the course and getting a degree. Some of them had been wondering, he continued, if the sum of $150 to be sent at the rate of fifteen dollars a month, would help pull me through the year. The words danced before my eyes. Out of the blue the exact amount that I needed had dropped miraculously into my lap!

By evening I had calmed down enough to compose a dignified reply to Griff Lewis, accepting the generous offer but only on condition that it be regarded as a loan to be repaid as soon as possible after my graduation. This arrangement was agreed upon, and as the monthly post-office orders began to arrive I became aware of a growing sense of obligation. There was Brother, for instance; he was past twelve now and getting to be a problem for Kitty's aging mother. It was only right that I should take over this responsibility as soon as my salary started.

I was reasonably sure of getting an appointment in some small-town school when I had a degree. It came a few days before Commencement. I was to teach Spanish and History in the Victor High School and my salary would be $1,080 a year. The notification was signed by Griff Lewis, president of the School Board of the Cripple Creek District. It was the last place I wanted to go, and I read it through several times, hoping to dispel the shadow of gloom. I dreaded ever returning to the camp. It seemed as though I were fated to repeat the pattern of Kitty's life.

On Commencement morning the academic procession had disbanded and graduates were beaming proudly, greeting their families and friends. A feeling of sadness had begun to steal over me when suddenly I heard a familiar, unmistakable voice calling my name, and looked up to see Uncle Si hurrying toward me. I hardly recognized him at first. His tall graceful figure had begun to stoop and his hair was almost white; deep lines marked his face. Only his quick smile and laughing voice were unchanged. For a moment I couldn't speak for the ache in my throat.

"Now looka here, honey, don't you start cryin'," he said, putting an arm around me and twirking my ear as if I were still a little girl losing at parchesi. "Your Uncle Si came to see you get that diploma, just like your dad woulda done— and every bit as proud, too!" Then he reached fumblingly into the frayed pocket of his vest. "Figure you could use a little extra chicken feed at a time like this," he said, slipping a gold piece into my hand. "Right?"

"Oh no, Uncle Si," I protested, fearing that it was his last. But he wouldn't listen and I turned away to hide my brimming eyes.

"Don't you try arguin' with your Uncle Si," he said, with a flash of his old spirit. "There's goin' to be lots more where that came from. I'm workin' now on the biggest deal yet. Won't be long 'til my ship comes in again and you an' Susie'll be wearin' seal skins. Just you keep the corners of your mouth turned up, my darlin'—that's your Uncle Si's motto!"

How like my father he sounded! I had learned from bitter

experience that his chances of ever striking another bonanza were slight. But he had left gold far richer than the Doctor Jack Pot in the heart of a little girl whose life he had touched and charmed and made different from what it might otherwise have been.

Early in September I sent for Brother and arranged for him to live and go to school in Colorado Springs. Then I went to Victor to begin my work as a teacher. After bills were paid, exactly seven dollars were left out of my first warrant; five were to go toward repaying the loan from Griff Lewis. He had gone home for lunch when I arrived at the pharmacy and wouldn't return for an hour. It was an unusually bright October day and I decided to stroll out to Golden Avenue. I had not been there for more than two years, not since my mother's death in the faded yellow house on the corner. Strange children were playing "kick the can" in the street and little girls I had never seen before traipsed up and down dressed in their mothers' long skirts, pretending to be ladies.

The neighborhood had changed completely since we had lived there. The ungainly clapboard place my father had built after the fires appeared much smaller. Now it was empty and dilapidated; the windows were broken and glass littered the ground. Most of the matched flooring—once Kitty's pride—had been ripped out and carried away. Strips of drab paper hung from the ceilings and flapped disconsolately in the breeze.

I sat for a while on the steps of the back porch, looking out over the camp. The air was acrid with the smell of decay and smoldering ash heaps. A stray burro nibbled at garbage tossed behind the privy across the alley. It was still a squalid, ugly town. Its only redeeming feature was in the kindliness of the human beings who had drifted there, by chance, in search of gold. "They're the salt of the earth," my father had often said. "A real Cripple Creeker stands by you

to the end, and never forgets you when he makes his stake—
no matter where he goes."

Somewhere behind the mountains a train whistle blew.
The rails of the Midland Terminal shone as they curved over
the trestle crossing Poverty Gulch. An endless chain of freight
cars loaded with ore crept cautiously around the grade toward Anaconda, bound for the reduction works in Florence.
Only a few years before, men with picks and shovels strapped
on their backs had tramped to the farthest mines. The trails
etched by their boots could be seen even yet, crisscrossing the
slopes.

The three o'clock train started slithering around the shoulder of Bull Hill on its descent into camp. I watched as it wove
in and out among the great mines, curving past the Anchoria-
Leland, the Gold King, the Abe Lincoln, zigzagging smoothly
back and forth until lost in the upper reaches of Poverty
Gulch. For a moment I was one of the passengers, returning
from a long, long journey. I got up quickly, remembering my
business with Griff Lewis, and hurried down the creaky steps
out of the yard.

He was thinner than when I last saw him and his hair
had turned gray at the temples. I started to introduce myself
as he held out his hand. "You don't have to tell me who you
are," he said. "I'd almost know you in the dark—you look so
much like John!" He took my arm and led me to his office at
the rear of the store. "Sit down," he said, pulling up a chair
near his desk. "I want to hear how things are going. It's
mighty nice to have you here in the District as a teacher; I
hope you've found a good place to live in Victor—rooms are
scarcer over there than they are in the Creek."

I reassured him that all was well but I felt strangely uncomfortable in spite of his warm friendly manner. "I'm very
glad to meet you again after so many years," I began awk-

wardly. "I was one of the little girls who used to flock in here and pester you for samples; and, of course, I've heard my father speak of you often. He admired you very much. If he could know about all that you have done for me he would be deeply grateful." My words sounded stilted, not as I had intended to say them. "I owe you a great debt—my position in the Victor High School as well as——"

"Now wait," he interrupted. "I must put you straight. I'll grant that as president of the School Board my approval carries a little wieght but not enough to secure the appointment of an inferior or poorly equipped candidate. You were well qualified and recommended. Otherwise, the position would have gone to someone else."

"But there is something more—perhaps I should have mentioned it first," I replied, determined to go directly to the point. "I mean the loan that made it possible for me to finish college. I've come to arrange to repay you."

He picked up a pencil and began to mark thoughtfully on a pad, as if trying to recollect something that had slipped his mind. "Was it called a loan?" he asked after a moment. "I've forgotten, but I confess that no credit is due me for lending you the money; I was only the lucky go-between." He got up suddenly and went into a wide alcove and began to fumble among the empty medicine bottles on a shelf. At last he brought out a large glass fishbowl and set it on the desk in front of me. On one side, printed in golden letters, was the inscription: FOR JOHN'S GIRL.

I felt mystified and wondered what this had to do with me or the loan. Then he grinned like a young boy with an exciting secret and tipped far back in his swivel chair, lacing his fingers over his head. "First, I want to say something about your father; it'll help you to understand the rest better," he began, looking through me with his narrowed eyes. "Everybody who knew John, and that meant most of the men in camp, respected him. Oh, he had his weaknesses along with all of us. For one thing, he drank too much and gambled when it brought hardship to his family, but that isn't uncommon in a mining camp. It's a man's life and his wife often shares it only on sufferance."

"I realized that a long time ago," I said, "but it didn't make it easier."

He reached for the fishbowl and polished the letters with his hand. "What you should always remember is that he had a consuming wish for you and never failed to speak of it to the friends who went to visit him. He told them that all he asked of the Almighty was to let him live long enough to know that you had finished your college education. 'If she turns out to be a fine woman,' he once said, 'fitted to stand up and look the world in the eye, then I guess she'll forgive my faults and my life won't have been for nothing.'

"The Bennett Avenue boys knew, of course, that John hadn't left a penny," Griff Lewis continued, "and that you'd have to give up school. Then a few of 'em came into my drugstore one night with a proposition. They wanted to finish the job for him and asked me how to go about it. None of 'em was acquainted with you but almost every kid in town had been in the drugstore at one time or another and they thought maybe I'd recollect you. Somebody suggested the idea of putting a fishbowl on my showcase where spare cash could be dropped now and then. I printed the gold letters on it and agreed to send you the money orders every month. That's all I had to do with it—I give you my word."

The truth had begun to dawn on me. "Then it really wasn't a loan from you?"

"Every cent came that way—from your father's friends." Griff Lewis nodded. "Miners, muckers, pugilists, bankers and lawyers—they all chipped in. He began to chuckle as if recalling something funny. "It beat all, the way the money rolled into that fishbowl! Poker winnings, lucky bets, overtime pay, extra dividends, unexpected royalties—even the purse for an impromptu prize fight at the Newport saloon. Nothing was too big or too small to put in the pot for John's girl. One day an old fellow came all the way from Victor. Blind Tom, we called him—sold shoelaces—lost his eyes years ago in an explosion at the Vindicator. Seems John had grubstaked him often and done him other favors. Well, sir, I watched him come in, grope his way to the showcase and feel around for something. 'What you looking for, Tom?' I asked, walking over. 'Where's that goddamn pot for John's girl?' he said. I pushed it toward him and I'll be darned if he didn't drop in two bits! Lord knows, he must have needed the money himself."

"I'd like to thank every one of them," I said, struggling for self-control. "Could you tell me their names?"

"You've got me there," he said, smiling. "I couldn't tell you if my life depended on it. Fact is, I never knew 'em all— impossible to keep track of everybody coming to the store. It's likely some have left camp; a couple were killed in a cave-in at the Ajax. We buried Blind Tom at Sunnyside graveyard over in Victor only a month or so ago—pneumonia finally caught up with 'im."

"But surely there must be somebody left to . . . to . . ." I couldn't finish the sentence.

"Not one of 'em ever expected a word of thanks," Griff Lewis said, putting his hand on my arm. "They wanted to make your father's dream come true. What they did was for John's girl."

The four o'clock whistles had blown when I left the Lewis Pharmacy and the sidewalk was crowded with miners just off dayshift. I scanned their faces eagerly, hoping to recognize some I had seen before who might have been among my father's friends. They were all strangers to me and oblivious to my gazing; and yet I felt an odd, tingling kinship with them. It seemed to me, as I hurried down Bennett Avenue, that I had come home, at last, to my father's world and had found warmth and human kindness beyond measure or understanding.

20

The City of Mines

ALTHOUGH Victor was only seven miles from Cripple Creek, I had seldom gone there as a child. The traditional rivalry between the two camps separated the people and seemed to give them a different character. In spite of the fact that most of the great mines were on Battle Mountain, either within or adjoining the town, it was not widely known outside of Colorado. Few stories were written about it; no popular songs originated on its dizzy slopes. Cripple Creek grabbed all the fame. In the eyes of the world even Battle Mountain's millionaires were identified with "the greatest gold-mining camp on earth," never with the City of Mines. After all, Cripple Creek had won her laurels fairly, its citizens said, as the first camp in the District, the metropolis and seat of Teller County.

Nowhere was this attitude of superiority more pronounced than among the school children. For an unlucky transfer pupil to admit that he had come from Victor was to risk social ostracism. It seemed an odd twist of fate that I had become a teacher here. But as I looked out upon it from my classroom window, high on a hill, the beauty of the land overwhelmed me. Famous gold-rich mountains rimmed the north with their tall smokestacks. A maze of roads wound in and out among the cribbings piled with waste rock. Small cabins were clustered around them in the open spaces, merging the camp with its mines. Absurd, cracker-box houses with tiny windows and crisscrossing stovepipes clung to the steep slopes of the lopsided streets exactly like the setting of a Humperdinck opera.

I recalled the day in 1893 when my father told me about the new camp that had been started over the hills to the south. He was bringing me home from Rocky Ford the spring after Brother was born. Frank and Harry Woods, two young Baptists from Denver, he said, had paid J. R. McKinnie a thousand dollars for his Mount Rosa Placer ground and plotted a townsite on it. "Looks like throwin' money away," he added. "It's so steep the houses'll have to be cabled to the mountainside."

Contrary to my father's opinion, the lots sold rapidly and sturdy buildings soon lined Victor Avenue. The brothers prospered and took great satisfaction in their creation. Among their first structures was a Baptist church where they taught Bible classes every Sunday. A little later Victor, which had been named after a friend, took on such stature that Frank and Harry decided the time had come to erect a fine hotel at the corner of Fourth Street and Victor Avenue. While grading the foundation, however, an incident occurred that forever changed the destiny of the Woods families. Almost at bedrock a slender vein of rich ore was uncovered which led three hundred feet up the hill to one of Battle Mountain's greatest bonanzas.

Before long, the Gold Coin, as their discovery was called, was producing $30,000 a month. Money poured in at such a rate that the newly organized Woods Investment Company almost ran out of investments. Rather than dump unsightly waste into Victor's main streets, they drove a tunnel three quarters of a mile through Squaw Mountain to Arequa Gulch. Then, realizing that ore as well as waste could be trammed out, they constructed an extravagant chlorination plant called the Economic Mill at the tunnel's exit. These buildings became the District's showpieces. Their pink roof tops could be seen for miles. The $250,000 Gold Coin shaft houses rose like guardian towers above the sprawling little town. Still the fantastic wealth grew and the Woods boys were beside themselves thinking up new ventures on which to spend it. They put up a costly hydroelectric plant at Skagway, on the slopes of Pike's Peak, to furnish power for the mill. So much was left over that they acquired the streetcar system of Pueblo, Colorado's second largest city. Finally, they bought controlling interests in some sixty of the District's producing mines, including one of the crown jewels—the Golden Cycle.

But Victor, the first-born, remained their pet. In four years it grew into a town of 6,000 people, living on the surface of two miles of underground workings. The benevolent founders possessed a rare social conscience and became distinguished as the only multimillionaires who had ever given anything back to the District that had enriched them. The Gold Coin Club House was built for the recreation of their hundreds of employees. When it burned down in Victor's disastrous fire, in 1899, another, of Romanesque design in terra-cotta brick, replaced it. The equipment included a fine gymnasium and a ballroom.

I recalled vividly the story in the *Times* about the grand opening on Christmas Eve, 1900. The magnificent arches and columns dazzled with incandescent lights. Inside, the club had been turned into booths, each one displaying replicas in miniature of the Woods brothers' famous mines. Small trams filled with Gold Coin ore slipped smoothly through a diminutive Economic Tunnel. Early-day prospectors panned for gold nuggets on the Mount Rosa Placer, with their tents, cooking utensils, and other paraphernalia near at hand.

An entertainment preceded the ball, the *Times* went on to say, with the Golden Cycle Band playing selections from *The Bohemian Girl*. Three Negro couples gave a strenuous exhibition of the cakewalk and the pretty little daughter of Mike Blake, foreman at the Cycle, "held the guests in rapt attention by her rendition of 'Floweret Say You'll Not Forget Me.'" The Woods brothers had been acclaimed by everybody present and would be cited for years to come, the newspaper account read, not only because of their many philanthropies such as the Gold Coin Club and Pinnacle Park at Cameron, but for their progressive and enlightened concern for the welfare of their employees.

Now it was only 1906; and as I gazed out at the imposing Gold Coin shaft houses I couldn't help thinking of the tragedies that had overtaken the Woods brothers. The endless flood of gold seemed to have ensnared them and changed their characters. From pious Sunday School teachers they developed into worshipers of Mammon, seeking more and more channels for their money; and increasing their power in the District. Leasers at their mines were forced to buy timbers as well as mining supplies from stores controlled by the Woods Brothers Investment Company; and every carload of ore had to be shipped over the Colorado Springs and Cripple Creek Railroad, known as the Short Line, in which the Woods company was a majority stockholder. Soon it became apparent that their goal was nothing less than control of the entire Cripple Creek District together with all its great producers.

Across the mountains in the county seat, however, a

group of other hardheaded manipulators, led by the Carlton brothers, Bert and Leslie, watched these developments with sharp eyes. They too proposed to corner the wealth of the District and had already made considerable gains in that direction. They followed the common practice, within the letter if not the spirit of the law, of buying large blocks of stock in a coveted property and then dumping them on the market, and thus cheapened the price. It followed, sooner or later, that the mine reduced or stopped paying dividends, banks cut off loans, and the new owners took over as creditors.

Such, in brief, was the method which brought about the chastening of Frank and Harry Woods. Their Victor Bank soon failed, the Economic Mill had burned down, the once brilliantly lighted tunnel was plunged into darkness and filled with debris. The hydroelectric plant at Skagway fell into disrepair, and the impractical, wooden sluice boxes rotted away. The community couldn't support Pinnacle Park; stray cattle and burros grazed among the teeter-totters and merry-go-rounds. The Gold Coin Club, the pride and joy of the brothers, was ultimately converted into a hospital.

Like other millionaires of the District, they had never built homes in Victor. Harry and his wife once lived for a year over the bank, but both men preferred to commute from their mansions in Colorado Springs. At last, these too were lost. Harry went to California, hoping, he told friends, to make a fresh start, but Frank stayed on in Colorado only to suffer further tragedies in the deaths of his wife and daughter. Before long the Carltons had taken over the Cycle, while the Gold Coin fell to the Tutt-Penrose-MacNeill interests.

Despite their broken lives and ill fortune, the founders of Victor had given it a distinctive atmosphere. People had settled there as if they expected to stay. They painted their small homes and hauled in wagonloads of topsoil to level off front yards for lawns, and flower beds of pansies and Iceland poppies. Here and there a rosebush could be seen flourishing in a cool, sheltered spot.

It had been fourteen years since I entered the log cabin school in Cripple Creek's Old Town. I was a child then, in the fourth grade. It was a far cry from that dirt floor to the fine two-story Victor High School where I had come as a new teacher. The responsibility weighed heavily on my mind.

The boys and girls in my classes, it struck me, were the smartest I had ever known. When I heard them come scuffling up the stairs into the room, I was seized by stage fright. One sophomore lad in particular loomed as a continuous challenge to my meager knowledge of modern history. He was quiet-mannered and fine-looking, with dark wavy hair and serious eyes that seemed to see through my thin pretensions. He was a hard though silent taskmaster. Before long I was immersed in cramming my head with world history, fortifying myself against his unexpected questions.

The name of the brilliant student was Lowell Thomas. He was the son of Dr. Harry Thomas, city physician, and one of the intellectual leaders in town. The Thomases were a simple, unobtrusive family, with the mother devoting her spare time to church and club work and the Doctor, in his free hours, sharing his vast knowledge with Lowell and Pherbia, his younger sister. Apparently no field of study had escaped the father's wide-ranging curiosity. The Thomas bookshelves were filled with great classics such as Boswell's *Life of Johnson*, *Pilgrim's Progress*, Milton's *Paradise Lost*, Dante's *Inferno*, and many others including a little-known volume called *Das Kapital*, by a German political philosopher named Karl Marx. Some of the books I had never read, myself, in college, but Lowell had pored over them, not once but many times.

The Thomas household didn't boast of much money but for

Dr. Thomas there were uncounted riches in earth and sky that were free for the asking. On clear, dark nights he often took Lowell for walks to point out the planets and the galaxies of stars. At other times they explored the land for rocks, and from their varied colors and contours the boy learned the timeless wonders of geology. From there it was a natural step to study the history of the people who inhabit the globe.

Dr. Thomas's professional duties frequently brought him in contact with the seamier side of camp life. It fell to him once to perform a post-mortem on the victim of one of the most gruesome murders ever recorded in the District. The corpse was none other than that of the notorious Jim Warford. After finally serving a short term in the penitentiary for killing the two constables on election day in Goldfield, he had returned to Independence and lived quietly in a hut above the Vindicator Mine on Bull Hill. He still carried the two ivory-handled revolvers whenever he went out, but he kept to himself much of the time. When, now and then, he showed up in one of the saloons, guilt-stricken, ex-members of the Citizens' Alliance who had helped send him to prison slipped out the back door, so it was said, and stole home through the alley.

One morning in April, while the ground was still covered with snow, a prospector stumbled over Warford's twisted, frozen body in a lonely spot on Battle Mountain, not far from an old shaft of the Portland Mine. It lay face downward. Fifteen bullets had riddled the chest, abdomen and internal organs. His heart was mutilated, and his head was split in two. Blood had oozed from his wounds and frozen in dark globules on the snow. Powder burns indicated that the shooting had been at close range. Dr. Thomas declared that in all his long career he had never seen a body in such frightful condition. Three thousand men visited the mortuary, as if to make sure that Jim Warford was dead; and then they carted him in a plain wooden box to the potter's field at Victor's Sunnyside graveyard.

Underworld activities in the City of Mines were among the most vicious in the District. Often they were of a highly specialized kind, such as the ghoulish frauds perpetrated on fraternal orders, where a body was sometimes disinterred four or five times and used over and over as evidence for collecting falsified insurance policies. The "deceased" was always a party to the crime and would disappear for a while to give his demise authenticity; and of course, his "grieving widow" always went into deep mourning.

Victor also had its tenderloin which boys and girls had to pass going to and from school. An effort was made to hide it from view by constructing a handsome, red-brick Grand Opera House which towered above and walled off the area. It failed that purpose, but the well-equipped, elegantly furnished theater became a popular amusement center. Touring road companies were not permitted to play on Sundays in Denver, but the District had no such religious scruples and that night a show was usually scheduled for the Victor Grand Opera House. Everybody who could muster the price of a ticket turned out in his best clothes to applaud such New York sensations as Sousa's Band, Primrose and Dockstader's Minstrels, Max Figman in *The Man on the Box*, Olga Nethersole in her shocker, *Sappho*, Ellen Beach Yaw, "with a range of nearly four octaves," and many other famous actors in plays and musical hits.

Victorites were known especially for their love of music. Pianos were numerous and children practiced their scales regularly. News of this musicians' paradise spread far. Occasionally an artist who had suffered a run of bad luck elsewhere would come to the City of Mines planning to open a studio. Or perhaps it was the "famous healthful climate" and scenic grandeur that attracted them. The most eminent of these artists was Hans Albert who had been acclaimed as the "world's third greatest violinist." He was subject to severe attacks of hay fever and asthma and once, in Omaha, he almost died and was forced to cancel the remainder of his tour. The day after his arrival in Victor, the *Daily Record* published the following announcement:

Professor Hans Albert, the world famous violinist, has come to make his home in the Cripple Creek District. He will open a studio in Victor and will consider taking a limited number of pupils. He will also be available for social, theatre and concert engagements. Professor Albert, formerly of Vienna, became a protégé of Emperor Franz Joseph, at the age of nine, and studied under Swedermann, the renowned maestro at the Royal Conservatory in Wurzburg. When the violinist was only sixteen, His Majesty the Emperor appointed him Konzertmeister with the Imperial Opera. Three years later he was called to America to become first violinist with the Theodore Thomas Symphony Orchestra of Chicago. Following a brilliant concert tour he had the honor to be invited by President and Mrs. Grover Cleveland to give a recital at the White House. . . .

Before long, Hans Albert became a conspicuous figure on Victor Avenue, with his bare head, long, unruly reddish-brown hair and short mustache. He always wore a frock coat far too large for his five-foot-two-inch frame. No matter how often people had seen him they seldom failed to turn and watch until he was out of sight. Even Victorites found it hard to get used to a long-haired musician and especially a violinist. This instrument was still regarded as an outcast, fit only for fiddling hillbilly tunes. No red-blooded miner would think of exposing his boy to ridicule by letting him be seen carrying a violin case through the streets; and few pupils went to Hans Albert's studio. He trudged over the hills from camp to camp, giving lessons and often not getting paid for them. But that didn't bother him, particularly if the pupil showed a little talent.

Trouble began to pile up for the virtuoso. Chronic asthma was bothering him again. He resorted to morphine which was easy to get at the drugstores without a prescription; and saloonkeepers were only too glad to fill him up with wine to cheer his spirit in exchange for a few lively tunes. He talked a great deal about his sweetheart, a pretty girl named Grace, back in Ottumwa, Iowa. If she were with him, everything, he was sure, would be all right. He had promised to send for her but her father strongly objected; and besides, Hans had never been able to make any money. Four years had passed and she was still waiting, ready to leave at the first moment, in spite of her wealthy father. If only he could get a windfall!

Then it happened in a surprising and unexpected way. Victor Herbert's popular light opera, *Mlle. Modiste,* starring Fritzi Scheff, was booked one Sunday night at the Victor Grand Opera House. I had gone with Howard Lee, an engineer at the Vindicator Mine and the son of David K. Lee, the carpenter-prospector with whom W. S. Stratton had often gone on prospecting trips.

The beautiful actress always toured with her own fifteen-piece orchestra, but shortly after reaching Victor the conductor suffered a mild heart attack and had to be rushed to Denver's lower altitude. Then, by some miracle, Hans Albert was asked to substitute for him. Fortunately he knew the musical score by heart, for he barely had time to run through it with the instrumentalists when the lights dimmed and the asbestos curtain began to go up.

The atmosphere of the packed house was taut and breathless, as if people feared that their local genius might embarrass or even fail them. But the moment Hans Albert tapped the music rack with his baton and nodded to the musicians, the audience burst into applause, forcing him to bow grandly before signaling the start of the overture. He seemed to be lifted into another world, a world that he had known well, and loved so long ago.

The red velvet curtain parted. The chorus had just finished the opening number, holding the final note to herald the entrance of Mlle. Modiste. For an instant the audience was spellbound. Fritzi Scheff floated lightly downstage, the center of all eyes, the darling of every heart. How exquisite she looked in her blue satin gown, petite silver slippers, with her golden curls brushed atop her head! The crowd clapped and shouted its approval. They couldn't get enough of her singing or her beauty.

Then at last came the cue for her famous ballad, "Kiss Me Again." I glanced at Hans Albert. Pride seemed to flow from his delicate fingers to the baton, as if he were aware that he and the lovely star shared the same mother tongue and had been nourished by the same musical traditions. What tenderness and artistry he drew from the orchestra! When she sang the finale, "Kiss Me, Kiss Me Again," and melted into her lover's arms, the enraptured audience broke into a frenzy, calling "More . . . more . . . more . . ."

Suddenly, without warning, the whole theater was plunged into darkness and when the lights failed to come on in a moment, people began to stir in their seats and mumble nervously. The dread of fire was always uppermost in everybody's mind. After what seemed eternity, a candle was lit somewhere behind the scenes and the asbestos curtain could be heard slowly dropping. Here and there in the auditorium matches flickered and the low hum of anxious voices grew louder. Many were pushing back their seats and stumbling toward the aisles. A feeling of strain and panic charged the air. One whisper of danger and hundreds would be fighting vainly for the exits!

Then, out of the inky black came strains of violin music, gay, lilting improvisations at first, that drifted into familiar ballads. The touch of Hans Albert was unmistakable. Some began to hum the tunes, then others joined in and within a few moments the crowd settled back to wait for the lights.

When they flashed on shortly, the show continued as if nothing had happened. As the curtain went down on the last act, the audience rose, clapping, cheering and yelling for Fritzi Scheff. She returned again and again, smiling, throwing kisses as if she had never before received such a heart-warming ovation. Stepping to the footlights after her last bow, she raised her hand to speak, stilling the enthusiastic crowd with difficulty. "We of the cast are most grateful for your wonderful reception," she said. "It has given us joy to play to such an appreciative audience." Then, looking at Hans Albert, she added, "I should like especially to thank your gifted maestro for showing such presence of mind in averting what might have been a disaster." She reached down and grasped his hand and I heard her say, "You are a true artist . . . *danke schoen . . . auf Wiedersehen!*"

The whole District was agog next day about Hans Albert and how he had checked a panic at the Victor Grand Opera House. But people were even more impressed by the way Fritzi Scheff had praised him and called him "a true artist." His stock in the community began to soar like that of a newly discovered jack pot. Friends went to his room to congratulate him, but he wasn't there—his bed hadn't been slept in. They searched his usual haunts, the Victor Pharmacy, the Silver Dollar Café, the Mint Saloon. No one had seen him. An alarm was sounded and gulches and prospect holes were scoured. But he had disappeared without a trace.

Late in the afternoon some small boys reported seeing "a crazy fellow" playing a violin high on the dump of an abandoned shaft on Carbonate Hill above Cripple Creek. When the deputy sheriff found him, Hans bowed and smiled and muttered something about playing for a vast audience "out there on the hillside." The tails of his dress coat were muddy and torn, and his long, narrow-toed, patent leather shoes were scuffed and unbuttoned. He was taken back to his room and a few days later committed to the Woodcroft Sanitarium in Pueblo. It was the first of many other experiences in and out of the hospital.

Finally, his loyal fiancée came west to join him. Her father had used every legal means possible to prevent the marriage, but without success. With the help of friends and the co-operation of saloonkeepers and pharmacists who agreed not to sell him liquor or drugs, he lived three years in Cripple Creek with his wife and two little daughters. Then another smothering attack of asthma led him to bribe a druggist for morphine. Almost immediately after taking it he became dangerously insane and was sent to a state hospital in Nebraska as incurable. His family never saw him again.

As the months passed, Howe and I seldom missed the Sunday night show at the Victor Grand Opera House. When the days lengthened into spring, we took long walks and sometimes climbed the highest hills to watch the setting sun arch the sky with rainbows, off toward the Sangre de Cristo Mountains.

I was drawn to him by the warmth of his nature, and his interesting way of telling stories, always with unexpected touches of humor that made me laugh as I had never laughed before. But when he spoke of his future, it was no joking matter. He planned to be a consulting engineer some day, like John Hays Hammond or Herbert Hoover, and travel all over the world. "But home base," he said, with a reminiscent shine in his eyes, "will be San Francisco, the most beautiful and fascinating city in the country and just close enough to Palo Alto to be almost perfect. He smiled and put his arm around me. "You'll notice I said *almost* perfect—if you were there with me, it would be a hundred per cent. How about it?"

His sudden, forthright proposal caught me by surprise and I hedged, trying to think of what to say. "I have to look after my brother," I replied, finally, "until he can take care of himself. I am really not free to marry anyone." He brushed this off as no obstacle at all. I grasped at another straw. Some of the girls I had known in college planned to become foreign missionaries in South America, Africa or India. It always struck me as being very romantic, and on the spur of the moment I decided that I too was going to adopt such a career. "When Brother is on his own," I said a bit self-consciously, "I shall probably go to China as a missionary."

He agreed that it was a noble idea but thought that the good work should start nearer home. "Take me, for instance," he said, "I doubt if there's a worse heathen anywhere in the world, and Lord, do I need saving!" He never gave up during the next few weeks of school. Every time we were together he always got around to the same question. It wasn't doubt of my love for him that caused me to hesitate, but memories of Kitty. I recalled how bitterly she had railed against Cripple Creek and all other mining camps, saying they were only for men, and that good women had to endure loneliness and neglect and make terrible sacrifices. I could hear her still urging me not to throw myself away on "a man of the mines."

But now I was old enough to make such a decision for myself. And somehow I couldn't imagine ever being lonely or afraid with Howe. One day I wrote and told him I would resign at the end of my two-year contract and we could be married in June.

21

The Beginning of a Dream
—and the End

THE wedding was at Howe's home in Denver; and after a short trip to Glenwood Springs, Colorado's spa for newlyweds, we left for Ouray at the north gateway of the San Juan Mountains. The Camp Bird Mine was eight miles farther and more than twelve thousand feet above sea level in Imogene Basin. We might have gone as far as the mill, two miles below the mine, in one of the big freighters that jogged up the narrow road skirting the high cliffs. But Howe said it would be more exciting to ride horseback over the trail.

"Do you know the way?" I asked, hesitating.

He admitted that he had only heard about it from others. "But there's just one direction—up," he said reassuringly. "It would be impossible to get lost; and you'll see some of the most magnificent scenery in the world!"

The country more than lived up to its billing, but the trail proved to be mostly crisscrossing animal tracks which often ended on top of a precipice or at the bank of a roaring stream. It was pitch-dark by the time we pulled into the Basin. My back ached and my knees felt numb. "That's our cabin," Howe said with a touch of concern, "the one with the light in the window. Evidently the boys got word and we have company."

As we came closer, hundreds of lanterns, it seemed, began to flash and the din of yelling, singing, banging dishpans and washtubs echoed and re-echoed across the bowl. It was wilder and more deafening than any shivaree I'd ever heard in Cripple Creek. "Speech! Speech!" the crowd shouted as Howe jumped down from the horse. But he apparently knew in advance that they would expect something more potent than words, and had laid in an ample supply. Soon they all went tearing off down the hill bellowing ribald singsongs never meant for a lady's ears.

Our one-room cabin with a small lean-to kitchen had to be cabled to a huge boulder to hold it together under a twenty-foot blanket of snow in winter. Three other similar shacks, unoccupied and weather-worn, crouched on the slightly level patches of ground. At the opposite side of the small Basin a log cabin squatted on a low granite knoll. In spite of its crumbling chinks and cracked window, it had a certain self-conscious air of gentility. Once Thomas F. Walsh, discoverer of the Camp Bird bonanza, dwelt there with his wife and children. The silver lode which he had sought turned out to be a fabulous deposit of gold and before long he moved to a fine mansion on Dupont Circle in Washington as Colorado's multimillionaire Senator.

Now an Italian miner named Jim Bartoli and his wife lived in the log cabin. I was delighted to find another woman in camp, but to my dismay she spoke only a few garbled words of English and spent most of her time washing the miners' socks and underwear. One day it occurred to me that I might offer to teach Mrs. Bartoli how to speak English. She was overjoyed with my suggestion and we had begun to make fine progress when the lessons came to an abrupt end. Jim, her "old man," had threatened to kill her if she ever had anything more to do with me. She said tearfully that he didn't want her to learn the ways of American women—they were no good—they wouldn't work or have babies.

The days were like eternity while Howe was at the mine. In my loneliness I often wept and wondered if, after all, Kitty hadn't been right. Surely there was no place for a woman in the Imogene Basin; one was allowed to exist Griff Lewis had once said, there only on sufferance. There was a big, comfortable boarding and bunkhouse for the several hundred miners and office workers just a few steps from the tunnel entrance. I never saw any of them except when Howe took me to the company store occasionally in the evening. It was always crowded with men warming their backs around the enormous stove, smoking, chewing, telling yarns that ended in raucous laughter. The only other pastime was the gramophone and its three cracked records, "Hello, Peaches," "In the Good Old Summer Time," and "Stop yer Ticklin', Jock!" played over and over by the clerk behind the counter.

I tried to keep my loneliness to myself but one afternoon Howe came home early and caught me sobbing on the bed. From that day on, my life at the Camp Bird became different. After work and on Sundays we began to explore some of the rugged peaks that rimmed the Basin. Along the way there were deep-blue and white columbines to gather in the quaking aspen groves, and wild raspberries on the burned-over slopes and luscious strawberries in the high meadows. When we ate our lunch on some grassy hummock, feather-footed ptarmigan in speckled summer garb nibbled at the crumbs in our hands.

But the most exciting trip of all was the short, steep hike to the jagged ridge of Chicago Mountain which towered almost thirteen hundred feet to form the south wall of the Basin. From there we could see the far pinnacles of the San Juan range shimmering in the afternoon sun, while directly below us, deep in shadow, lay the Camp Bird on one side; and on the other, the little town of Silverton, famous for its Gold King and Sunnyside mines. "Some day," Howe said, "we'll go on over to the Sunnyside; it's not much farther—you can see the tip of the smokestack above the crest yonder."

Howe left the Camp Bird Mine before long to become a field engineer for a large international mining and smelting company. Brother had been sent to a boarding school in the East; and I went to Los Angeles where Howe returned every few weeks to write his reports. He advanced rapidly and within a year was sent to eastern Oregon to take charge of operating the Rainbow Mine on which his company held an option. It was located in the arid, sagebrush-covered Malheur Mountains, twenty-five miles west of Huntington, the nearest railroad station.

The camp consisted of a commodious house where we lived, a small boardinghouse for miners and a dozen or so cabins. The altitude was less than a mile and as soon as water had been piped down from the mountainside, we planted a garden. The natives warned us that nothing would grow in that soil, but by the following summer people came from faraway to see the beautiful sweet peas, twelve feet tall, Shasta daisies, poppies and corn flowers splashing color over the hillside. Some of the men had sent for their families and soon they too caught the gardening fever and the turnover in employees was cut drastically in an area where miners had never been known to stay long.

When the population grew to three hundred, a school was started and a pretty, blond teacher came up from Salt Lake City. But she soon married one of the young engineers. From then on, the turnover in schoolteachers rose or fell according to the number of eligible bachelors in camp. Next, arrangements were made for a minister from Baker City to preach twice a month at the boardinghouse. Then someone suggested that we take up a collection of books for a library.

The co-operative efforts led to others such as grading land for a tennis court and a baseball field. Someone got the idea of making over an abandoned mill into a recreation hall. The company covered it with a new roof and put in a dance floor. Nothing gave the community so much endless amusement as the miners' Sunday-night boxing exhibitions and wrestling matches, alternating with Pearl White in *The Perils of Pauline*. The monthly dances were frequently enlivened by fights, especially in summer when the office men put on airs and enraged the miners by sporting "ice cream" pants.

It was a serious matter, among Rainbow miners, to violate their social code. No decent married woman, for instance, would ever be seen alone with a man other than her husband; nor would she dance twice with the same partner or deny her spouse the first and last waltzes. Once, an attractive young wife defied the customs, not only by two-stepping three times with the same admirer, but also by gliding dreamily with him in the "Home, Sweet Home" waltz. The humiliated, jealous husband went to his cabin for a shotgun and when the couple appeared, killed them both and committed suicide.

But despite occasional murders and stage robberies, the Rainbow Mine was a paradise for Howe and me. It was while we were here that our daughter, Barbara, was born; and it was here that we learned some of the ingredients necessary to a full, rich life, regardless of surroundings or circumstances. We had time to listen to fine recorded music, to read books. But what was more important, we had time for each other and for the people whose lot had been cast with ours, on a remote, isolated mountainside.

The mine, however, failed to come up to expectations, and

253

after four years we said farewell to our friends and drove away for the last time to the station in Huntington. It was the beginning of many travels, to Alaska, Mexico and the bush country of Cobalt and Porcupine, far north of Toronto in Canada.

From time to time, during our travels, we heard news about the Cripple Creek District. As the mines deepened, underground water had become an increasing problem. The El Paso drainage tunnel had been driven in 1904 to channel the run-off from Bert Carlton's Doctor-Jack Pot as well as that of the El Paso on Beacon Hill. It proved to be inadequate and another, called the Roosevelt Deep Drainage Tunnel, was started in 1907 on the initiative of Bert Carlton. Meanwhile, he continued to acquire many of the former bonanzas in the area of Raven Hill and Battle Mountain, with the idea of finding large deposits of low-grade ore and possibly other jack pots at deeper levels. He had driven his last formidable rival, John T. Milliken, out of the mining and milling business and was well on the way toward realizing his ambition to become the invulnerable kingpin of Cripple Creek.

Frank Woods, his one-time opponent in the struggle for power, had suffered another deadly blow. He had turned his lease on the fourth level at the Golden Cycle Mine over to his son, Frank, Jr., and had gone to Boulder County to do assessment work on a claim. Winter was late that year of 1913. Dark, threatening clouds overhung the sky, the morning of December first, and within a few hours a foot of snow lay on the ground with no signs of a letup; and old-timers predicted a hard blizzard.

It was about three o'clock in the afternoon when word of a cave-in at the Golden Cycle Mine flashed through the District. A roaring slide of earth and rock two hundred feet wide and a thousand feet thick, the reports said, had torn loose above the fourth level and buried everything in its path, including four men, among them young Frank Woods.

Cripple Creek and Victor had experienced many mine accidents but none of them equaled in violence that slide at the Golden Cycle. One of our Victor friends sent us clippings from the *Record,* giving details. The concussion shook adjoining properties within a radius of several thousand yards. Mines in the lowest workings of the Vindicator, a quarter of a mile away, felt the tremor and dishpans, skillets and dishes rattled in Elkton, the other side of Squaw Mountain. The storm, meanwhile, had developed into a howling, pitiless blizzard, pounding at communication lines, blocking all traffic and hampering efforts to rescue the entombed men.

Because of the cramped quarters underground, only three or four workers could be used at a time. They groped down slippery ladders with rocks crashing around their heads, and splashing in the black depths of a sump, far below. Finally, one of the men was found alive, pressed tight against the side of a drift and almost completely buried, but miraculously he had escaped serious injury. "I'd just trammed out a load and was standing on my car," he said, "coasting back to the stope when suddenly a blast of air hit me and rolled me like a ball down the drift. I could hear the ground cracking and booming, and feel the muck squeezing up around my neck. I thought I was done for!" Then he told how he grabbed hold of the side wall and was hanging on desperately when another slide thundered past, snapping timbers and tumbling boulders; and cutting off the three men in the raise.

It had been seventy hours since the start of the blizzard. Drifts were twenty feet high; cabins, windows and doorways were buried, and streets impassable. Not an ore team moved; fire trucks were immobilized and several houses burned. Landslides filled railroad cuts, snow plows worked in vain to cut through ice. Over at the Joe Dandy Mine the smokestack was carried off, and up on Bull Hill the galvanized tin roof at the Lee Mine was torn loose and blown a half-mile away. All together, eight locomotives with their crews were stalled in the mountains surrounding the District.

But the rescuers at the Golden Cycle fought on, five, six, nine days; and still the mine's secret was locked in its vitals. It began to seem hopeless. Cots for the men were snaked up the trail, and women in Victor filled kettles with hot food to send to the shaft on sledges. The talk everywhere was about "poor Frank Woods waiting helplessly in Colorado Springs for a train to get through to camp." It was the evening of the tenth day before his son's body was finally uncovered, together with the torsos of the other two victims. They were all crushed beyond recognition.

Among the passengers who stepped down from the first train to reach Victor was a slender man with stooped shoulders and a deeply lined face. Crowds had gathered on the platform to touch his hand in sympathy. He smiled, unseeingly, as he walked slowly to a friend's waiting car; he seemed dazed, as if he had come to a strange place. Frank Woods had no room of his own in the City of Mines, which he and his brother Harry had founded, and apparently no recollection of the fabulous Golden Cycle, once the proud boast of the Woods family. Now, feeble and bereft, he seemed aware only that all his loved ones were gone and that, somehow, he must face the last mile alone.

But if fortune had turned against the Woods brothers, it showered unexpected blessings on another persistent old-timer who never gave up hope. The lucky man was Richard Roelofs, who had paid me a dollar long ago to wash the mountain of moldy dishes piled in his kitchen. I had seen him once or twice when I was teaching in Victor. He had been leasing for many years, he said, with indifferent success, "making just enough extra to send young Dick east to a good school." Now, at last, he had made a magnificent strike.

In a way, the Cresson Mine's history was like that of the Doctor-Jack Pot. Both were located in the upper gulches that skirted either side of Raven Hill and both were considered more or less washed up by their absentee owners who, for some reason, couldn't quite let go. In one respect, however, the Cresson differed sharply from its neighbor over the hill. Never in its palmiest days had it enriched anybody. Richard Roelofs must have been near the end of his rope, the wiseacres said, to undertake the management of such a worthless hole in the ground.

But he hadn't spent twenty hard years in the District whittling his name on aspen bark, and like Josiah Winchester and the Jack Pot, he staked his last cent on the hunch that unimaginable gold lay somewhere in the depths of the discounted Cresson. Being Dutch, he also knew how to keep his counsel until the property was clear of debt. After a few years, when the Cresson began to pay small dividends, Richard Roelofs became known as one of the most astute mining experts in the District. It was just too bad, one prominent man said, that Dick hadn't sunk his teeth into something better than the Cresson in years past when all the bonanzas weren't yet discovered.

Then one day in the late fall of 1914 news broke that Richard Roelofs had run into a vug of sylvanite ore, off a drift on the twelfth level, that would have made Jason's Golden Fleece look like tin foil. The jeweled cave was said to be forty feet high, twenty feet long and fifteen feet wide; and the crystal walls were beyond estimate in gold values. Howe and I met the fortunate Cripple Creeker not long afterward on Seventeenth Street in Denver and we lunched together at the Brown Palace Hotel. He told us the fascinating story of his discovery and how unreal it had seemed at first. The interior of the vug sparkled with leafy, prismatic crystals which fell on his clothing with the slightest movement of air. When he came to his senses he realized the importance of letting only two or three of his most trusted associates in on the find. Steel doors were built across the entrance, against high graders, and armed men guarded the collar of the shaft day and night. Then he straightened himself with a glow of satisfaction and said, "I am confident that within a month this one vault alone will produce more than a million dollars!"

It wasn't likely that another bonanza would ever be uncovered in the Cripple Creek District, the knowing ones had declared. The camp's youth was spent; its years of making headlines were ended. But not quite. The Cresson had made fools of the prophets, at least for a while longer, and poured new wealth into the coffers of stockholders, including Richard Roelofs.

But other factors, far beyond the District's borders, were conspiring to squeeze the last ounces of lifeblood from what had once been "the greatest gold-mining camp on earth." A war had broken out in Europe in midsummer of 1914. When the United States joined the Allies in the spring of 1917, the small towns and cities were emptied of young men.

Cripple Creek suffered a mortal blow. In spite of the boost in mine production, by the late discovery of the Cresson, the population had been steadily shrinking from its peak of 50,000 in 1900 to around 6,000 in 1917, just before the start of the war. The biggest drop came within five years after the labor strike ended in 1904, when 15,000 left camp. It began to look as though only a miracle could save the Cripple Creek District from complete disintegration.

The miracle turned out to be Bert Carlton. The finish of

the Roosevelt Deep Drainage Tunnel after ten years, largely through his money and persistence, made it possible to un-water the deepest mines. He controlled most of them now, including the Cresson, under a syndicate listing such familiar names as Spencer Penrose, Charlie MacNeill, Eugene Shove and Richard Roelofs. With the backing and promise of so many millions, Cripple Creek would surely stage a revival, the people said, and there would be good jobs in the mines waiting for their sons "when the shooting was over, over there." From that time on, few could be found around camp who would ever say a disparaging word against Bert Carlton. He had stood by the District loyally in its darkest hour.

Howe and I had been living in Leadville during the early years of the war. His company sent him there to take charge of unwatering Fryer Hill, where several of that camp's rich-est mines were located. Brother was in France as a master air mechanic with the Army. In 1918 I had gone to Denver while Howe went to Boston for a conference with company officials. He had no idea where he might be sent next, but the company had taken an option on the Sunnyside Mine near Silverton, and I dreaded the possibility of going to live in a remote cabin on that bleak mountainside.

Then, influenza which had broken out in Spain a few weeks before swept through Europe and crossed the Atlantic. A thousand cases had been reported in New England in the last ten days and within twelve hours it had struck Chicago, then Kansas City. Now it had reached Denver and other towns in Colorado, and deaths were mounting.

Twenty-five cases were reported in the Cripple Creek Dis-trict, and each day the lists grew. All public meetings were forbidden. Even dogs and cats, suspected of being carriers, were not allowed to run loose. Women from the row on Myers Avenue, led by a bristling redhead known as "the Boilermaker," were volunteering as nurses. Exhausted doctors died along with their patients. Bodies jammed the mortuaries; there were no more coffins. Within six weeks over four hundred people in the District had died. Gravediggers worked in relays and at night Pisgah cemetery was bright with the flares of their bonfires. It seemed as if Cripple Creek were gasping for its last breath.

Denver, with lower altitude and wider facilities, fared a little better. But everybody wore gauze masks on the streets, and the dead lay in sealed coffins for fear of spreading the infection. Howe returned home the latter part of October with such good news that I forgot, momentarily, the tragedy that had afflicted so many of our friends. He had been promoted to the position of assistant consulting engineer for all of the company's western properties; and his headquarters were to be in San Francisco! "But we'd better hold up shipment of our furnishings," he said, "until I return from a short inspection trip to Sunnyside."

"Oh, Howe," I interrupted, suddenly gripped with terror. "Why do you have to go now—can't you wait a while—until the worst of the epidemic is over?"

"It's already subsided in the East," he said, "and I figure that if I weathered it in Boston I ought to hold out in that fine, pure air at the Sunnyside. Anyhow, there's no alternative. I'll only be gone four or five days."

He barely had time to reach the mine when I saw in the paper one morning that miners at the Sunnyside were fleeing across the mountains, panic-stricken because of the virulent influenza epidemic that had killed six men, the night before, within thirty minutes. Shaking like a leaf, I called long distance. It was difficult to make connections through to Silverton; few operators were working. Finally, a man answered at the mine. I asked for Howe and after another long delay the man returned to say that Mr. Lee was sick and couldn't come to the telephone just then but not to worry; he'd be all right soon; under no circumstances should I come. A telegram arrived from Howe that afternoon assuring me that he was in no immediate danger and again urging me to stay in Denver with Barbara.

The next morning, at daybreak, I was wakened by the desperate ringing of a bell. It was long distance calling me. A dim, far away voice said that Howe had passed away shortly after midnight.

22

The Return

I t had been more than thirty years since Howe died; and
five decades had passed since the memorable day my father
enrolled me at Cutler Academy. I was getting on, as Kitty
used to say; and my responsibilities had eased. More and more
lately my thoughts had been reverting to Cripple Creek.
Stories had reached me from time to time about its disintegration. Soon it would be a ghost town, they said, a skeleton
rattling its bones. Only a few old-timers were left in the
whole District; newcomers from Texas and Oklahoma were
buying up the best of the old houses for a few dollars, to
use for a month or two in summer. It was difficult for me to
imagine the throbbing, lustful camp of my childhood grown
decrepit; and I became obsessed with the idea of going back
again before it crumbled in ruins.

When Howe died I had myself and a young child to support,
and after a few years trying to get my bearings I returned to
the field of education as Dean of Women at my Alma Mater,
Colorado College. Then followed administrative positions at

Radcliffe, Harvard Summer School, Bennington, Whitman, and finally the University of California in Berkeley.

Before I realized it, 1951 had brought me to another milepost. The time had come to say good-bye to the college campus, and the signs at the crossroads were indistinct. I was conscious only of a longing to go home, back to the house on Golden Avenue in Cripple Creek. It was reported that a multimillionaire had bought up the town with the intention of restoring and making it into a famous tourist attraction. I would have to hurry if I hoped to find the old mining camp as I recalled it.

The bus was crowded when it left Colorado Springs but gradually emptied as we stopped at the summer resorts up Ute Pass. I was the only passenger when we pulled out of Woodland Park. The road climbed west from there, skirting the lower slopes of Pike's Peak. Although it was the last of June, patches of snow still clung to the gulches. Nearby lupine, mustard and candytuft tossed on the sunny hillsides, and meadowlarks sang from the telephone wires.

"How far is it from here?" I asked the driver eagerly. "Will it be much longer?"

"'Bout three quarters of an hour," he replied, without looking around. "You a stranger in these parts?"

"Not exactly. I lived in Cripple Creek as a child and taught school in Victor."

He seemed unimpressed. "Lotsa old-timers coming back these days. Guess they find good many changes. Sure ain't what it used to be."

I asked him if he would drive past the National Hotel. "I went to the big opening in 1896. It was a memorable event. Is it still there?"

He gave me an amusing glance. "It was tore down in 1919. Only hotel today is the Imperial up on Third, across from the old telephone buildin'. Kinda hard gettin' a room there 'less you've got a reservation."

"What's going on?" I asked, a little apprehensive.

"The mellerdrama show in the basement, a real rootin', tootin' tear jerker. Tenderfeet flock up here by the hundreds, in Cadillacs an' Lincolns, to take it in an' do the other sights like goin' down the Molly Kathleen Mine. Gives 'em a big kick." He was silent a moment. "Come to think of it, though, today bein' Thursday they ain't usually so many. Maybe there'll be room for you. Hotel manager's a nice fella, real accommodatin'."

Apparently Cripple Creek had already become a museum piece. Luckily a room was available for one night. After a dinner in the hotel's dining room, I telephoned around for another place to stay and finally found one over an undertaking parlor in Victor.

This camp, still more fascinating and interesting to me than Cripple Creek, had evidently been passed up by most of the sight-seers in favor of a tour through the new Carlton cyanide mill that lay halfway between the two rival towns. For a fee of one dollar they could watch the huge stamps crushing the ore and gaze at synthetic gold bricks. Then they were apt to hurry back for lunch by François and the matinee in the Imperial's basement.

Bert Carlton had died in 1931 leaving two of his major plans unrealized. Ethel, his widow—the beautiful young girl I had first seen at the National Hotel's inaugural ball—and his brother Leslie took over the projects. By then, another drainage tunnel was necessary to unwater the Carlton properties which included every old producer in the District, except the Strong just above Victor. It took ten years to complete the six-and-a-quarter-mile bore which Ethel named for her husband. Later the Carlton cyanide mill was erected to extract the last grains of gold from the vast dumps.

I puffed up and down Victor's hilly streets, seemingly steeper than ever, chatting with the few remaining pioneers. The weather-worn high school still stood nobly on its hilltop, with rooms to spare. But the Opera House had burned down many years before and the Gold Coin Club had undergone still another transformation. Teller County's one physician, Dr. A. C. Denman, and his wife had remodeled the front part, upstairs, into an attractive apartment; and the doctor, a pioneer himself, commuted to the District's only hospital on Church Hill in Cripple Creek.

Some of the landmarks were posted with large numerals for the benefit of stray sight-seers, and one day I noticed the number eight on a gray clapboard house that looked familiar to me, but the neighborhood had changed and I couldn't recall who had lived there. It was unoccupied but not run down, and had not suffered the usual fate of shattered windows. I climbed several stairs to the ell porch to read the notation alongside the number. It said: "This was the boyhood home of Lowell J. Thomas, a graduate of the Victor High School, class of 1910, and later famous as newscaster, author and world explorer. He was the son of Dr. and Mrs. Harry Thomas, for many years active and respected citizens of Victor." I recalled, then, that the doctor had served as a surgeon in the British and American armies in World War I and became a professor in universities abroad as well as in the United States. A tireless scholar, he did special work at Oxford at the age of eighty.

I thought about the others who had lived here for a while, on their way to fame. There was the fourteen-year-old scrapper, Julius Marx, better known as Groucho; and a well-scrubbed little boy named Robert M. Coates who grew up to write stories for the *New Yorker* magazine about his childhood in Goldfield. It wasn't surprising when Cripple Creek's gifted young high-school orator, Ralph Carr, became Colorado's governor or that pretty Jacqueline Logan later starred in movies, but certainly nobody expected nineteen-year-old Wallace Irwin, once an assayer's helper in Anaconda, to achieve future distinction as a poet, novelist and man of letters. And it seemed incredible that Roland Farley, handicapped by blindness, would some day be honored in Europe as well as in his own country for his compositions in music, while Ruth, his devoted sister would make a place for herself as a teacher of the blind.

There were still others, such as Jack Dempsey, once a mucker at the Portland Mine who won the World's Heavyweight Championship—acclaimed by many as the greatest of all pugilists—and the first fighter ever to draw a million-dollar gate. I recalled too that Bernard Baruch, the precocious young college graduate who had roughed it in some of Battle Mountain's mines, returned east to make his mark as a financier, pundit and counselor to the nation's Presidents.

Some, unknown and unsung, had gone out from these rugged camps to become heroic soldiers, successful lawyers, engineers and business men. A few had the courage to stay on, still treasuring the home to which they had belonged for so many years.

By chance, after three or four weeks, I heard of a place in Cripple Creek called the "Hoot Mon," just across from the Imperial Hotel. In my day it had been the telephone building, but two elderly Scots, Agnes and Jack Dewar, had remodeled it some forty years ago into three apartments. I still had vivid recollections of Jack dressed in his kilties and playing the bagpipes in all the big Labor Day parades. Agnes, his sister, was now a tidy, buxom woman in her late sixties, whose chief amusement was to put on a clean apron and stand in her front doorway watching the tourists get out of their grand automobiles and go into the Imperial Hotel.

Bennett Avenue, except for the south or shady side, where half-demolished structures had left gaping cavities, bore some of the earmarks of its past heyday. Many of the buildings, although looking tired and beaten, still flaunted their fading names—Burnside, Welty, Shockey, Phenix (the spelling had been shortened for lack of space), and Pullen. The Midland Terminal depot at the eastern end dominated the street, as always, aloof and dignified in spite of its sagging steps and boarded-up windows. It was planned to make it into a museum where relics of Cripple Creek's glorious history would be exhibited.

I cut across lots from the depot to Myers Avenue. It had been dubbed Julian Street, after the author by that name wrote a scurrilous article for *Collier's* magazine picturing Cripple Creek as a vast tenderloin presided over by one Leo the Lion, a denizen of Myers Avenue. Now it was nobody's street. Not a saloon, crib or dance hall remained in the two blocks that had once pulsated with music and gusty laughter. Only the two-story, pink brick lair of sin—the Old Homestead —stood there naked and alone, a monument to Cripple Creek's most profligate and debauched era. It was rumored that somebody had bought it recently, intending to put in extra baths and rent rooms named after former madams, Pearl, Hazel, Grace, Georgia, Belle, as added spice for the tourist trade.

I set out down Bennett Avenue one day, looking for very old men who would surely remember my father. Expensive cars were parked, bumper to bumper, along the street. Visitors sauntered on the sidewalk and stopped to gaze occasionally at the souvenirs in the small-shop windows. Several taverns enlivened the air with popular jukebox records.

Through the open doors customers could be seen, dressed in wide sombreros, highboots and levis, and sipping drinks, affecting the manner of the wild, gold-rush years.

All of a sudden I caught sight of an aged fellow leaning against the front of a vacant store. I hurried over to speak to him, confident that the mere mention of John Barbee would bring a smile to the wrinkled, unshaven face. "Have you been in Cripple Creek many years?" I asked brightly.

"Since the spring of '96," he replied, chewing his gums. "Came in as a kid after the big fires.

"Oh," I said, feeling let down. "You were too young then to know my father, John Barbee."

"Nope; never heard of 'im."

I went on to another feeble codger dozing in a sunny doorway. "I beg your pardon," I began politely. "I'm trying to find someone who might have known my father in the early days. John Barbee was his name—sometimes he was called "Honest John."

He squinted at me with watery eyes. "You his girl?"

My spirits rose. "Yes; I'm Mabs. I used to go prospecting with him, summers, over on Beacon Hill."

"I'm gettin' so my hearin's not much good. What'd you say his name was—Beacon?"

"Barbee—John Barbee," I shouted.

"Nope; ain't seen 'im 'round lately; fact never heard of a fella named Tom Barley."

I made one or two further attempts and then gave up, convinced that my father had vanished from Cripple Creek's memory as completely as if he had never existed. I started up First Street past the County Court House toward Golden Avenue. For a moment it was hard to get my bearings, so many buildings had been torn down. In the block where we lived only one house remained—the Baltzells', which the neighbors had helped to build after the great fires. Children were playing in the yard but I had no desire to knock on the door. Instead, I decided to take a short walk through vacant lots to Pisgah graveyard.

The cemetery had spread out fantastically, as the town shrank closer in the basin. It stretched like a patched blanket over the saddle where Mount Pisgah sloped into the adjoining ridge. It was early September and the quaking aspens on the higher reaches had begun to turn yellow. I climbed to the topmost point and sat down on the sun-browned grass. How still the world seemed! Not a breeze stirred, no sign of life anywhere, not even a chipmunk or a blue jay.

Fragments of scenes long forgotten began drifting at random through my mind. The arrival of the first train; Brother's small pockets spilling over with gold pieces he had won at faro; Pearl de Vere's funeral and Joe Moore's heart-rending "Good-bye, Little Girl, Good-bye;" Kitty all dressed up in her new blue cashmere, in a dead faint on the floor when Mrs. Fitz had threatened to whip Jim Corbett; Uncle Si's return from Denver loaded with presents; and Teddy Roosevelt at the Finns' reception. Today no vestige was left of those happy, romantic, tragical years.

The sun had begun to go down and the air was getting chilly. I picked my way among the rocks, fallen headboards and sunken mounds; and stood for a moment in farewell beside my father's grave. Beacon Hill rose to the south and the El Paso lay in full view. The great mine, too, was dead, together with the prospector who discovered it.

I quickened my step down the dusty road to camp, so lost in thought that it startled me to hear someone speaking. It was a gray-bearded man wearing a corduroy coat that looked as if it had come in with the gold rush. I forgot to ask if he had known my father; somehow it didn't matter any more.

"Nice day for a walk," he was saying. "Don't see strangers footin' it 'round here often."

"Are you prospecting in this vicinity?" I asked, noticing the small canvas ore sack in his coat pocket.

"Yep; up on Mineral Hill," he said, pointing in that direction.

"Most of the big strikes, I understand, were at the opposite end of camp on Battle Mountain and Beacon Hill," I said. "What makes you think you'll find gold on Mineral Hill?"

"Say! You talk just like them other old-timers!" he chuckled. "Well, let me tell you somethin'. See that flat bit a land yonder? In the early days it was a placer—Freeman's placer. I seen nuggets panned outa there big as chestnuts. Couldn't come from nowheres, I figger, 'cept Mineral Hill—washed down hunderds a years ago. I gotta claim that'll prove it. Won't be long 'til I open up the biggest bonanza ever found in the District. Take it from me, this ol' minin' camp's a long ways yet from cashin' in its chips. Come back again pretty soon," he added, turning to go, "when things are boomin'. Could be any day now!"

The shine of hope and faith in the old fellow's eyes followed me long after he had disappeared from sight. And it came to me, as it had once long ago, that it wasn't the gold he wanted. It would likely slip through his fingers in no time, or be given away for the asking. It was the enticing hunt that led him on, the elusive chase, the everlasting love of the game.